NABOKOV'S THEATRICAL IMAGINATION

Drawing on a wealth of unpublished archival material, this study offers a comprehensive assessment of the importance of theatrical performance in Vladimir Nabokov's thinking and writing. Siggy Frank provides fresh insights into Nabokov's wider aesthetics and arrives at new readings of his narrative fiction. As well as emphasising the importance of theatrical performance to our understanding of Nabokov's texts, she demonstrates that the theme of theatricality runs through the central concerns of Nabokov's art and life: the nature of fiction, the relationship between the author and his fictional world, textual origin and derivation, authorial control and textual property, literary appropriations and adaptations, and finally the transformation of the writer himself from the Russian émigré writer Sirin to the American novelist Nabokov.

SIGGY FRANK is Lecturer in Russian Studies at the University of Nottingham.

NABOKOV'S THEATRICAL IMAGINATION

SIGGY FRANK

CAMBRIDGE
UNIVERSITY PRESS

CAMBRIDGE UNIVERSITY PRESS
Cambridge, New York, Melbourne, Madrid, Cape Town,
Singapore, São Paulo, Delhi, Tokyo, Mexico City

Cambridge University Press
The Edinburgh Building, Cambridge CB2 8RU, UK

Published in the United States of America by Cambridge University Press, New York

www.cambridge.org
Information on this title: www.cambridge.org/9781107015456

First published 2012

Printed in the United Kingdom at the University Press, Cambridge

A catalogue record for this publication is available from the British Library

ISBN 978-1-107-01545-6 Hardback

Contents

Acknowledgements

I would like to thank the University of Oxford for awarding me a Scatcherd European Scholarship which funded the doctoral research on which this book is based. I would also like to thank the Leverhulme Trust for granting me an Early Career Development Fellowship which allowed me to rethink large parts of my doctoral project and to undertake archival research in Russia and the United States. A research grant from the School of Modern Languages and Cultures, University of Nottingham, facilitated further archival research at the Library of Congress.

Earlier versions of parts of Chapter 3 and Chapter 4 have appeared as 'Exile in Theatre/Theatre in Exile: Nabokov's Early Plays *Tragediia Gospodina Morna* and *Chelovek iz SSSR*', *Slavonic and East European Review*, 85/4 (October 2007), 629–57. I am grateful for the permission to use this material here. Excerpts from various materials held at the New York Public Library, Henry W. and Albert A. Berg Collection of English and American Literature, Astor, Lenox and Tilden Foundations, Vladimir Nabokov Papers, are reprinted here by arrangement with the New York Public Library and the Estate of Vladimir Nabokov. All rights reserved. I am also grateful for the permission granted by the Estate of Vladimir Nabokov to reproduce the photo on page 31.

Much of this book is about notions of authorial property, and in some ways this study is a vivid illustration of individual and shared authorship, as I have benefited from discussions with colleagues and friends, all of whom have made some direct or indirect contribution to this study. First, I owe a large debt to Jane Grayson who has been an exceptionally generous friend and colleague over many years. Her inspiration, ideas and insights have been invaluable for this study. I would also like to thank the following people: Andrei Babikov, David Bethea, Andy Byford, Neil Cornwell and Julie Curtis. I wish to thank the staff at the Taylor Institution Slavonic and Modern Greek Library, University of Oxford; The Berg Collection at the New York Public Library; The Nabokov Collection at the Manuscript Division at the Library of Congress, Washington, and the Bakhmeteff Archive, Columbia University.

A very special thank you goes to my husband Matthew for being my best reader and re-reader throughout this project. I am also indebted to my parents, Peter and Eva Golpon, and my parents-in-law, Stephen and Sue Frank, for their continuous support. This book is dedicated to a most remarkable, courageous and inspiring woman, my grandmother Charlotte Golpon (1912–2004), and her love for everything Russian.

Note on transliteration and translation

For transliteration of Russian texts, I adhere to the Library of Congress system without diacritical marks. For the sake of readability, however, I use common Anglicised spellings of Russian names of both historical and fictional persons: for instance, Cincinnatus (instead of Tsintsinnat), Dreyer (instead of Dreier), Franz (instead of Frants), Hermann (instead of German), Gogol (instead of Gogol'), Liubov (instead of Liubov'), Meyerhold (instead of Meierkhol'd), Stanislavsky (instead of Stanislavskii), Waltz (instead of Val's) and so on.

For English translations of Nabokov's work, I rely mostly on the standard English translations prepared or authorised by Nabokov himself. All other translations are mine, unless otherwise indicated.

Abbreviations

The following abbreviations are used throughout this book.

BAR	Bakhmeteff Archive of Russian and East European Culture, Columbia University, New York.
BS	Vladimir Nabokov, *Bend Sinister* (London: Penguin, 1974).
Despair	Vladimir Nabokov, *Despair* (London: Penguin, 1981).
IB	Vladimir Nabokov, *Invitation to a Beheading* (London: Penguin, 1963).
KQK	Vladimir Nabokov, *King, Queen, Knave* (London: Penguin, 1993).
NWL	*Dear Bunny, Dear Volodya: The Nabokov–Wilson Letters, 1940–1971*, ed. Simon Karlinsky, revised edn (Berkeley: University of California Press, 2001).
Plays	Vladimir Nabokov, *The Man from the USSR and Other Plays*, trans. Dmitri Nabokov (San Diego, New York and London: Bruccoli Clark, Harcourt Brace Jovanovich Publishers, 1984).
'Playwriting'	Vladimir Nabokov, 'Playwriting', in *The Man from the USSR and Other Plays* (San Diego, New York and London: Bruccoli Clark, Harcourt Brace Jovanovich Publishers, 1984), 315–22.
P'esy	Vladimir Nabokov, *Tragediia Gospodina Morna: P'esy, lektsii o drame*, ed. Andrei Babikov (St Petersburg: Azbuka, 2008).
RLSK	Vladimir Nabokov, *The Real Life of Sebastian Knight* (London: Penguin, 1995).
Sobr. soch.	Vladimir Nabokov, *Sobranie sochinenii russkogo perioda v piati tomakh*, 5 vols. (St Petersburg: Simpozium, 1999–2000).

SM	Vladimir Nabokov, *Speak, Memory: An Autobiography Revisited* (London: Penguin, 1969).
Stories	Vladimir Nabokov, *The Collected Stories* (London: Penguin, 1997).
SO	Vladimir Nabokov, *Strong Opinions* (New York: Vintage, 1990).
VN Berg	Vladimir Nabokov Papers, New York Public Library, Henry W. and Albert A. Berg Collection of English and American Literature, Astor, Lenox and Tilden Foundations.
VNLOC	Vladimir Nabokov Papers, Library of Congress, Manuscript Division, Washington, DC.
'Tragedy'	Vladimir Nabokov, 'The Tragedy of Tragedy', in *The Man from the USSR and Other Plays* (San Diego, New York, London: Bruccoli Clark, Harcourt Brace Jovanovich Publishers, 1984), 323–42.
WI	Vladimir Nabokov, *The Waltz Invention*, trans. Dmitri Nabokov (New York: Phaedra, 1966).

Introduction

'By nature I am no dramatist', Nabokov confessed in the foreword to his screen adaptation of *Lolita*.[1] He wrote only four plays and a handful of short closet dramas during his Russian period – a rather meagre amount in comparison to the numerous novels and short stories which span both his Russian and English-language period. On the few occasions when Nabokov talked about theatre, it consistently emerges as a minor, inherently flawed art form. Initial unease seems to have finally turned into outright disgust when he equates theatre with 'group activity, that communal bath where the hairy and the slippery mix in a multiplication of mediocrity'.[2] Nabokov's statements, however, are challenged by his own practice as a writer of dramas and fiction. His plays are clearly written for the stage, imagining the stage space and utilising and interrogating the formal properties of theatrical performance. His novels are populated by characters who, although hardly ever setting foot into a theatre, are constantly involved in theatrical performances; some in such crude theatricals as the one Cincinnatus is caught in, others in more haunting and alluring illusions which keep them enveloped for the duration of the novel. Nabokov may condemn and deride the theatre as a concrete art form, but as metaphor, structural principle, theme and context, the theatre becomes an essential and pervasive element of his fiction.

Nabokov's playwriting coincides with points of rupture in Nabokov's life and work. His dramas frame his European period, marking the beginning and the end of his career as a Russian émigré writer. His first experiment in drama *The Wanderers* (*Skital'tsy*, 1923), written in 1921, was followed by the brief closet dramas *Death* (*Smert'*, 1923), *The Grandfather* (*Dedushka*, 1923) and *The Pole* (*Polius*, 1924), which eventually resulted in his first full-length drama, *The Tragedy of Mr Morn* (*Tragediia Gospodina*

---

[1] Vladimir Nabokov, *Novels 1955–1962* (New York: The Library of America, 1996), 673.
[2] *Ibid.*, 673.

Morna, written 1923–4). All of them belong to the initial stages of exile in Cambridge and Berlin. Artistically, they prepare and accompany Nabokov's transition to prose. The publication of Nabokov's first novel, *Mary* (*Mashen'ka*, 1926) – a turning point in his artistic career – is dovetailed by his second play *The Man from the USSR* (*Chelovek iz SSSR*, written 1926). Although Nabokov would later call 1926 'one of the happiest years of [his] life' (*Stories*, 648), the play articulates darker sentiments, namely the anxieties and uncertainties of the Russian émigré community in Berlin as it witnesses its own disappearance. It is around the same time that exile changes for Nabokov (and most Russian émigrés) from a temporary to a permanent condition. Nabokov would return to drama only in the late 1930s during another period of transition in his personal and artistic life. *The Event* (*Sobytie*, 1938) and *The Waltz Invention* (*Izobretenie Val'sa*, 1938) were written shortly after the move from Nazi Germany to France and with yet another departure, this time to an English-speaking country, already on the horizon. A period of radical changes encompassing linguistic, cultural and geographic moves was imminent. This is not to say that personal and artistic crises generate dramatic work, but periods of transition leave their stamp on Nabokov's plays. Drama with its inherently transitional nature (always looking ahead to its metamorphosis in the theatre) becomes a formal equivalent to wider questions of transition which are explored in the related themes of border crossing, exile and translation in Nabokov's work.

Theatrical subtexts pervade to a greater or lesser extent the whole of Nabokov's work, just as questions of exile and transition underlie directly or indirectly most of Nabokov's writings. *The Man from the USSR* continues the theme of émigré life and the exile condition from *Mary*, but as a theatrical form it feeds into the puppet theatre of *King, Queen, Knave* (*Korol', dama, valet*, 1928), a specific form of theatre which would be varied and developed in Hermann's comedic and almost perfect performance in *Despair* (*Otchaianie*, 1934). This thread of theatricality which has only occasionally surfaced in the 1920s becomes clearly visible during a phase of intense and continuous interest in theatre, which somewhat overlaps with a period of linguistic and geographical transition in Nabokov's life. Nabokov's most overtly theatrical novel, *Invitation to a Beheading* (*Priglashenie na kazn'*, 1935–6) had been prepared in a brief étude on theatrical reality in the short story 'The Leonardo' ('Korolek', 1933). *The Event* and *The Waltz Invention* trigger the theatrical short story 'Lik' (1939) about a Russian émigré actor. The close association of theatre and transition becomes once more manifest in Nabokov's subsequent novel, and his first in English, *The Real Life of Sebastian Knight* (1941), which marks a crucial turning point in Nabokov's fate as an exile. To the loss of Russia is now added the loss of language, the last firm link with his native country. This self-imposed linguistic exile informs the explicitly theatrical shape of this novel of loss, emigration and twin identities. *The Real Life of Sebastian Knight* is thus an integral part of this series of 'theatrical works'. Nabokov's theoretical ideas on drama, which he articulated after his move to the United States in his lectures on theatre at Stanford in 1941, were subsequently reworked in '"That in Aleppo Once..."' (1943) and in *Bend Sinister* (1947), both thoroughly theatrical works which are shaped by Nabokov's exilic concerns, thematising the transition between different cultures and languages. While the emergence of the theatrical theme in Nabokov's work during the 1930s and 1940s is the focus of this study, this is not to suggest that theatricality is a chronologically limited phenomenon in Nabokov's work. Nabokov's novels sustain a strand of theatricality long after he has left his dramatic work behind. Theatrical structures and themes also inform his later American novels, in the gruesome nightmare realities the amateur actress Lolita has to endure, and notably in the tragicomedy *Pnin* (1957), in Kinbote's rather creative reworkings of Shakespeare's plays or in the comedic performance which Nabokov's last published novel, *Look at the Harlequins!* (1974), puts on.

The ambiguity of Nabokov's response to the theatre – his anti-theatrical stance in lectures and interviews on the one hand and the integration of theatricality into his fiction on the other – is directly related to the essential properties of theatre, which are both points of fascination and causes of anxiety for Nabokov. Some of the aesthetic requirements of theatrical performance are difficult to reconcile with the insistence on individual authorial control, one of the fundamental principles of Nabokov's art. Theatre is an inherently collaborative art form and the consequent absence of one organising principle runs contrary to Nabokov's notion of the author as 'the perfect dictator in that private world [of fiction]' (*SO*, 69) or as the commander of his fictional 'galley slaves' (*SO*, 95). The fleeting and fickle reality of a medium which exists only for the short time of its performance and which is unable to reproduce itself exactly is a further point of contention for an artist who subscribes to a notion of eternal and absolute art and beauty. The theatricality of Nabokov's work, however, is established not only in regard to questions of concrete production, but also in the specific representational mode of theatre.

Theatre is unique among all art forms in its capacity to let the real and the imaginary (the reality of the auditorium and a fictional stage reality) physically coincide in the same space. In what one theatre semiotician has called the 'iconic identity' of theatre, the young man on stage is present as both an actor and a Danish prince trying to avenge his murdered father.[3] A piece of material on stage exists both as a painted backdrop and as a blossoming cherry orchard which is to be sold off for summer cottages. In contrast to fiction which is conditioned by the inherent absence of the object it conjures up, theatre transforms actually physically present objects and realities into something else. This is what Peter Handke describes as objects pretending to be other objects or brightness pretending to be another brightness.[4] Theatre creates a twofold vision of reality in which a location is both here and somewhere else or where time is both now and then. The gap between the here and the somewhere else is an essentially theatrical characteristic. The theatricality of Nabokov's work is located in precisely this transitional zone, in the gap between something present and its representation. It is here that Nabokov's interrogation of theatricality takes place, in transit on the famous magic carpet which is folded in such a way as to enable a simultaneous vision of different times, places and realities.

This contrapuntal perception facilitates the immediacy of a theatre production, which presents a striking contrast to the mediated reality of a book. Literature, through the necessity of having been written, records a past event, as Susan Langer points out: 'Literature projects the image of life in the mode of virtual memory', while theatre presents 'a perpetual present moment … filled with its own future'.[5] Jacques Derrida also locates the written text in the past, displacing the author from the text in the process: 'Tout graphème est d'essence testamentaire' (Every piece of writing is in essence a testament).[6] The same distinction can be made between cinema and theatre. As a markedly visual medium, theatre has naturally certain affinities with the cinema, another mode Nabokov frequently emulates in his fiction. Both theatre and cinema convey a narrative through visual representation and share the consequent reliance on actors, costumes, make-up and props. Their strong visual element makes

[3] Keir Elam, *The Semiotics of Theatre and Drama* (London: Methuen, 1980), 22–3.
[4] Peter Handke, *Publikumsbeschimpfung*, in his *Theaterstücke* (Frankfurt am Main: Suhrkamp, 1992), 18.
[5] Susanne K. Langer, *Feeling and Form: A Theory of Art Developed from Philosophy in a New Key* (London: Routledge and Kegan Paul, 1953), 306 and 307.
[6] Jacques Derrida, *De la grammatologie* (Paris: Éditions de Minuit, 1967), 100.

them especially suitable for a vivid depiction of the sudden collapse of a fictional world. At the end of *Bend Sinister*, for example, theatrical and cinematic imagery are fused in the exposure of the novel's world as artifice. Theatre and film are also combined in *Mary*, where the protagonist works as a film extra in a crowd scene set in a theatre. In the subsequent play *The Man from the USSR*, a film set exposes the illusionary nature of the stage reality which encloses it so that cinematic and theatrical reality cancel each other out. Yet, like literature, cinema presents a mediated reality from some point in the past, while theatre is exclusively bound to the present tense, as Peter Brook notes:

There is only one interesting difference between the cinema and the theatre. The cinema flashes on to a screen images from the past. As this is what the mind does to itself all through life, the cinema seems intimately real. Of course, it is nothing of the sort – it is a satisfying and enjoyable extension of the unreality of everyday perception. The theatre, on the other hand, always asserts itself in the present. This is what can make it more real than the normal stream of consciousness. This also is what can make it so disturbing.[7]

Cinema's past mode, in contrast to theatre's present mode, positions it much closer to narrative fiction than theatre. Like a book, the medium itself becomes transparent during its reception. The cinematic mode essentially emulates the mode of narrative fiction, replacing the film which runs before the inner eye of the reader, with an actual visualisation of the narrative.[8]

The immediacy of the theatrical performance conditions the inherent imperfection of the theatrical illusion. The overlap of production and reception in the theatre exposes the concrete production of a fictional reality. In this process, theatre points to itself as an artistic medium, laying bare its own devices. In contrast, 'the printed text is largely "transparent" as a medium, indicating an imaginative world from which the book itself recedes during the reading process'.[9] The theatrical illusion is therefore never absolute unlike the fictional worlds of literature or cinema. The process of fictional construction is frequently an integral part of Nabokov's

[7] Peter Brook, *The Empty Space* (London: McGibbon and Kee, 1968), 99.
[8] In her study on Nabokov and cinema in the wider context of modern American literature, Barbara Wyllie demonstrates cinematic influences on specifically narrative techniques in Nabokov's fiction, i.e. narrative perspective (the point of view as a camera eye), narrative pace, narrative control and narrative tone (*film noir* and screwball comedy), which implicitly confirm the closeness of cinema and narrative fiction (see her *Nabokov at the Movies: Film Perspectives in Fiction* (Jefferson, NC and London: McFarland, 2003).
[9] Stanton B. Garner, Jr, *The Absent Voice: Narrative Comprehension in the Theater* (Urbana: University of Illinois Press, 1989), xi.

novels, as in *Despair* or *The Gift* (*Dar*, 1937–8), novels which are in the process of being written while being read. Vladislav Khodasevich, a fellow émigré and one of Nabokov's most perceptive critics, was the first to notice the specifically theatrical dimension of these devices in Nabokov's fiction:

> [Nabokov's] works are populated not only by his fictional characters, but also by a great multitude of devices, reminiscent of elves or gnomes, who dashing back and forth among the characters, perform a gigantic task: before the spectators' eyes they saw, cut, nail and paint, erecting and changing the settings between which the play is staged.[10]

The audience's interaction with the stage is an integral part of the theatrical performance. The spectators in the theatre constitute an essential other against which the actual performance is defined. The audience therefore establishes and maintains a different reality, which sustains the inherently twofold reality of theatre. An essential entity in the creative process, the audience corroborates the performance, as Carlson points out: 'Performance is always performance *for* someone, some audience that recognizes and validates it as performance even when, as is occasionally the case, that audience is the self.'[11] The recognition of the performance relies on the distance between self and other, in both the audience and the performers, which sustains the theatre's peculiar double vision throughout.

Richard Bauman suggests that performance is conditioned by a twofold perception which differentiates between 'the actual execution of an action' and the 'capacities, models, or other factors that represent the potential for such action or an abstraction from it'.[12] Richard Schechner thinks along similar lines when he defines performance as 'restored behaviour', implying like Bauman a pre-existing model which is re-enacted in performance.[13] Nabokov sees the theatre primarily in its relation to the scripted drama text. Central to his thinking is the implied notion of the theatrical performance as relying on a pre-existing, original drama text which is enacted in the theatre. Taking the Western stage tradition of modern drama as a paradigm of theatre, this notion ignores, of course, the whole

[10] Vladislav Khodasevich, 'O Sirine', *Vozrozhdenie*, 13 February 1937, 9. Reprinted in his *Sobranie sochinenii v chetyrekh tomakh* (Moscow: Soglasie, 1996–7), vol. II, 388–95 [391].
[11] Marvin Carlson, *Performance: A Critical Introduction* (London and New York: Routledge, 1996), 5–6.
[12] Richard Baumann, 'Performance', in Erik Barnow (ed.), *The International Encyclopedia of Communications* (New York and Oxford: Oxford University Press, 1989), 262–6 [262].
[13] See Richard Schechner, *Between Theater and Anthropology* (Philadelphia: University of Pennsylvania Press, 1985), 35–116.

area of possible performances without a drama text as their base which can be found in, for instance, experimental or non-Western theatre forms. Within this rather conventional concept, theatre emerges as an ambivalent art form which negotiates its position between the scripted drama and the performance in the theatre. Closely connected with the split of the theatrical process into a dramatic written text and a theatrical performance is the absence of the playwright from the actual theatrical performance in the theatre. The drama text is removed from the playwright's control and translated into a new artistic medium. In the process, the theatrical performance becomes de-centred and loses a clearly discernible origin. In Nabokov's mind this issue of what could be termed 'theatrical translation' is associated with the wider question of faithful translation of a text and the author's control or lack of control over his texts. Theatre thus crystallises pivotal concerns of Nabokov's art, questions of authorial control and textual property in relation to linguistic, cultural and theatrical translation.

The theatricality of Nabokov's work is framed by wider concerns of exile as a personal experience and an artistic condition. The fleeting reality and impermanence of the exile existence corresponds with the unique and temporary nature of theatre performances, while the 'contrapuntal vision' characteristic of the exile condition, which Edward Said and other theoreticians of exile have noted, finds a formal equivalent in the twofold perception of a theatre performance.[14] The playwright's dependence on the theatrical performance to realise his or her work provides an analogy for the exiled writer's reliance on linguistic and cultural translation to give a (strange) voice to his or her work. Removed from the immediate control of their creators, theatrical performance and translation develop a certain degree of autonomy. The exiled author and the playwright remain in the wings, the marginal spaces off the centre, conspicuous only by their absence.

The absent author is a commonplace in much of twentieth-century literary theory. Expelled from the text by Formalists and New Critics, the author was allowed a cautious return in the ghostly figure of the 'implied author', only to be eventually assassinated (in the heady days of 1968) by Barthes. The author has vanished (at least in theory) from the text as a source of origin or a source of intention. The text has thus become uprooted, a de-centred autonomous entity the coherence and unity of which is determined by itself or by its readers. Nabokov's work

---

[14] See, for instance, Edward Said, 'Reflections on Exile', in his *Reflections on Exile and Other Essays* (Cambridge, MA: Harvard University Press, 2000), 173–86; Michael Seidel, *Exile and the Narrative Imagination* (New Haven: Yale University Press, 1986).

shapes and is shaped by this literary discourse about the status of the author. With fierce insistence on his privacy, Nabokov denied any form of discernible personal presence or traces in life or text: 'I hate tampering with the precious lives of great writers and I hate Tom-peeping over the fence of those lives ... and no biographer will ever catch a glimpse of my private life.'[15] Elsewhere he insisted that it 'is pretty useless to deduce the life history and human form of a poet from his work; and the greater the artist the more likely it is for us to arrive at erroneous conclusions'.[16] Paradoxically though, it is this very absence which produces the God-like invisible presence of some form of authorial control beyond and above Nabokov's texts. The rather crass appearance of Nabokov himself at the end of his second novel, *King, Queen, Knave*, is only one of many authorial manifestations which become ever more complex during the course of his career. It is somewhere between the implied author, who is a largely ideological category, and the fictional author, who is part of the fictional world, that Nabokov locates glimpses, reflections, shadows of himself and his fictional representatives, in the form of an authorial principle or an artistic structure which interacts with and consciously shapes the text. A large part of Nabokov's work rests on this tension between the absence of the empirical writer and the presence of some authorial principle in the text, between Nabokov's absence and the traces of what in *Lolita* (1955) would become McFate's presence in the text. In the later stages of Nabokov's career, with increasing public exposure, the space 'in between' is taken over by the stylised, thoroughly theatrical persona VN. Nabokov's enactment of the conceited, strongly opinionated, sharp and witty author-figure extends the space of the fictional and shields the real author from preying eyes. Theatricality emerges yet again from a gap, the no-man's-land between reality and fiction, self and persona, the actor and his role, Nabokov and his fictional or implied representatives.

It would be going too far to say that Nabokov's plays are *terra incognita*, but until very recently they have occupied a forgotten niche in what is otherwise the thoroughly explored and classified territory of Nabokov studies. Although Nabokov had most of his Russian works translated into English after *Lolita* brought him worldwide fame, he was much less successful with the translation of his dramas, apart from *The Waltz Invention* which

---

[15] Vladimir Nabokov, *Lectures on Russian Literature*, ed. Fredson Bowers (San Diego, New York and London: Bruccoli Clark Layman, Harcourt Brace and Company, 1981), 138.
[16] *The Song of Igor's Campaign*, trans. Vladimir Nabokov (Woodstock, NY and New York: Ardis, 1988), 79.

was translated into English by his son Dmitri Nabokov in the mid-1960s.[17] During his lifetime, *The Event* was not published in English translation, while his first two plays, *The Tragedy of Mr Morn* and *The Man from the USSR*, remained unpublished. Of *The Tragedy of Mr Morn* only an incomplete manuscript, given by Nabokov to the Library of Congress for mere tax reasons, survives.[18] In 1990, Ardis still planned to publish one volume of Nabokov's complete dramas as part of the collected works in Russian, to be supervised by Véra Nabokov.[19] This project was, however, abandoned after the collapse of the Soviet Union, when Nabokov's work began to be published in his native country. The Russian plays available from émigré journals were collected into one volume in 1990, but the collection included only the first act of *The Man from the USSR*, while *The Tragedy of Mr Morn* was left out.[20] The latter appeared in print in *Zvezda*, the accuracy of which was compromised by a number of mistakes and misprints.[21] Until very recently, Nabokov's complete dramatic works had been published only in German translation as part of the Rowohlt edition of Nabokov's collected works.[22] A distinct turning point in this state of affairs was the recent publication of an excellent edition of Nabokov's plays in Russian, prepared by Andrei Babikov.[23] As the first and only comprehensive, accurate edition which contains all of Nabokov's available dramatic works in the original, this volume has opened the way for a thorough assessment of Nabokov's dramatic work. For the English reader, *The Man from the USSR*, *The Event* and the early verse plays *The Pole* and *The Grandfather* were published in translation by Dmitri Nabokov.[24] This edition was the first to include also two of the thematically related lectures on drama.

---

[17] An English translation of *The Waltz Invention* was initially unsuccessfully offered to the *Playboy*. See A. C. Spectorsky to Carmen Pomroy, 16 April 1965, VN Berg.

[18] See Brian Boyd, *Vladimir Nabokov: The American Years* (London: Vintage, 1991), 367.

[19] See Dieter E. Zimmer, 'Nachwort des Herausgebers', in Vladimir Nabokov, *Gesammelte Werke*, vol. XV/i (*Dramen*), ed. Dieter E. Zimmer (Reinbeck: Rowohlt, 2000), 563–78 [578]; Dmitri Nabokov, 'Nabokov and the Theatre', in *The Man from the USSR and other Plays*, trans. Dmitri Nabokov (San Diego, New York and London: Bruccoli Clark, Harcourt Brace Jovanovich Publishers, 1984), 3–26 [26].

[20] Vladimir Nabokov, *P'esy*, ed. Ivan Tolstoi (Moscow: Iskusstvo, 1990). The same material was also published in the Simpozium edition as part of Nabokov's collected works in Russian (Vladimir Nabokov, *Sobranie sochinenii russkogo perioda v piati tomakh* (St Petersburg: Simpozium, 1999–2000)).

[21] Vladimir Nabokov, 'Tragediia Gospodina Morna', *Zvezda*, 4 (1997), 9–98.

[22] Nabokov, *Gesammelte Werke*, vol. XV/i (*Dramen*). The translations are mainly based on the Russian galley proofs of the envisioned Ardis edition, as well as on some manuscripts.

[23] Vladimir Nabokov, *Tragediia Gospodina Morna: P'esy, lektsii o drame*, ed. Andrei Babikov (St Petersburg: Azbuka, 2008).

[24] Nabokov, *Plays*.

Given that Nabokov's dramas are not widely read, it is perhaps unsurprising that they are not very popular with stage performers either. During Nabokov's lifetime, *The Tragedy of Mr Morn* was never realised on stage, while *The Man from the USSR* was limited to only two productions in Berlin in 1927. *The Event* is the only play which could be considered a relative success, with four performances in a Paris émigré theatre in 1938. In the following years it became known also outside of Paris, but only in Russian émigré circles, while *The Waltz Invention* was not staged for thirty years.[25] *The Waltz Invention* reached a rather limited Western audience for the first time at the end of the 1960s in student productions.[26] The interest in Nabokov's plays and the staging of his novels has been more manifest in Russia, especially during *perestroika*, when formerly forbidden authors and playwrights gained prominence on the stage.[27] More recently, *The Event* was staged at the Nabokov Museum in St Petersburg and has also been adapted for the cinema by Andrei Eshpai.[28] Through the publication of the recent Russian edition of Nabokov's plays, the script for *The Man from the USSR* became for the first time available to Russian theatre practitioners and the play was performed at the Sfera Theatre in Moscow in 2009. Yet it has been the adaptations of Nabokov's novels which have been widely staged in Russia rather than his actual plays.[29]

---

[25] *The Event* was staged by Russian émigré theatres in Prague, Warsaw and Belgrade.

[26] The world premiere of *The Waltz Invention* was a rather modest affair at the Oxford University Russian Club under the direction of David Bellos in 1968 (see Véra Nabokov and David Bellos, misc. correspondence (1967–8), VN Berg; author's personal correspondence with David Bellos, 27 March 2002; Boyd, *American Years*. 529). A year later the play had its English premiere in Hartford, Connecticut (see Boyd, *American Years*, 576; 'Repertory: Nabokov in Embryo', *Time*, 24 January 1969). Since then the play has been staged only once more outside of Russia. In 1998, *The Waltz Invention* was taken up by the Strawdog Theatre Company, Chicago, under the direction of Nic Dimond (see Richard Christiansen, 'A Bizarre but Problematic Tragifarce', *Chicago Tribune*, 7 May 1998, 2).

[27] *The Waltz Invention* was directed, for instance, by Adolf Shapiro at the 'TIUZ' in Riga in 1988. For reviews see: G. Karpalov, '"Izobretenie Val'sa"', *Pravda*, 20 December 1988, 3; E. Matsekha, 'Nekto v serom zadaet zagadki: V. Nabokov na stsene Rizh. TIUZa', *Izvestiia*, 2 May 1989, 4; Roman Timenchik, 'Chitaem Nabokova: "Izobretenie Val'sa" v postanovke Adol'fa Shapiro', *Rodnik* 10 (1988), 46–8. *The Event* was staged, for instance, under the direction of Lev Rakhlin at the theatre studio 'Narodnyi dom' in Leningrad in 1989. For reviews see: T. Putrenko, 'Bednyi Nabokov', *Literaturnaia gazeta*, 14 December 1988, 8; Ivan Tolstoi, 'Preodolenie steny: P'esy Vladimira Nabokova "Sobytie" i "Izobretenie Val'sa" v Leningrade i Rige', *Zvezda*, 7 (1989), 203–6.

[28] See Christine Engel, 'Andrei Eshpai: *The Event* (*Sobytie*, 2007)', *KinoKultura: New Russian Cinema*, 26 (2009) (www.kinokultura.com/2009/23r-sobytie.shtml).

[29] Andrea Tompa, 'Staging Nabokov', *Nabokov Online Journal*, 2 (2008) (http://etc.dal.ca/noj/volume2/articles/09_Tompa.pdf).

With few exceptions, contemporary reviewers and more recent critics have been noticeably unenthusiastic about Nabokov's dramatic work.[30] One of the points of criticism after the staging of his first play, *The Man from the USSR*, was that it distinctly lacked dramatic action.[31] Similar charges were made against the much later *The Event* which received mixed reviews after its premiere. While some praised what they saw as dramatic innovation, others voiced their puzzlement and disappointment at a play that seemed to lack any dramatic development. In his first review of *The Event*, even Khodasevich, usually one of Nabokov's most admiring critics, concluded that 'from a literary point of view, [the play] does not belong to the best works of this author'.[32] Nabokov's next play, *The Waltz Invention*, was almost completely debunked by most critics. Georgii Adamovich, for instance, implied that the play was written hastily and carelessly and called it a 'tritely utopian story'.[33] One might explain Adamovich's dismissal as being just another dig at Nabokov in their long-standing feud, but Edmund Wilson in 1943, long before the disagreement over the translation of Pushkin's *Evgenii Onegin* would make him and Nabokov enemies, offered a similar opinion:

Mary [McCarthy, Wilson's wife] and I have both read it [*The Waltz Invention*] and think it not one of your best productions. I doubt whether you could get it produced. The first scenes amused me, but I don't think there is enough to the idea to make it last through three acts – also, the unreality of everything gets on the reader's nerves before he understands that it is all a fantasy in the madman's mind; when he does find that out, he feels sold. (*NWL*, 108)

More recent critics have echoed these negative assessments of *The Waltz Invention*.[34] As a general assessment of Nabokov's playwriting skills, Diment states that 'Vladimir Nabokov will probably not be remembered

---

[30] Only two critics maintain that Nabokov is an outstanding dramatist who still has not been given the recognition he deserves. See René Guerra, 'Vladimir Nabokov v neprivychnoi ipostasi: Zametki o dvukh poslednikh p'esakh Nabokova-Sirina "Sobytie" i "Izobretenie Val'sa"', *Kontinent*, 45 (1985), 367–79; René Guerra, 'Ob odnoi zabytoi p'ese Vladimira Nabokova', in Vsevolod Sechkarev (ed.), *Otkliki: Sbornik statei pamiati Nikolaia Ivanovicha Ul'ianova (1904–1985)* (New Haven, 1986), 97–119; Andrei Babikov, '*The Event* and the Main Thing in Nabokov's Theory of Drama', *Nabokov Studies*, 7 (2002/3), 151–76.

[31] Boris Brodskii, 'Chelovek iz SSSR (Na postanovke p'esy V. Sirina)', *Rul'*, 5 April 1927, 5.

[32] Vladislav Khodasevich, '"Russkie zapiski", aprel' – iiul', *Vozrozhdenie*, 22 July 1938, 9.

[33] Georgii Adamovich, 'Rets.: *Russkie zapiski*, 1938, no 11', *Poslednie novosti*, 24 November 1938, 3. Reprinted in N. G. Mel'nikov and O. A. Korosteleva (eds.), *Klassik bez retushi: Literaturnyi mir o tvorchestve Vladimira Nabokova* (Moscow: Novoe literaturnoe obozrenie, 2000), 175–6 [176].

[34] See Brian Boyd, *Vladimir Nabokov: The Russian Years* (Princeton University Press, 1990), 491; Galya Diment, 'Plays', in Vladimir E. Alexandrov (ed.), *The Garland Companion to Vladimir Nabokov* (New York: Garland, 1995), 586–99 [594].

by posterity as a great playwright',[35] while Boyd sums up Nabokov's difficulties as a dramatist memorably: 'For Nabokov writing for the stage was
like playing chess without his queen.'[36] Elsewhere Boyd offers the following explanation: '[Nabokov] is a novelist, a poet, a master of the hidden
resonances and the delayed inferences that the printed page can accommodate but stage or screen cannot ... his respect for fact means that in
drama he adheres to the limitations of real conversation: he will not per-
mit characters to speak with the eloquence he can achieve with pencil
and eraser and time.'[37] Nabokov's wider work tends to be viewed through
the prism of his brilliance as an experienced novelist, the author of works
such as *The Gift* which for some would be one of the greatest Russian
novels of the twentieth century. There seems to be a sense of disappointment among Nabokov's contemporary reviewers and more recent critics,
as if his novels raised expectations which his dramas cannot fulfil.

This generally negative assessment has done little to encourage any sys-
tematic analysis of Nabokov's dramatic art to date. There are only a handful of articles which deal with Nabokov's plays. The first critic to turn to
Nabokov's plays was Simon Karlinsky.[38] His analysis of Russian subtexts
in the plays seems to have set the tone for subsequent studies in that it
treats the dramas as literary texts in dramatic form. Subsequent criticism
related to Nabokov's dramatic oeuvre also tends to concentrate on charac-
terisation, ethical and metaphysical problems, and dramatic and literary
subtexts – in short on mimetic rather than performative features of the
plays. The drama script is therefore treated in the same way as other literary texts, without considering the theatrical performance, projected and
inscribed into Nabokov's drama texts.[39] Babikov goes so far as to state
that 'the real spectator of Nabokov's *The Event* and *The Waltz Invention*
is, strange as it may seem, a reader'.[40] This approach to Nabokov's dramas
seems to have become all-pervasive in that it even influences the evaluation of an actual theatre performance. Roman Timenchik's review of

[35] Diment, 'Plays', 586.   [36] Boyd, *Russian Years*, 482.
[37] Boyd, *American Years*, 413.
[38] See Simon Karlinsky, 'Illusion, Reality and Parody in Nabokov's Plays', in L. S. Dembo,
Nabokov: The Man and His Work (Madison: University of Wisconsin Press, 1967), 183–94.
[39] See, for instance, Boyd, *Russian Years*, 222–6; 263–7; 480–5; 489–92; Aleksandr Dolinin,
'Istinnaia zhizn' pisatelia Sirina: Posle "Dara"', in *Sobr. soch.*, 5, 9–39; Guerra, 'Zametki o dvukh
poslednikh p'esakh'; Guerra, 'Ob odnoi zabytoi p'ese Vladimira Nabokova'. A more recent study
chooses a similar approach, suggesting all sorts of literary subtexts for Nabokov's *The Event*,
which would remain inaccessible to any spectator in the immediacy of a theatrical performance
(see Babikov, 'The Main Thing').
[40] Andrei Babikov, 'Izobretenie teatra', in *P'esy*, 5–42 [39].

Alfred Shapiro's staging of *The Waltz Invention* is telling in its praise of the distinctive 'literary' quality of the production:

The production itself behaves like a reader: it obediently follows the blind alleys of meaning, conscientiously announces those passages which have not been fully understood but are intriguing, re-reads again particularly interesting bits and only cursorily glances at those which seem to hold no mystery. In other words, the theatre emphasises its respectful yet not subservient attitude towards the text.[41]

An exception in this general trend is Dmitri Nabokov's excellent introduction to his father's plays.[42] Coming from the perspective of a former opera singer, he has an acute sensitivity to the performance potential of Nabokov's dramas.

This focus on the literary and textual aspects of his plays has left Nabokov's wider theatrical side unexplored. That his essentially theatrical imagination inhabits not only his plays and his overtly theatrical novel *Invitation to a Beheading*, but also his other fiction, has been largely neglected in discussions to date. While Nabokov's engagement with art forms other than fiction has recently been given increasing attention, there is no study which concentrates on the theatricality of Nabokov's narrative fiction.[43] If noted at all, the theatricality in Nabokov's work tends to

---

[41] Timenchik, 'Chitaem Nabokova', 46.

[42] Nabokov, 'Nabokov and the Theatre', 3–26.

[43] There are four monographs focusing on Nabokov's interaction with other art forms: Alfred Appel, Jr, *Nabokov's Dark Cinema* (New York: Oxford University Press, 1974); Wyllie, *Nabokov at the Movies*; Gerard de Vries and Donald Barton Johnson, *Nabokov and the Art of Painting* (Amsterdam University Press, 2006); Gavriel Shapiro, *The Sublime Artist's Studio: Nabokov and Painting* (Evanston, IL: Northwestern University Press, 2009). A collection of interdisciplinary essays, edited by Lisa Zunshine, while performing the valuable service of highlighting Nabokov's interaction with other art forms does not contain a single piece on his theatre (see *Nabokov at the Limits: Redrawing Critical Boundaries* (New York and London: Garland, 1999)). Apart from studies on music, ballet and pictorial art in that volume, there are several individual articles dealing with similar issues. For Nabokov and music, see Nora Bukhs, 'The Novel Waltz (On the Structure of *King, Queen, Knave*)', zembla (www.libraries.psu.edu/iasweb/nabokov/forians.htm) (trans. from the French: 'Sur la structure du roman de Vl. Nabokov *Roi, Dame, Valet*', *Revue des études slaves*, 59/4 (1987), 799–810); Nassim W. Balestrini, 'Art and Marriage in Vladimir Nabokov's "Music" and Lev Tolstoy's "The Kreutzer Sonata"', in Steven G. Kellman and Irving Malin (eds.), *Torpid Smoke: The Stories of Vladimir Nabokov* (Amsterdam and Atlanta, GA: Rodopi, 2000), 53–73. For Nabokov and painting, see Neil Cornwell, 'Paintings, Governesses and "Publishing Scoundrels": Nabokov and Henry James', in Jane Grayson, Arnold McMillin and Priscilla Meyer (eds.), *Nabokov's World*, vol. II: *Reading Nabokov* (Basingstoke: Palgrave, 2002), 96–116; Susan E. Sweeney, 'Looking at Harlequins: Nabokov, The World of Art and the Ballets Russes', in Grayson, McMillin and Meyer, *Nabokov's* World, vol. II, 73–95; Gavriel Shapiro, 'Nabokov and Early Netherlandish Art', in Gavriel Shapiro (ed.), *Nabokov at Cornell* (Ithaca, NY and London: Cornell University Press, 2003), 241–50. For Nabokov and cartoons, see Clarence Brown, 'Krazy, Ignatz, and Vladimir: Nabokov and the Comic Strip', in Shapiro (ed.), *Nabokov at Cornell*, 251–63. For Nabokov and ballet, see Sweeney, 'Looking at Harlequins'.

be mentioned only in passing, with the implication that Nabokov uses theatre to denote the topos of the world as stage.[44] In this view, theatre becomes a means to emphasise the artifice of the (fictional) world and its crafty deception, which in turn implies the existence of a stable creator behind this world.[45] Ivan Tolstoi, in his introduction to the Russian edition of Nabokov's plays, chooses a different angle when he considers the explicitly visual quality of Nabokov's novels as a stage-like feature: 'Essentially his whole prose is staged [*mizanstsenirovana*] and theatricalized. It is a stylistic particularity of his books that the text, just like a decorated stage, is full of those characteristic details which bring the world to life.'[46] Elsewhere he sees the fourth-wall convention as a paradigm for the strict separation into objective and imagined reality, which Nabokov applies from the illusionist theatre to his novels.[47] Tolstoi is the only critic who considers the integration of a feature of a theatrical performance in Nabokov's work, albeit without developing it in any detail.

The deployment of theatricality in the novel has recently attracted increasing interest in literary criticism.[48] In particular, in regard to the Victorian novel, theatricality has been widely examined in its function as a metaphor for the discrepancy between a person's internal emotional state and external behaviour, or as a model for self-fashioning and self-definition.[49] Attention has also been paid to the interaction between the novel and the theatre as socio-historical and cultural phenomena.[50] In this

---

[44] See Drury Pifer, 'Le théâtre et le monde', *Europe: Revue littéraire mensuelle*, 791 (March 1995), 57–63.

[45] See, for instance, Alfred Appel, Jr, 'Introduction', in Vladimir Nabokov, *The Annotated Lolita*, ed. Alfred Appel, Jr (London: Penguin, 1995), xvii–lxvii [xvii–xxxiii]; Vladimir Alexandrov, *Nabokov's Otherworld* (Princeton University Press, 1991), 138, 232–3; Guerra 'Zametki o dvukh poslednikh p'esakh', 389.

[46] Ivan Tolstoi, 'Nabokov i ego teatral'noe nasledie', in Nabokov, *P'esy*, ed. Tolstoi, 5–42 [42].

[47] See Tolstoi, 'Preodolenie steny'.

[48] See, for instance, Linzy Erika Dickinson, *Theatre in Balzac's* La Comédie humaine (Amsterdam and Atlanta, GA: Rodopi, 2000); Albert Ettinger, *Der Epiker als Theatraliker: Thomas Manns Beziehung zum Theater in seinem Leben und Werk* (Frankfurt am Main: Peter Lang, 1988); Christopher Greenwood, *Adapting to the Stage: Theatre and the Work of Henry James* (Aldershot, Burlington: Ashgate, 2000).

[49] See, for instance, Charlene E. Bunnell, *'All the World's a Stage': Dramatic Sensibility in Mary Shelley's Novels* (New York and London: Routledge, 2002); Paula Byrne, *Jane Austen and the Theatre* (London: Hambledon and London, 2002); Penny Gay, *Jane Austen and the Theatre* (Cambridge University Press, 2002); Joseph Litvak, *Caught in the Act: Theatricality in the Nineteenth-Century English Novel* (Berkeley and Oxford: University of California Press, 1992).

[50] Jeffrey J. Franklin, *Serious Play: The Cultural Form of the Nineteenth-Century Realist Novel* (Philadelphia: University of Pennsylvania Press, 1999), 80–131; Deborah Vlock, *Dickens, Novel Reading, and the Victorian Popular Theatre* (Cambridge University Press, 1998); Martin Huber, *Der Text als Bühne: Theatrales Erzählen um 1800* (Göttingen: Vandenhoeck und Ruprecht, 2003).

book, I address a different set of questions by focusing on the interaction between two distinct art forms, theatre and literature. In the chapters that follow, I trace the various forms and guises under which theatrical performance enters Nabokov's work and examine how Nabokov integrates the theatrical mode as a structural device into his novels, how his novels negotiate their position in the border region where they meet another art form, theatre, and how they emulate, appropriate and resist theatrical properties.

The first chapter ('Trying theatre') maps Nabokov's encounters with theatrical art, tracing the contours of his engagement with the theatre as theatre-goer, playwright and, to a lesser extent, performer during his formative years in Silver Age St Petersburg and later in the context of Russian émigré theatre in the 1920s and 1930s. Traces of Nabokov's fascination with theatrical art appear in the margins of contemporary émigré newspapers and in some of his personal letters, which have survived in archives. At the same time, long periods during which Nabokov did not show any pronounced interest in the theatre testify to little interest and perhaps even indifference, which only changes once playwriting offers a way of adding a bit of income during the financially desperate situation of the late 1930s. The complex historical and cultural conditions which shaped Nabokov's own playwriting and the fragmented nature of his engagement with the theatrical art thwart a clear outline of a consistent or coherent attitude towards drama during this time. Nabokov's experience of the theatrical life of pre-revolutionary St Petersburg and perhaps more important of Russian émigré communities in Berlin and Paris provides the backdrop against which Nabokov's more theoretical considerations of the theatre can be assessed in the next chapter ('Theatre on trial'). The various forms of Nabokov's interest in the actual performance of at least his own plays have disappeared in the lectures in which Nabokov polemicises against contemporary theatre practice and the eclipse of the playwright in the actual performance. Taken together, these two chapters explore Nabokov's contradictory views as a playwright and as a critic in relation to the competing ways of perceiving a drama in print and in performance.

This discrepancy is highlighted by Nabokov's practice as a dramatist. His plays are written for performance not only in their reliance on the stage for enactment or effect, but in the exploration of their own medium, theatrical performance. Despite their different tones and subject matters, all of his plays are concerned with the instability of reality and its precarious, illusory nature. The confrontation of different realities which challenge and subvert each other is a central theme in all of his plays. Theatre, as a place where illusion and disillusionment, fiction and reality are placed so closely together, becomes a suitable artistic form which reflects metaphorically the protagonists' (self-)delusions and deceptions. Chapter 3 ('Thresholds and transgressions') and 4 ('Theatre dreams') examine the different and in some respect contradictory functions Nabokov ascribes to theatrical performance in his four plays, the theatre as a 'disenchanting' art which exposes its own artificial devices in a necessarily imperfect illusion and theatre as a captivating dream which achieves a certain level of independence, evoking the Romantic myth of the autonomous existence of art outside the control of its author. Both chapters observe and contrast the translation of these different functions into Nabokov's theatre novel *Invitation to a Beheading* and related short fiction.

The last two chapters focus exclusively on Nabokov's way of integrating theatricality into his novels and short stories – literary forms which have little if any apparent link with the performance side of theatre. Nabokov shifts the focus here from the twofold reality of the stage to the potentially competitive duality of script and stage. Chapter 5 ('Puppets and masks') looks at specific theatrical forms, the puppet theatre and the *commedia dell'arte*, as models through which Nabokov explores the relationship between the dramatic script and theatrical performance. The puppets in *King, Queen, Knave* and the commedia masks in *Despair* are employed to examine the different ways in which the author's script is followed, challenged or subverted in the characters' performance. While Nabokov's interest in and creative reworkings of puppets and masks is by no means limited to these two novels, in *Despair* and *King, Queen, Knave*, he probes the aesthetic properties and conventions of two distinct theatrical forms, before theatre would become a wider, less clearly defined theme in Nabokov's work. By the time he writes his first English novel, the disappearance of the author Sirin seems to prompt the writer Nabokov to undertake ever more subtle and intricate explorations of authorship and authorial control in his fiction. The vanishing author, whether real or imagined, finds a precise reflection in the equally mysterious figure of Shakespeare. The final chapter ('Shakespeare's ghost') traces instances of Shakespeare's presence in Nabokov's early English works. Zealous biographers, editors and translators take the place of ever more receding authors, who lose control over their work and its performance.

Rejection and fascination, textual control and textual autonomy, the commander of the 'galley slaves' and the absent author, the historical

writer and the authorial principle, Nabokov and VN, dangerous delusion and alluring illusion, the permanence of the written text and the
ephemeral nature of theatre, the belonging of printed matter and the
uprooted theatre performance – these, then, are the poles between which
Nabokov's engagement with theatre and theatricality is played out. In
some way, this book is also a study in gaps or a study in thresholds marking the blurred transitional spaces between different realms in Nabokov's
fictional worlds.

1

Trying theatre: Nabokov's playwriting

Nabokov introduced his lectures on theatre by declaring that 'the art of staging and acting [is] a great art … which I love ardently' ('Tragedy', 323), but it is difficult to find evidence of this passion in Nabokov either as theatre-goer or as playwright. Nabokov was neither passionately in love with the stage nor seduced by its masks, costumes and performers. Nabokov's 'ardent love' was of a more fleeting nature, flaring up only to fizzle out shortly afterwards. His initial verse dramas were not even written for the stage; they are closet dramas marking a period of artistic transition from poetry to prose. Only three of his plays were written clearly for theatrical performance, in the mid-twenties and the late thirties. In between these periods Nabokov showed little interest in theatrical performance. To some extent, this wavering attitude can be explained not so much by personal or artistic indifference but by the temporary and impermanent existence of the Russian émigré theatres in Berlin and Paris. Nabokov did not actively seek but rather responded to opportunities for the staging of plays, which arose at irregular intervals. More than any other art form, the Russian theatre abroad closely mirrored the psychological, artistic and financial uncertainty of the émigré condition. Removed from its native country, Russian theatre became a most fragile art form, costly to maintain, and with only limited prospects for artistic and financial rewards.

Artistically, the plays written for performance are closely linked to the Russian émigré theatre of the 1920s and 1930s. Nabokov's dramas are firmly grounded in the Russian drama and stage tradition. During his time in exile, Nabokov remained rather detached and aloof from the theatrical cultures of his host countries. Nabokov's plays have to be seen within the confines of the Russian emigration and its collective nostalgia for pre-revolutionary Russian culture, in particular Russia's Silver Age. The preference for this cultural era in the Russian emigration emerged from the notion of its 'authentically Russian character', which had not yet been corrupted by avant-garde art or Constructivism, both of which became associated with Soviet culture.

Nabokov grew up in a highly educated and cultured family that played an active role in St Petersburg cultural life. From an early age onwards, he was exposed to contemporary painting, music and the performing arts. Nabokov's father, V. D. Nabokov, was a keen theatre-goer who was eager not to miss any theatrical event.[1] Boyd states that 'as a young parent [V. D. Nabokov] continued to frequent the theatre and opera regularly, often with his children in tow'.[2] Yet, like many Russian children of his generation, Nabokov's first contact with the theatre was probably not through high culture, but through the Petrushka puppet play or *balagan*, the Russian version of Punch and Judy, a popular entertainment at Russian fairs, which by the late nineteenth century had become a widespread entertainment for children of all social classes with puppeteers being frequently employed to perform at children's parties.[3]

Rejecting conventional realism, the cultural life of pre-revolutionary St Petersburg was pervaded by a spirit of self-conscious theatricality.[4] Popular theatre, like the Petrushka play and the Italian *commedia dell'arte*, was appropriated by and reworked into Russian high culture to explore the world of dreams, fantasies and illusions. In a celebration of nostalgia, elegance and aesthetic refinement, the Petrushka play and the commedia were taken up and developed in a variety of art forms including literature, painting, ballet and theatre by the somewhat overlapping artistic

---

[1] V. D. Nabokov's sister, Nadezhda, remembered that her brother used to go to the theatre every evening (see Boyd, *Russian Years*, 44). In the early 1920s, V. D. Nabokov wrote a series of articles in which he remembered the performing arts, including the theatre, ballet and opera of pre-revolutionary Russia for the émigré journal *Theatre and Life* (*Teatr i zhizn'*). He also belonged to the Russian émigré committee in Berlin which welcomed a splinter group of the Moscow Art Theatre under the leadership of Vasilii Kachalov (see Michaela Böhmig, *Das russische Theater 1919–1931* (Munich: Otto Sagner, 1990), 74).

[2] Boyd, *Russian Years*, 40.

[3] Catriona Kelly, *Petrushka: The Russian Carnival Puppet Theatre* (Cambridge University Press, 1990), 55.

[4] Savely Senderovich and Elena Shvarts argue that the theatricalised culture of Russia's Silver Age remained manifest in Nabokov's work in the recurring motif of oranges, an allusion to Gozzi's *The Love for Three Oranges* which came to epitomise the appropriation of the *commedia dell'arte* and the related Russian *balagan* in pre-revolutionary St Petersburg (see their 'The Juice of Three Oranges: An Exploration in Nabokov's Language and World', *Nabokov Studies*, 6 (2000/1), 75–124).

movements of the World of Art (Mir iskusstva) circle and Symbolism.[5] It was naturally in the theatre that this playful theatrical mood was epitomised. Nikolai Evreinov, for instance, staged in 1912 a meta-theatrical parody of different theatrical performance styles, including an exaggerated depiction of the excessive realism of Konstantin Stanislavsky's Moscow Art Theatre.[6] In 1943, Nabokov still remembered its comic effect: 'the idea was that the first act [of Gogol's *The Government Inspector* (*Revizor*, 1836)] must be on a Sunday morning because otherwise the officers could hardly have been able to gather at the Mayor's house, and if it were a Sunday morning *then* the bells of the neighboring church would be pealing. And if they pealed then they would drown the voices on the stage – which they did. Oh it was very amusing.'[7] The search for alternatives to the Realist theatre was most visible in the pre-revolutionary work of one of Russia's leading theatrical innovators, the 'stylised' or 'conditional' theatre (*uslovnyi teatr*) of Vsevolod Meyerhold. By foregrounding the traditional conventions of the theatre, Meyerhold probed the theatrical reality, creating a detailed theatrical illusion only to shatter it by laying bare the theatrical devices. Like other artists of his time, he was fascinated by the Petrushka theatre and the commedia. Meyerhold directed, for example, the first performance of Alexander Blok's *The Fairground Booth* (*Balaganchik*) in 1906 at Vera Komissarzhevskaia's theatre, a variant of the commedia which in Meyerhold's production became a self-conscious exploration of the aesthetic limits of theatre. In his last production before the revolution in 1917, Meyerhold would leave the Petrushka play behind but retain the self-conscious theatricality of the *commedia dell'arte* in his lavish production of Lermontov's *Masquerade* (*Maskarad*, 1842), a culmination of the pre-revolutionary celebration of theatricality and fascination with masks and puppets.

In Nabokov's case, Russia's Silver Age overlapped with his formative years. Nostalgia for a lost culture coincided with nostalgia for the lost world of childhood and youth. As if in defiance of these artistic and personal experiences of loss, Nabokov would retain the sometimes almost child-like playfulness and theatrical mood of the Silver Age not only in

---

[5] For a detailed survey of possible influences of the Mir iskusstva circle on Nabokov, see Sweeney, 'Looking at Harlequins'; Gavriel Shapiro 'Vladimir Nabokov and "The World of Art"', *Slavic Almanach: The South African Year Book for Slavic, Central and East European Studies*, 6/9 (2000), 35–52.

[6] See Spencer Golub, *Evreinov: The Theatre of Paradox and Transformation* (Ann Arbor, MI: UMI Research Press, 1984), 161–8.

[7] Quoted in Boyd, *Russian Years*, 103.

some of his plays, but also in his novels up to his last published work whose title, *Look at the Harlequins!*, invokes the colourful theatre of Pierrot and Harlequin. The strong interest in theatrical performance and theatricality on the stage in Russia's Silver Age resonates in Nabokov's own plays which, after the initial closet plays, are written with an eye to performance.

For Nabokov, the commencement of exile coincided with his early experiments with drama. His first play 'In Spring' was written while in the Crimea where the Nabokov family had taken temporary refuge after the October Revolution. Nabokov later recalled that it was a 'lyrical something', based on a heavy-handed, somewhat Symbolist plot as Boyd's summary of the drama suggests.[8] The Crimea at that point had become the waiting room for a large part of the future Russian emigration, biding time while hoping for a possible restoration of the Provisional Government in Petersburg. In hindsight, Nabokov aligned the feverish hothouse atmosphere of those days with Pushkin's experience of exile in the South of Russia:

Many young people were always around, brown-limbed braceleted young beauties, a well-known painter called Sorin, actors, a male ballet dancer, merry White Army officers … and what with beach parties, blanket parties, bonfires, a moon-spangled sea and a fair supply of Crimean Muscat Lunel, a lot of amorous fun went on; and all the while, against this frivolous, decadent and somehow unreal background (which I was pleased to believe conjured up the atmosphere of Pushkin's visit to the Crimea a century earlier) Lidia and I played a little oasal game of our own invention. (*SM*, 191)

In the Russian version of his autobiography, he would add to this the mushrooming of theatrical initiatives in Yalta.[9] He later remembered his role as Fritz Lobheimer, a student who has an affair with a married woman, in an amateur production of Arthur Schnitzler's play *Flirtations* (*Liebelei*, 1895).[10]

The move to England came as a slight shock. Cambridge, where Nabokov studied Russian and French from 1919 to 1922, showed him if not the cold then at least a rather cool shoulder. It was a place so much

---

[8] Quoted in *ibid.*, 141. 'In Spring' remains unpublished, and Boyd's summary of the play gives the impression of a somewhat confused plot without any clearly discernible direction (*Russian Years*, 141–2).

[9] Vladimir Nabokov, *Drugie berega* (Ann Arbor, MI: Ardis, 1978), 215.

[10] Andrew Field, *Nabokov: His Life in Part* (London: Hamish Hamilton, 1977), 131. See also Boyd, *Russian Years*, 148. This performance would be reworked with variations and changes in *Pnin* (see Vladimir Nabokov, *Pnin* (London: Penguin, 1997), 148–9).

stranger and more alienating than Nabokov would have expected after a childhood spent with English tutors. He later thought of his initial joining of college life with its many unwritten rules and dress codes as 'indulging in some weird theatricals' (*SM*, 199). The difficulties he experienced with becoming part of this 'mild masquerade' (*SM*, 201) of Englishness sharpened his sense of himself as Russian. He set out 'trying to become a Russian writer' (*SM*, 201). Yet in hindsight he saw that the English context proved to be inescapable and left an ineradicable imprint on his writing: 'It would have horrified me at the time to discover what I see so clearly now, the direct influence upon my Russian structures of various contemporaneous ("Georgian") English verse patterns that were running about my room and all over me like tame mice' (*SM*, 205).

The process of merging different literary traditions is equally evident in his initial verse plays of the early 1920s. It was written drama rather than performed theatre which left a mark on Nabokov's work of that time. The theatrical life of Cambridge after the First World War had a predictably provincial character. While the Barnwell Theatre Royal was not reopened until 1926,[11] both the New Theatre and the Amateur Dramatic Society, Cambridge's most prominent student theatre, specialised primarily in light comedies, farces and melodramas, a repertoire which was only occasionally varied by performances of the Benson Shakespeare Company at the New Theatre.[12] Nabokov's time at Cambridge is less important as a source of direct theatrical influences than as a period of engagement with English classical drama and poetry, threads of which are woven into the plays he wrote during and shortly after his time in Cambridge. Whether he took the opportunity to see some of the Elizabethan dramas in performance, perhaps at the Marlowe Dramatic Society at Cambridge which specialised in Elizabethan dramas, is impossible to say.[13] Later he remembered Cambridge suffused with English Renaissance literature, including one of the Elizabethan playwrights: 'I thought of Milton, and Marvell, and Marlowe, with more than a tourist's thrill as I passed beside the

---

[11] See F. A. Keynes, *By-Ways of Cambridge History*, 2nd edn (Cambridge: W. Heffer, 1956), 124.

[12] See the 'What's On' pages of *The New Cambridge* for the years 1920–1, which lists for the New Theatre, for instance, productions of: *Come Out of the Kitchen: A Comedy in Three Acts* (19–21 February 1920), *Kissing Time: A Musical Comedy* (8 and 12 March 1920), *A Southern Maid: A Musical Play in Three Acts* (25–30 October 1920), *Lord Richard in the Pantry: A Farcical Comedy* (24–29 January 1921), *The Ruined Lady: A Comedy* (10–12 February 1921) and *Oh Julie: A Musical Comedy* (14–19 March 1921); Keynes, *By-Ways of Cambridge History*, 135.

[13] Their performances included the first part of Shakespeare's *Henry IV*, John Webster's *The White Devil*, Beaumont and Fletcher's *The Triumph of Death*, and *Arden of Feversham* (see Keynes, *By-Ways of Cambridge History*, 143). Nabokov refers to just such a student production of *Hamlet* in his 'University Poem' ('Universitetskaia poema', 1927).

reverend walls. Nothing one looked at was shut off in terms of time, every-thing was a natural opening into it' (*SM*, 207). Elsewhere he expressed his admiration specifically for Elizabethan drama: 'in Shakespeare's oak-shade Ben Johnson and Fletcher and a number of other dramatists grew – a dense undergrowth of talent'.[14]

The Elizabethan playwrights offered a convenient model for the next stage in Nabokov's artistic development, providing an almost natural stepping stone from poetry towards prose. Nabokov's verse dramas retain the lyrical form but combine it with some sort of narrative and more com-plex plot constructions. Nabokov wrote his first play (after 'In Spring'), *The Wanderers*, in 1921 during his time at Cambridge. The play, written under the anagrammatic pseudonym Vivian Calmbrood, purports to be a translation of the first act of an eighteenth-century English drama into Russian.[15] Later, while working on his first full-length play, *The Tragedy of Mr Morn*, Nabokov considered taking up *The Wanderers* again: 'After Mr Morn [*sic*] I will write a second – a final – act for "The Wanderers". Suddenly felt like it.'[16] But the play remained in its fragmentary form. The reworking of the Robin Hood legend in the figure of the outlaw Robert as well as the choice of iambic pentameter, the staple measure of English verse drama, add authenticity to this mock translation of an English play. Neither the critics of the published version nor Nabokov's father doubted that the translation was genuine. Although the metre and the subject matter of Nabokov's *The Wanderers* lean towards English drama, its qual-ity as a mock translation from English to Russian links it back to one of Pushkin's 'Little Tragedies', which purports to be a Russian translation of 'Scenes from Shenstone's tragicomedy: The Covetous Knight'. Nabokov returned to this little hoax much later in a poem which continues the initial prank in another alleged translation of Vivian Calmbrood. In the poem 'Vivian Calmbrood. "The Night Journey"' (1931), the narrator meets another poet who turns out to be no other than Shenstone, the alleged author of Pushkin's hoax.[17]

The 'English theme' recurs in three brief verse plays written two years later, *Death*, *The Grandfather* and *The Pole*. Like *The Wanderers*, they are written in iambic pentameter and for two of them, Nabokov's time

[14] Vladimir Nabokov, *Lectures on Don Quixote*, ed. Fredson Bowers (San Diego, New York and London: Bruccoli Clark, Harcourt Brace Jovanovich Publishers, 1981), 6.
[15] Vivian Calmbrood is an anagram of 'Vladimir Nabocov' (with the *c* replacing the *k*).
[16] Vladimir Nabokov to Véra Nabokov, 8 January 1924, VN Berg.
[17] See Richard A. Gregg, 'Pushkin and Shenstone: The Case Reopened', *Comparative Literature*, 17/2 (Spring 1965), 109–16.

at Cambridge provided again a source of material. *Death*, a contemplation on the nature of a possible afterlife, is set in Trinity College, where
Nabokov himself studied, while *The Pole*, a dramatisation of the last days
of Robert Falcon Scott's failed expedition to the South Pole in 1912, was
inspired by Nabokov's visit to the British Museum, where he had seen
Scott's diaries.[18] *The Pole* was included in a public reading Nabokov gave
at the Union of Russian Theatre Workers in the spring of 1924.[19] Probably
in the hope of finding a German publisher, he also had the play translated
into German.[20] Almost devoid of physical action and essentially poems in
dialogical form, Nabokov's verse plays were in effect closet dramas, meant
to be disseminated in print rather than on the stage.[21]

This conflation of Russian and English tradition foreshadows a similar strategy in Nabokov's first ever extensive piece of work, *The Tragedy
of Mr Morn*, written from 1923–4 in Berlin and Prague. *The Tragedy of
Mr Morn* retains the English meter (blank verse) of the preceding closet
dramas but develops a far more complex dramatic plot line about a kingdom won and lost and a king in exile. It is a transitory piece of work
located between literatures, cultures and literary forms. Boyd points to
the clearly Shakespearean overtones in 'its five acts, its three thousand
lines of blank verse, its mongrel names … and above all in the atmosphere of its plot'.[22] And while this is certainly true, the play is at the same
time dreamier, more Romantic and lyrical, in places far slower, than any
of Shakespeare's dramas. Its Romanticism is far closer to Lermontov's
Masquerade, especially in Meyerhold's elegant and lavish production
on the eve of the Russian revolution. Thematically, *The Tragedy of Mr
Morn* recalls Pushkin's *Boris Godunov* (1831), a play about revolutions and
royal impostors set in Russia's Time of Troubles. Pushkin's drama itself
is strongly influenced by Shakespeare's history plays just as Lermontov's
Masquerade reworks Shakespeare's *Othello* in a Russian context. In tune
with their Shakespearean themes, both plays are written in unrhymed

---

[18] See Nabokov's article on Rupert Brooke, in which he states that 'The rough copy [of Brooke's
sonnet] is kept under glass at the British museum between Dickens' manuscript and Captain
Scott's notebook' (Vladimir Nabokov, 'Rupert Bruk', *Grani*, 1 (1922), 212–31. Reprinted in *Sobr.
soch.*, I, 728–44 [733]). I. N. Tolstaia argues that Nabokov was also well acquainted with Scott's
diaries, which were published in 1913 (see '"Polius" V. Nabokova i "Posledniaia ekspeditsiia
Skotta"', *Russkaia literatura*, 1 (1989), 133–6).

[19] Boyd, *Russian Years*, 230.

[20] See 'Polius' ('The Pole'), German translation ('Der Pol'), draft, VNLOC, Box 12, Folder 12. The
translation is likely to have been prepared between August 1924 and April 1925 when Nabokov
lived at Trautenaustraße 9 in Berlin, as the address is given at the top of the draft.

[21] Diment also considers the verse plays to be closet dramas (see 'Plays', 587).

[22] Boyd, *Russian Years*, 222.

iambic pentameter, which, following *Boris Godunov*, became a standard measure for Russian drama.[23] In this way, Nabokov's play points to both English and Russian predecessors. Nabokov manages to bring together two literatures and at the same time to place himself as a poet and play-wright firmly in the tradition of Russia's Golden Age.

The Tragedy of Mr Morn occupies an indeterminate position, some-where between a closet drama and a play intended for performance. Just like a closet drama, *The Tragedy of Mr Morn* was first presented to an exclusive and private circle, as an announcement in *Rul'*, the Russian émi-gré daily in Berlin, indicates: 'V. Sirin read his recently finished verse tra-gedy … at an evening by invitation only. In the near future V. Sirin will also give a public reading of the play.'[24] Initially, the Russian director Ivan Schmidt and his wife, the actress Elena Polevitskaia, had been envisaged as part of the selected audience at this reading, in the hope of attracting them to stage *The Tragedy of Mr Morn*.[25] In the first half of the 1920s, Schmidt regularly staged both Russian and German performances at Max Reinhardt's theatres, including the Deutsches Theater, while Polevitskaia was one of the most popular actresses of the Russian emigration who also gave guest performances at the Deutsches Theater and toured other European countries with much success.[26] Given their artistic distinction and popularity, it seems almost presumptuous that Nabokov should have hoped Schmidt and Polevitskaia would consider the play of an unknown writer, but that might have been an irrelevant consideration for a poet who had self-published a collection of poems at the tender age of seven-teen.[27] In the end, neither Schmidt nor Polevitskaia attended the reading. The actual audience included the critic Iulii Aikhenvald and the writer Mark Aldanov, who were not directly involved in any theatrical enter-prises. The transition to a wider audience was made three weeks later in a public reading. This second reading was followed by a detailed review of the reading of the play.[28] Over the next months, the status of *The Tragedy of Mr Morn* appears to have finally changed from a merely literary text to a fully-fledged play with the potential for performance. In the spring, Nabokov reported to his mother that *The Tragedy of Mr Morn* 'is being sent to the German Theatre (in Königsberg [today: Kaliningrad]) for

[23] See Barry P. Scherr, *Russian Poetry: Meter, Rhythm, and Rhyme* (Berkeley: University of California Press, 1986), 53.
[24] *Rul'*, 16 March 1924; See Boyd, *Russian Years*, 228.
[25] See Boyd, *Russian Years*, 228.
[26] See Franz Horch (ed.), *Die Spielpläne Max Reinhardts 1905–1930* (Munich: R. Piper, 1930), 51–62.
[27] See Boyd, *Russian Years*, 118–19.
[28] See E(vgenii) K(annak), '"Tragediia Gospodina Morna"', *Rul'*, 6 April 1924, 6.

translation and performance'.[29] Nothing ever came of this, but it reflects Nabokov's interest in having the play performed in a theatre rather than in one of those dramatic readings which he later remembered as rather pathetic events:

> Quite a feature of émigré life, in keeping with its itinerant and dramatic character, was the abnormal frequency of those literary readings in private houses or hired halls. The various types of performers stand out very distinctly in the puppet show going on in my mind. There was the faded actress, with eyes like precious stones, who having pressed for a moment a clenched handkerchief to a feverish mouth, proceeded to evoke nostalgic echoes of the Moscow Art Theatre.[30] (*SM*, 216)

Nabokov's verse plays are transitional pieces between literatures and literary forms, accompanying Nabokov's search for his own voice as a writer. In his autobiography the merging of English and Russian literature becomes a roaring fire (not a pale one) of English texts, which sets free the Russian Sirin: 'Then the flaming sheet [of the London *Times*], with the whirr of a liberated phoenix, would fly up the chimney to join the stars. It cost one a fine of twelve shillings if that firebird was observed' (*SM*, 205).

PLAYING WITH THEATRE: THEATRICAL COLLABORATIONS

In Nabokov's next drama, *The Man from the USSR*, written almost three years later in the autumn of 1926, Nabokov moved away from verse drama and produced a far more contemporary and realistic drama than *The Tragedy of Mr Morn*. With the increasing politicisation of the German theatre in the 1920s, classic as well as contemporary plays received a politically didactic or socially engaged interpretation. Neither the 'New Objectivity' (*Neue Sachlichkeit*) nor the later interest in Constructivist experiments in theatre left any clear traces in Nabokov's drama, whose responses to this kind of theatre were predictably derisive. The agitprop productions by Erwin Piscator, one of Berlin's most famous directors in the mid-1920s, for instance, were labelled 'trashy concoctions' ('Tragedy', 327). Yet Piscator's montage technique of integrating cinematic elements into the theatre seems to resonate in Nabokov's second play, *The Man*

---

[29] Vladimir Nabokov to Elena Nabokov, 14 June 1924, VN Berg.
[30] A more excruciating instance of dramatic readings occurs in *The Gift* where the reading of an earnest Symbolist play inadvertently causes a suppressed storm of hilarity in the émigré audience (see Vladimir Nabokov, *The Gift* (London: Penguin, 1981), 67–70).

from the USSR, where in the first act the silhouette-like, two-dimensional background of a basement window evokes the impression of a screen onto which a film is projected, while the fourth act takes place on a film set.[31]

During the early 1920s the theatrical life of the émigré community in Berlin was thriving. Although plans to set up a permanent Russian theatre failed as the itinerant émigré community did not represent a reliable permanent audience, there was a great variety of theatre productions and dramatic enterprises initiated by members of the émigré community.[32] This vibrant theatrical scene was complemented by guest performances of Soviet ensembles, most notably the different Moscow Art Theatre studios and the Moscow Art Theatre itself under the direction of Stanislavsky in 1922 and 1923. Nabokov's cousin, Nicolas Nabokov, recalled that '[the] Stanislavsky company performed in Berlin to full houses, and all of us [the Nabokov family] went to see their Chekhov, Tolstoy, Dostoevsky, and Gorky productions'.[33] This flourishing period of Russian theatre in Berlin, however, only lasted as long as inflation in Germany remained high and costs low for Russian immigrants. Theatrical activities among émigrés in Berlin reached a peak in 1922, which was, however, followed by a steady decline thereafter.[34] When, in 1924, the German mark stabilised and expenses for émigrés increased, a large number of Russians moved to Paris. Alongside this drain of Russian émigrés and the consequent decrease of a potential theatre audience, émigré theatres folded and the tours by Soviet ensembles dried up. The generally low standard of Russian émigré productions in Berlin was a further obstacle in attracting a permanent audience. The theatre critic Iurii Ofrosimov, for instance, complained about the lack of talented actors, many of whom pretended to be closely associated with the prestigious pre-revolutionary theatres. Apart from these artistic failures, he ascribed the problems of émigré theatre also to the general lack of finances and the consequent shortage of ensembles, rooms and equipment.[35] An exception to this was the relatively

---

[31] Piscator used this technique of mixing film and theatre, for instance, in his productions of Alfons Paquet's *Sturmflut* (February 1926), a play about the Russian revolution which in turn had been influenced by Eisenstein's *Potemkin*, and Paul Zech's *Das trunkene Schiff* (May 1926) (see John Willett, *The Theatre of Erwin Piscator: Half a Century of Politics in Theatre* (London: Eyre Methuen, 1978), 59–62; John Willett, *The Theatre of the Weimar Republic* (New York: Holmes and Meier, 1988), 108–9).

[32] See Böhmig, *Das russische Theater*, 56–67.

[33] Nikolas Nabokov, *Bagázh: Memoirs of a Russian Cosmopolitan* (London: Secker and Warburg, 1975), 109.

[34] See Böhmig, *Das russische Theater*, 46–8.

[35] See Iurii Ofrosimov, *Teatr: Fel'etony* (Berlin: Volga, 1926), 159–61.

stable establishment of Iakov Iuzhny's Bluebird Cabaret ('Siniaia ptitsa'), a colourful, Modernist variety theatre which enjoyed great success and reached European and American audiences beyond the small circle of Russian émigrés.[36] One of the last significant events in the theatrical life of Russian Berlin was Meyerhold's production of Gogol's *The Government Inspector*, which was performed in April 1930.[37] Instead of a social satire, Meyerhold presented the whole play as the Mayor's dream or nightmare. Much later Nabokov would single this performance out in his book on Gogol: 'Meyerhold, in spite of all his additions and distortions, offered a stage version of *The Government Inspector* which conveyed something of the real Gogol.'[38]

Despite his self-professed dislike of groups and associations, Nabokov took an active part in the cultural life of the Russian emigration. This also included his participation in some minor theatrical events in the 1920s. In 1925, he played a part in two Boccaccio-inspired pantomimes for the opening of Lidiia Ryndina's Balagan Theatre.[39] A year later he acted the role of Pozdnyshev from Tolstoy's *Kreutzer Sonata* (*Kreitzerova Sonata*, 1891) in one of the literary mock trials which were so popular among the Russian émigrés.[40] Staged at the Writers' Union, the literary trial was to judge Pozdnyshev, who had to justify the murder of his wife and her lover against two prosecutors, played by Iulii Aikhenvald and N. Volkovysky. A reviewer in *Rul'* considered Nabokov to have great acting talent, remarking that:

the evening organised by the Union of Journalists and Writers turned out to be genuinely pleasant and genuinely literary. It was the participation of V. Sirin, who masterfully staged and read the declaration of the accused Pozdnyshev, which lent great and unexpected interest to this evening. Although the young writer seriously deviated from Tolstoy's character, in his creative, inspired interpretation, Tolstoy's murderer-philosopher became a real and suffering human being.[41]

The speech Nabokov wrote for the event, a somewhat long-winded retelling of Tolstoy's tale, is entirely in tune with Tolstoy's text – contrary to the claims in the newspaper and Nabokov's own estimation that he

---

[36] See Böhmig, *Das russische Theater*, 101–30.

[37] See *ibid.*, 226–31.

[38] See Vladimir Nabokov, *Nikolai Gogol*, corrected edition (New York: New Directions, 1961), 38.

[39] The sketches were entitled 'The Jealous Husband', 'Love and Love's Ways' (see 'Balagan', *Rul'*, 17 March 1925, 4).

[40] Literary trials came into fashion in the early 1920s in the Soviet Union and were later adopted by the Russian emigration (see 'Literaturnyi sud', *Dni*, 26 January 1923, 5; N[ikolai] Volkovyskii, 'O skvernykh zrelishchakh', *Dni*, 6 Feb 1923, 5).

[41] R. T., 'Sud nad "Kreitserovoi sonatoi"', *Rul'*, 18 July 1926, 8.

had considerably deviated from Tolstoy's original.[42] Nabokov's theatrical involvement continued in another charity event, the revue 'Quatsch' ('Kvatch'), where he played the part of the theatre director and dramatist Evreinov ('in great make-up', according to one reviewer), one of the notable directors of pre-revolutionary Russia, who continued his theatrical work untiringly in the emigration.[43]

During this time, Nabokov also worked in close collaboration on several scenarios together with his friend and fellow-writer, Ivan Lukash, for the Bluebird Cabaret. Nabokov would later dismiss all of them as minor youthful ventures.[44] The work on the scenarios grew less from some sort of creative impulse, than from the necessity to earn money.[45] This practically minded approach to writing is suggested by a contract between Lukash, Nabokov and the composer Yakobson regarding a scenario with the title 'The Fiery Crown' ('Ognennyi venets').[46] The contract gives Yakobson full rights to change the title and even the text of the scenario (a yielding of authorial and creative control which is unthinkable in regard to the older Nabokov), but stipulates in detail royalties and other payments to Nabokov and Lukash, including an immediate one-off payment of $200 to the authors. Money played indeed such a major role that two years later, after the end of their collaborative work, Lukash who had meanwhile moved on to the newspaper *The Salamander* (Salamandr) in Riga, encouraged Nabokov in a letter that he 'take that son of a bitch Yakobson by the scruff of the neck'.[47] And Nabokov remembered more than fifty years later that The Bluebird Cabaret still owed him money.[48] These minor pieces represent Nabokov's first significant experience of

---

[42] See Vladimir Nabokov, 'Rech' Pozdnysheva. Holograph draft of mock trial, unsigned and dated July 1927, VN Berg. It is tempting to trace the development of Nabokov's enactment of a murderer addressing a jury to justify his crime all the way to Humbert Humbert's literary trial.

[43] See *Rul'*, 1 June 1927, 4. The German word *Quatsch* means 'nonsense'.

[44] He dismissed them, for example, in an interview with Alfred Appel: '"all this [the scenarios] is not really very interesting, is it?"' (*Nabokov's Dark Cinema*, 155).

[45] Boyd, *Russian Years*, 231. For a description of the scenarios see Appel, *Nabokov's Dark Cinema*, 154–5.

[46] See *Masterworks of 20th Century Russian Literature and Illustration* [Bloomsbury Auction Catalogue: Auction 21 May 2008, New York], 46–7.

[47] Ivan Lukash to Vladimir Nabokov, 1 February 1926, VNLOC, Box 1, Folder 31. In 1939, Lukash would return to dramatic work with another émigré playwright, Ilya Surguchev (who wrote a review of Nabokov's *The Event* after its Paris performance in 1938). Lukash and Surguchev collaborated on an adaptation of Lukash's novel *Mussorgsky's Poor Love* (*Bednaia Liubov Mussorgskogo*) (see Surguchev to Lukash, 1 June 1939; 9 June 1939; 11 June 1939, BAR, Ilya Surguchev Papers, Box 1). Lukash died of tuberculosis in 1940 (see 'Skonchalsia I. S. Lukash', *Novoe russkoe slovo*, 29 May 1940, 2).

[48] Andrew Field, *VN: The Life and Art of Vladimir Nabokov* (London: Futura, 1988), 123.

collaboration in both theatrical productions and theatrical writing, which would shape and determine his understanding of theatre and prepare his engagement with the theatrical production of his next play.

In contrast to *The Tragedy of Mr Morn*, *The Man from the USSR* was written with a far clearer idea of its eventual performance in mind, as the play was commissioned by Ofrosimov, who had recently brought together the theatre troupe 'The Group' ('Gruppa'). Long past the heyday of Russian theatres in Berlin, Ofrosimov's initiative was another attempt to breathe some life into the theatrical scene of Russian Berlin. The depiction of the daily life of the Russian emigration in Berlin was a subject which clearly appealed to Nabokov's fellow émigrés, as the positive review of the play in *Rul'* suggests: 'This is the first play from émigré life and one has to say that it is a successful one.'[49] In a letter to his mother, Nabokov is clearly at ease with the collaborative nature of a theatre production, presenting the playwright and director as different entities who work towards a common goal: 'I am about to write a play with Offrozimov [*sic*], or actually, I will write it and he will stage it.'[50] Considering Nabokov's later declared hostility towards any group activity, the close collaboration which continued during the preparations for the performance is rather surprising. Nabokov regularly attended the rehearsals and helped choose the costumes, at least for the female parts, as he reported to his mother: 'Today I am going shopping with my two actresses to choose dresses, hats and coats for them.'[51] A photograph which has survived from that time shows Nabokov amid the cast – the playwright as an integral part of the theatre performance (see Figure 1).

Only the first act of *The Man from the USSR* appeared in print in *Rul'*[52] For public reception, the play depended therefore entirely on its performance on stage. Even before the premiere on 1 April 1927 at the Grotrian-Steinweg-Saal in Berlin, it was met with great interest as Nabokov reported to his mother: 'Everybody is talking about my man from the USSR.'[53] Although this might have been the exaggeration of a budding writer, an announcement in *Rul'* confirms that after the first performance there was sufficient interest to merit an additional (and final) performance: 'Due to the great interest in the production of V. Sirin's drama *The Man from the USSR*, [the theatre troupe] Gruppa will repeat its performance on

49 Brodskii, 'Chelovek iz SSSR', 5.
50 Vladimir Nabokov to Elena Nabokov, 6 April 1926, VN Berg.
51 Vladimir Nabokov to Elena Nabokov, 8 March 1927, VN Berg; See Boyd, *Russian Years*, 272.
52 Vladimir Nabokov, 'Chelovek iz SSSR [Act One]', *Rul'*, 1 January 1927, 2–3.
53 Vladimir Nabokov to Elena Nabokov, 8 March 1927, VN Berg.

Figure 1 Nabokov (with pipe) with members of the theatre troupe that staged
The Man from the USSR, Berlin 1927

Tuesday.[54] Nabokov's dependence on the actual staging for disseminating
the play was a risky and ultimately unsuccessful strategy in the impoverished cultural and theatrical life of the Russian emigration in Berlin at
that time. The long break Nabokov took from any dramatic work might
be explained, at least in part, by the almost impossible situation that émigré theatrical life presented to Russian playwrights.

BOX OFFICE DREAMS: *THE EVENT* AND *THE WALTZ INVENTION*

The late thirties were a time of crisis for Nabokov on a personal, financial, linguistic and artistic level. Nabokov was in limbo, between places,
between cultures, between languages and between relationships. From
1936 onwards Nabokov tried to find work in an English-speaking country. In the medium term, however, the Nabokovs were about to leave
Nazi Germany and move to France at the beginning of 1937. During this

---

[54] 'Teatr i musyka', *Rul'*, 30 March 1927, 5.

time while waiting for Véra and his son to join him in Paris, Nabokov challenged the security of his marriage through his affair with Irina Guadanini. Financially the Nabokovs were in a desolate situation and forced to stay in the South of France, which presented a cheaper option than costly Paris.[55] It was here that Nabokov wrote his last two plays, *The Event* and *The Waltz Invention*.

In 1930s Paris, conditions for the establishment of Russian émigré theatres were more favourable than in Berlin. With the shift of the cultural centre of the émigré community from Berlin to Paris in the mid-1920s, the Russian population of the French capital had grown to roughly 50,000 by 1930.[56] A great variety of Russian émigré theatres were established in Paris, some of which were short-lived initiatives, as in Berlin, but some of which turned out to be more stable ventures.[57] What could be termed the preliminary phase of émigré theatres in Paris produced some fairly stable enterprises (Dina Kirova's Intimate Theatre, Boris Espe's Chamber Theatre Abroad).[58] From the onset of the economic depression, the protective labour policy of the French government had made life for the Russian émigrés increasingly difficult. These economic pressures on both the potential audience and the financial reserves of the theatres had a strong impact on the theatrical scene, which stagnated during this period.[59] From the mid-1930s onwards, however, there were again a number of theatrical initiatives, the success of which proved the continued interest in Russian theatrical events among the émigré community in Paris. This phase concluded in what must be seen as the most successful and most stable of all Russian theatres abroad, the Russian Theatre in Paris, which was brought to life in 1936 through a collaborative effort of artists and public and cultural figures. Evreinov recalls that a number of well-known émigré actors and directors founded the Russian theatre together with Ilya Fondaminsky, co-editor of *Sovremennye zapiski* and key figure in the

---

[55] See Boyd, *Russian Years*, 486.
[56] See James E. Hassele, *Russian Refugees in France and the United States Between the World Wars* (Philadelphia: American Philosophical Society, 1991), 58. Referring to an estimate by Jean Delage, Robert Harold Johnston cites a similar number of 52,750 Russian émigrés in Paris in the early 1930s ('Paris: Die Hauptstadt der russischen Diaspora', in Karl Schlögel (ed.), *Der grosse Exodus: Die russische Emigration und ihre Zentren. 1917 bis 1941* (Munich: Beck, 1994), 260–78 [263]).
[57] The following information on the history of émigré theatre in Paris is partly based on the second chapter of Nikolai Evreinov, *Pamiatnik mimoletnomu (iz istorii emigrantskogo teatra)* (Paris, 1953), 18–38; M. G. Litavrina, *Russkii teatral'nyi Parizh* (St Petersburg: Aleteiia, 2003), 105–50.
[58] See M. G. Litavrina, 'Russkie dramaticheskie teatry v Parizhe (1924–1943 gg.)', in E. A. Shulepova (ed.), *Kul'turnaia missiia rossiiskogo zarubezh'ia: Proshloe i sovremennost'* (Moscow: Rossiiskii institut kul'turologii, 1999) 70–7 [74].
[59] See Litavrina, 'Russkie teatry v Parizhe', 74.

political and cultural life of the Russian emigration, his friend Vladimir Zenzinov and the poet Sophia Pregel'.[60]

With the exception of some cautiously experimental theatrical initiatives during the 1930s, Russian theatres were on the whole rather conservative backward-looking artistic enterprises.[61] They were seen as cherished national and cultural institutions which were to guard an authentic Russian heritage against Soviet corruption. Their repertoires and productions were shaped entirely by cultural practices, assumptions and values from pre-revolutionary times. The majority of Russian émigré theatres shared rather traditional programmes in regard to the actual choice of plays and performance styles. Russian theatres abroad performed almost exclusively Russian plays by pre-revolutionary playwrights, with Alexander Ostrovsky and Anton Chekhov being the most widely played ones. Plays which could be used to project the image of an idealised Russia which in reality had never existed were favoured. Ostrovsky especially with his portrayals of the nineteenth-century Russian merchant classes in the Moscow area and the provinces, and not Westernised Petersburg must have touched a special nerve in the Russian émigré community, evoking the image of a quintessentially Russian life untouched by corrupting influences from the West. Chekhov, on the other hand, with his melancholic portrayal of an internally displaced intelligentsia in the Russian provinces longing for the real life somewhere else provided an obvious mirror for the Russian intelligentsia in Paris. Productions like *The Cherry Orchard* (*Vishnevyi sad*, 1904) and its theme of expulsion from paradise, whether imagined or real, became an obvious topos for the Russian émigré condition, which was also quickly picked up by most reviewers. The productions themselves were hardly innovative, adhering for the most part to Realist theatre of the turn of the century in the tradition of Stanislavsky's Moscow Art Theatre. Performances in émigré theatres were marked by a strong reluctance to experiment with theatre, or even just to imitate the Symbolist or avant-garde experiments from the decades before and after the revolution. The cultural life of the Russian emigration was thoroughly politicised, and any form of avant-garde or Formalist innovation became quickly associated with Soviet culture and hence tainted by accusations

---

[60] See Evreinov, *Pamiatnik mimoletnomu*, 36.

[61] In 1933, M. Oksinaia and O. Iuzhakova founded a theatre company that concentrated primarily on contemporary Soviet dramas. Two years later the Wandering Comedians ('Brodiachie komedianty'), with Evreinov as their artistic director, worked with the expressed aim of theatrical innovation. In 1935, two theatre companies, Associated Russian Actors ('Ob''edinennye Russkie Artisty') and Zeling's and Skokan's troupe were set up.

of pro-Soviet sympathies.[62] Khodasevich, for instance, complained about the low standards of émigré audiences and the consequently retrospective, provincial and unchallenging repertoires of Russian theatres abroad.[63]

When Nabokov arrived in France in 1937, the theatrical life of the émigré community was thriving. The Russian Theatre had successfully concluded its first season (1936), which had been in tune with the general demand for Russian classic plays and initiated a more progressive repertoire in the following season including the work of Soviet and émigré authors. The next season was to introduce the work of younger contemporary Russian playwrights to the stage. Fondaminsky played a central role in this change of the theatre's concept, as Iosif Gessen emphasised in his memoirs: 'The Russian Theatre owes its existence to [Fondaminsky], he prompt[ed] émigré writers to write new Russian plays for the theatre.'[64] Responding to Fondaminsky's appeal to younger émigré writers, Nabokov wrote *The Event* at the end of 1937 in anticipation of a theatrical performance. Babikov has shown that Nabokov had been working on a play for the Russian Theatre already at the beginning of the year with concrete expectations for its eventual production, as a letter to his wife indicates:

I am meeting with actors and actresses (my *leading lady* [in English] Bakhareva is enchanting, yesterday I had lunch at hers with Iliusha [Fondaminsky] and V.M. [Zenzinov]) … the playwriting is torturous (I told you about the play's topic: a cheerful, sweet young lady appears together with her mother in a spa town – and all this is only an interv[al] luc[id] – it ends –inevitably – with her returning to her ('theatrical') insanity). (*P'esy*, 584)

A few days earlier he had met some of the actors of the Russian theatre and the actress Elizaveta Kedrova had 'shamelessly begged [him] for a role [in his new play]' (*P'esy*, 585).

The Russian Theatre's attempt at innovation was almost from the start condemned to failure. Neither the actors nor the audience were prepared for the meta-theatrical phantasmagoria which *The Event* plays out. Referring to the Realist tradition of the Moscow Art Theatre which dominated the Russian Theatre in Paris, the Russian émigré director

[62] In his excellent study on Russian émigré literature of the younger generation, Leonid Livak discusses in detail the correlation between negative attitudes towards experimental art and anti-Soviet views in émigré circles (see *How it Was Done in Paris: Russian Émigré Literature and French Modernism* (Madison: University of Wisconsin Press, 2003), 28–38).

[63] Vladislav Khodasevich, '"Sobytie" V. Sirina v Russkom teatre' *Sovremennye zapiski*, 66 (1938), 423–7 [423–4]. Reprinted in Mel'nikov and Korosteleva (eds.), *Klassik bez retushi*, 169–73.

[64] Iosif Gessen, *Gody izgnaniia: Zhiznennyi otchet* (Paris: YMCA-Press, 1979), 256.

Evreinov, for instance, reported to a friend during the time of rehearsals: 'In regard to Sirin's play [*The Event*], there is a slight confusion here at the Russian Theatre [in Paris]. They say, the play is not topical and demands a grotesque performance, which is completely out of place [*kak korove sedlo*] at the Russian Theatre.'[65] Nina Berberova states that in 'their youth [Russian] actors were coached in [Stanislavsky's] Method'.[66] In the Russian version of her memoir, she also remembered that in the performance of *The Event*, 'a former actress from the Moscow Art Theatre [M. Kryzhanovskaia in the role of Madame Vagabundova] did not know how to perform [her lines which were written in verse]'.[67] The theatre critic of *Vozrozhdenie*, Ilya Surguchev, criticised the director and the actors for not understanding how to stage the play appropriately.[68] When the play was performed in Belgrade, Vsevolod Khomitsky, the main actor, also complained bitterly to his friend Evreinov about the difficulties in playing the drama's main character: 'Now we're staging (to my utter horror) Sirin's *The Event*, in which I play … Troshcheikin. I understand and take on roles which have only *one character trait*, but a role which has only *one emotion* can be horrifying [to perform]' (emphasis in original).[69] The émigré audience in Paris had problems adapting to Nabokov's play. Berberova remembers that the 'public wanted a realistic theatre, it dreamt of seeing on the stage people drinking tea from a samovar, but Nabokov gave it *The Event* and *The Waltz Invention* (where Waltz turned out to be not a dance but a man and one of the female roles was written in verse). When at the end of my play [*Madame*], part of the cast of characters doubted the existence of the other, no one understood it.'[70] She also remembers that Surguchev, who was also the author of the melodrama *The Violins of*

---

[65] 'Iz dvukh uglov: Perepiska Nikolaia Evreinova s Iuriem i Iuliei Rakitinymi 1928–1938', in V. V. Ivanov (ed.), *Mnemozina: Dokumenty i fakty iz istorii russkogo teatra xx veka* (Moscow, GITIS, 1996–), vol. III, 243–78 [Evreinov to Iurii Rakitin, 8 Feb 1938, p. 276]. Ereinov probably got hold of the play in one of the copies which were made for the rehearsals at the Russian Theatre.

[66] Nina Berberova, *The Italics Are Mine*, trans. Phillipe Radley (New York: Alfred A. Knopf, 1992), 350.

[67] Nina Berberova, *Kursiv moi: Avtobiografiia* (Moscow: Soglasie, 1996), 403. Khodasevich also thought that actors trained at the Moscow Art Theatre had difficulties with verse plays: 'The actors of the [Moscow] Art Theatre were able to find and convey the most complex nuances in everyday speech, but they were unable to deliver speeches of a higher register. None of them, with the exception of M. N. Germanova, was able to speak lines in verse' (Vladislav Khodasevich, 'Teatr Stanislavskogo', in his *Sobranie sochinenii*, vol. II, 438–43 [442]).

[68] See I[lya] S[urguchev], '"Sobytie", p'esa Sirina', *Vozrozhdenie*, 11 March 1938, 12. Surguchev thought that the play itself was interesting but full of dramaturgical mistakes.

[69] Vsevolod Khomitskii to Nikolai Evreinov, 23 December 1938, BAR, Nikolai Evreinov Papers, Box 2.

[70] Berberova, *Italics Are Mine*, 350–1. The character who speaks in verse is Vagabundova from *The Event*. *The Waltz Invention* was not staged by a Russian émigré theatre.

Autumn (Osennie skripki) which had been staged in 1915 at the Moscow Art Theatre, 'lectured me on my lack of *realism*' (emphasis in original).[71]

To some extent Nabokov's play easily fitted the bill of specifically Russian themes which were favoured in the émigré theatres of the time. The first act in particular poses as a Realist play close in spirit to Chekhov, and the subsequent play turns gradually into an intertextual palimpsest of Russian canonical plays and productions, including Gogol, Chekhov and Stanislavsky's and Meyerhold's theatre productions. Although Iurii Annenkov, the director, claimed that '[w]ith a change of names, Sirin's plays could be played in any country and in any language with the same success', it is doubtful whether *The Event* could be detached from the context of Russian culture, or even from the context of Russian émigré culture.[72] The play demands an ease with the Russian dramatic and theatrical tradition which would have been hard to find outside of Russia or the émigré communities at the time. In this way, Nabokov clearly claimed the Russian theatrical tradition as his own, but appropriated it in an unconventional fashion which was calculated to shock. This ambiguous strategy recalls *The Gift*, which is both Nabokov's tribute to the traditional canon of Russian literature and a serious assault on some of its most cherished traditions.

Before the premiere Khodasevich poked fun at the very idea of Nabokov as dramatist: 'Is it true that you have written a play? Will you come [to Paris] and see the premiere, as befits a playwright? Will you come out for the curtain call? Will you fall in love with the main actress? In any case I have decided to go to the first performance, out of love for you and to spite everybody, because I refused to go and see Aldanov's and [Nadezhda] Teffi's plays.'[73] Closer to the play's premiere, he asked Berberova to organise free tickets for him via the actor Konstantinov who was closely involved with the Russian Theatre.[74] In a more concrete variation of the playwright's absence in the theatre, Nabokov himself did not attend the premiere of his play at the Russian Theatre in March 1938, under the direction of Annenkov.[75] Instead, he received letters from Vladimir Zenzinov,

[71] Berberova, *Italics Are Mine*, 351.
[72] N. P. Vakar, "Sobytie" – p'esa V. Sirina (beseda s Iu. P. Annenkovym)', *Poslednie novosti*, 12 March 1938, 4. Reprinted in Mel'nikov and Korosteleva, *Klassik bez retushi*, 165–6 [165].
[73] Vladislav Khodasevich to Vladimir Nabokov, 25 January 1938, VNLOC, Box 1, Folder 27. Also in Khodasevich, *Sobranie sochinenii*, vol. IV, 532–3.
[74] Vladislav Khodasevich to Nina Berberova, n. d. 1938, Beinecke Rare Book and Manuscript Library, Yale University Library, Nina Berberova Papers, GEN MSS 182, Box 12, Folder 305.
[75] See Boyd, *American Years*, 27. V. S. Ianovskii recalls Fondaminsky's despair about Nabokov's absence at the premiere of *The Event* (see his *Polia elitseiskie: Kniga pamiati* (St Petersburg: Pushkinskii fond, 1993), 230). This absence from the premiere of his own play would be echoed in

Georgii Gessen and Iosif Gessen giving detailed accounts of the production and its reception.[76] The premiere (4 March 1938) was clearly a disaster. Zenzinov admitted that the acerbic review of the first performance faithfully reflected the mood among the audience.[77] While the first act had been received well, the following acts (which develop into an increasingly fantastic and grotesque spectacle) produced a disturbing and unpleasant effect ('the applause was no longer friendly'). Both Zenzinov and Georgii Gessen explained this negative reaction by the conservative orientation of the audience.[78] After the second performance (6 March), which produced a more positive response, Nabokov's friends made use of their excellent connections and persuaded Pavel Miliukov, the editor of the Russian daily *Poslednie novosti* and of *Russkie zapiski*, to print not only their letter to the editor ('from a spectator from the 14th arrondissement'), but also to revise the newspaper's stance and publish a more positive review.[79] In the end, Miliukov not only published the letter but went so far as to add another remark 'from the editor', which shrewdly recommended that the play had to be seen at least twice to be fully understood.[80] It was to a large part thanks to his friends' 'strategic plan', as Zenzinov called their undertaking, that Nabokov's play was performed twice more and received at least a neutral review in *Poslednie novosti* (from Nabokov's long-standing literary adversary Adamovich).[81]

Instead of just a simple failure, the play became the source of a prolonged controversy. Of the reviews, five were outright negative, one by Khodasevich was luke-warm, and Adamovich's first review deferred judgement until the later publication of the play text. The only outright positive responses were the 'letter to the editor' and an interview with Annenkov, who as the director of the play predictably praised the drama and its

his 'Paris Poem' ('Parizhskaia poema', 1943), where the non-existent author is linked with a sense of existential forlornness : 'Death is distant yet [...] but now and then / one's heart starts clamoring: Author! Author! / He's not in the house, gentlemen' ['Смерть еще далека [...], но иногда / сердцу хочется «автора, автора!». / В зале автора нет, господа' (*Sobr. Soch.*, V, 424–5)] (Vladimir Nabokov, *Poems and Problems* (New York and Toronto: McGraw-Hill Company, 1970), 121; 120).

[76] See Georgii Gessen to Vladimir Nabokov, 7 March 1938, VNLOC, Box 1, Folder 16; Vladimir Zenzinov to Vladimir Nabokov, 7 March 1938, VNLOC, Box 1, Folder 58; Iosif Gessen to Vladimir Nabokov, 8 March 1938, VNLOC, Box 1, Folder 17.

[77] See P[archevskii], K., 'Russkii teatr: "Sobytie" V. Sirina', *Poslednie novosti*, 6 March 1938, 5. Reprinted in Mel'nikov and Korosteleva, *Klassik bez retushi*, 163–4.

[78] Adamovich called the audience of the first performance 'snobs', though counted himself among them (see 'Rets.: "Russkie zapiski". 1938. No. 4', *Poslednie novosti*, 21 April 1938, 3. Reprinted in Mel'nikov and Korosteleva, *Klassik bez retushi*, 166–9).

[79] See '"Sobytie", p'esa V. Sirina (pis'mo v redaktsiiu)', *Poslednie novosti*, 10 March 1938, 4.

[80] See '"Sobytie" (pis'mo v redaktsiiu)'.

[81] See Sizif [G. Adamovich], 'Otkliki', *Poslednie novosti*, 10 March 1938, 3.

performance. Boyd states that '[n]othing else in the history of émigré the-ater had stirred such controversy – nothing else had so boldly defied the-atrical convention – and as the newspapers rushed to remark, *The Event* had become *the* event of the season'.[82] Boyd is surely correct in placing the effect the play produced within the context of Russian émigré theatre, without which the ensuing controversy is almost impossible to understand. Looked at against the backdrop of Modernist twentieth-century theatre, Nabokov's play is hardly groundbreaking. Blok's *The Fairground Booth*, Luigi Pirandello's seminal *Six Characters in Search of an Author* (1921) and Evreinov's *The Most Important Thing* (*Samoe glavnoe*, 1921), which was play-ing all over Europe in the 1920s, had already introduced the meta-theatre Nabokov tried out in *The Event*.[83] Evreinov suggested that *The Event* was rather derivative and called it privately a 'pirandellism', a connection which was also made by several reviewers.[84] Khodasevich also relativised the seeming innovation of the play's production by placing it in a wider cultural context: 'Even the novelty and boldness of the theatrical devices [used to convey Nabokov's play] is relative, because they are absolutely new only on the émigré stage.'[85] In the much narrower context of émigré cul-ture with its conservative cultural values shaped by pre-revolutionary art and drama, however, it is easily conceivable why this experimental play by Nabokov, who had already made himself a name as a Formalist *enfant ter-rible*, would be rejected outright. On balance, the play was received badly, as Evreinov reported to a friend: 'the play of the talented Sirin has just ter-ribly failed [at the Russian Theatre]'.[86]

As before, with *The Man from the USSR*, Nabokov was counting on the actual performance of *The Event*, yet this time for entirely different reasons. It was written at a time when he was especially desperate to find a new source of income. In this precarious situation Nabokov turned to drama, which had a distinct advantage over prose writings as a possible source of income. Whereas short stories and the serialisation of novels

[82] Boyd, *Russian Years*, 485.
[83] Nabokov later professed that he 'never cared for Pirandello' (*SO*, 74).
[84] 'Iz dvukh uglov: Perepiska Evreinova s Rakitinymi' [Rakitin to Evreinov, 3 Feb 1938, 275]. Evreinov's dismissal did not prevent the Russian director Rakitin from worrying about get-ting hold of the play before his competitors in Belgrade. The majority of reviewers of *The Event* noted traces of Pirandello in Nabokov's play. See, for instance, Sizif [G. Adamovich], 'Otkliki', 3; S[urguchev], '"Sobytie", p'esa Sirina', 12; M. Zheleznov, '"Sobytie" V. V. Sirina', *Novoe russkoe slovo*, 6 April 1941, 4.
[85] Khodasevich, '"Sobytie" V. Sirina', 424.
[86] Nikolai Evreinov to unknown, 9 May 1938, Département des Arts du spectacle, Bibliothèque nationale de France, Fond Nicolas Evreinoff (4 – Coll 22/309).

brought in a one-off payment, the same drama could be sold several times to different theatre companies, as Aldanov's advice on selling *The Event* indicates:

I haven't read your play yet. Only two copies have been made and both are with the actors. I heard that your play will be printed in Miliukov's new journal [*Russkie zapiski*]. I was very glad to hear that, the more so as they are known to pay well. I think your play will ease your financial difficulties. My [play] *Brunhilda's Line* [premiere 18 February 1937 at the Russian Theatre] brought in more than I had thought, even if it has not been translated yet into another language (and it's no good for that anyway) and although I have not yet received the royalties from several countries. It seems that there are a number of Russian theatres about. The majority of them stage a play once or twice, but in Warsaw, apparently, my play has run already twelve times (the Poles attend there too) – by the way, namely from Poland I have not received any money yet. When we see each other next, after the first performance of *The Event*, I will give you all the addresses.[87]

Nabokov's response to Aldanov indicates his despair: 'I really, really hope that the play will bring in at least something, because my financial situation is absolutely desperate; it's a mystery to me how I can exist at all.'[88] The Paris production of *The Event* earned him a modest 315 FF.[89] Nabokov even managed to secure some additional income from the play's publication in *Russkie zapiski* (April 1938), although editors were reluctant to pay for dramatic works which were generally deemed unpopular with readers – another favour by Miliukov as Aldanov reminded him in a reprimanding letter.[90]

During this time Nabokov took Aldanov's advice and sold the play to several other theatre companies. In May 1938, *The Event* was staged in Prague. The second performance of *The Event* abroad by the Association of Russian Actors in Belgrade (Udruženje ruskih glumaca u Beogradu) was not very promising, financially. The company reported that the premiere of *The Event* had taken place on 15 January 1939 and asked Nabokov to name his price, but not without drawing his attention to the fact that the performance had brought in only 2710 dinars.[91] An added difficulty was

---

[87] Mark Aldanov to Vladimir Nabokov, 29 January 1938, VN Berg.
[88] Vladimir Nabokov to Mark Aldanov, 3 February 1938, VN Berg. See also Boyd, *Russian Years*, 480.
[89] Financial receipt for performance of *The Event*, VNLOC, Box 21, Folder 9. Reproduced in *P'esy*.
[90] See Mark Aldanov to Vladimir Nabokov, 30 April 1938, VNLOC, Box 1, Folder 3.
[91] See Tat'iana Iablokova[?] to Vladimir Nabokov, 24 January 1939, VNLOC, Box 1, Folder 22. In earlier correspondence they had agreed on a twelve percent cut for Nabokov (see Tat'iana Iablokova[?] to Vladimir Nabokov, 3 March 1938, VNLOC, Box 1, Folder 22).

the problem of wiring money from Belgrade to France. It was Berberova, Nabokov's fellow playwright at the Russian Theatre a year earlier, who secured the couriering of the money for him via a friend from Belgrade.[92]

Shortly after the Paris performance of *The Event*, Nabokov turned to a potential new audience for his play, in response to a request by his New York agent Altagracia de Jannelli: 'Please send the play as soon as you get it translated. Don't bother with a good or bad translation, for it may need adaptation in any case, if it is good for America.'[93] The subsequent rejection of the play is explained at least in part by the specific Russian audience for which the play was originally written and its incompatibility with American tastes. Nabokov's agent told him that '[my] judgement [of *The Event*] is adverse. It starts with tragedy, since it is a tragedy to lose a son, turns to farce that is not funny. It is not witty. Turns then to [a] species of dream. Then back to witless farce … Besides this, the story is nothing. You are going to tell me that you wrote this for a joke. That is all very well, but in America they don't want a joke for a play.'[94] A French translation of the play under the title 'Catastrophe', prepared by Jarl Priel at the end of the 1930s, was neither published nor staged.[95]

Instead of an American production, the Russian version of *The Event* was performed again to a Russian émigré audience at the Heckscher Theater in New York under the direction of G. Ermolov (4 April 1941). It is a singular coincidence that it was *The Event*, a play about a painter, that brought Nabokov and his old drawing teacher Mstislav Dobuzhinsky together again shortly after Nabokov's arrival in the United States. Dobuzhinsky designed the theatre set for the New York production and the Nabokovs kept Dobuzhinsky's reproduction of a cracked plate and counterfeit photography during their frequent moves in the United States and even took these pieces of scenery to Montreux.[96] It was the first and only time Nabokov saw his own play performed.[97] The review in *Novoe*

[92] See Vladimir Nabokov to Nina Berberova, 17 May 1939, Beinecke Rare Book and Manuscript Library, Yale University Library, Nina Berberova Papers, GEN MSS 182, Box 15, Folder 409; Nina Berberova to Vladimir Nabokov, 29 June 1939, VNLOC, Box 1, Folder 6.
[93] Altagracia de Janelli to Vladimir Nabokov, 9 May 1938, VN Berg.
[94] Altagracia de Janelli to Vladimir Nabokov, 14 March 1939, VN Berg.
[95] French translation of *Sobytie* (Catastrophe), draft, VNLOC, Box 12, Folder 13.
[96] See Dmitri Nabokov, 'Introductory Note [to *The Event*]', in *Plays*, 125; 'Perepiska Vladimira Nabokova s M. V. Dobuzhinskim', ed. V. Stark, *Zvezda*, 11 (1996), 93–108 [99].
[97] This might have been also the last time Nabokov went to the theatre, although in an interview with the French newspaper *L'Express* in 1959, he did not even seem to remember the American premiere of his own play when he stated that 'I don't often go to the theatre. Last time was in 1932' ('The Good Mr. Nabokov: Lolita's Father Neglects the Nymphets for Pushkin and

russkoe slovo by the theatre critic Zheleznov was generally positive in regard to the play and its staging.[98] Nabokov, however, managed to take issue with Zheleznov's innuendo that one of the characters in *The Event* was a parody of Ivan Bunin.[99] In a letter to the editor, Nabokov complained that while the Paris performance might have given reason to speak of a literary parody (although against his intention), in New York there was no hint or allusion to any prototype in the actors' performance.[100] Perhaps it was the generous letter of recommendation which Bunin signed for Nabokov shortly before his departure to the United States ('a novelist of quite exceptional talent', 'a teacher of Russian literature and thought of quite exceptional quality') which made Nabokov deny the obvious and unkind parallels between Bunin and the pretentious Famous Writer of the *Event.*[101]

Nabokov's last play, *The Waltz Invention*, was written while Nabokov's financial situation was still dire. In September 1938, he wrote to the Russian Literary Fund in the United States: 'I can't say how much a small monthly support would help. My material situation has never been so terrible, so desperate. My literary income is not even half of a very modest budget.'[102] In these circumstances, 'Nabokov turned to another play, not in expectation of stupendous wealth but merely in the hope of adding to the small payment from the play's periodical publication another small payment if the Russian Theatre took it for the coming season.'[103] In September 1938, *The Waltz Invention* was written, like *The Event*, in only four weeks and with the Russian Theatre in mind. In November, Nabokov read the play to actors of the Russian Theatre, including Grigorii Khmara who was to play the role of Waltz.[104] The play, however, was never staged. A disagreement

Robbe-Grillet', trans. Maurice Couturier, *L'Express*, 5 November 1959 [posted on NABOKV-L, 'An interesting interview of Nabokov in French', 19 January 2011]).

[98] See Zheleznov, '"Sobytie" V. Sirina', 4.

[99] Babikov has convincingly shown that it is indeed Bunin who inspired the character of the Famous Writer in *The Event* (see *P'esy*, 597–8 [note to page 392]).

[100] Vladimir Nabokov to *Novoe russkoe slovo*, 7 April 1941, VNLOC, Box 1, Folder 65. The letter was published a few days later (V. Sirin, 'Pis'mo v redaktsiiu: po povodu retsenzii M. Zheleznova', *Novoe russkoe slovo*, 11 April 1941). Nabokov retained a cutting of the letter's publication in his archive (VNLOC, Box OV1).

[101] See 'V. V. Nabokov i I. A. Bunin: Perepiska', ed. M. D. Shrayer and R. Davis, in R. Davis and V. A. Keldysh (eds.), *S dvukh beregov: Russkaia literatura xx veka v Rossii i za rubezhom* (Moscow: IMLI RAN, 2002), 167–219 [202–5]. Nabokov retained the letter of recommendation which he had written himself as part of the archival material which he passed on to the Library of Congress (Ivan Bunin to Vladimir Nabokov, 1 April 1939, VNLOC, Box 1).

[102] Quoted in Boyd, *Russian Years*, 488–9.

[103] *Ibid.*, 489.

[104] See *P'esy*, 608.

between the proposed director Annenkov and the theatre management delayed the scheduled premiere of the play (10 December 1938) indefinitely.[105] Once more, Nabokov turned to an English-speaking audience, perhaps in expectation of moving to the United States or England and had *The Waltz Invention* translated.[106] Yet any hopes he might have had for an American production were disappointed and the play was performed only thirty years later by an amateur group in Oxford.

DEPARTURES AND ABANDONED PROJECTS

Some sort of engagement with the theatre continued during Nabokov's first years in the United States. Once more, drama offered a source of urgently needed income, albeit this time in the form of lectures on drama rather than playwriting itself. In 1939, Aldanov had secured an invitation for Nabokov to give a number of guest lectures at Stanford University in the summer of 1941. Encouraged by Professor Henry Lanz of the Slavic department to put a strong emphasis on drama in his lectures on Russian literature, Nabokov filled at least two notebooks with his ideas on drama and dramaturgy. Nabokov put in hours at the New York Public Library, reading (and possibly re-reading) contemporary playwrights and several theoretical texts on theatre. In his lectures he analysed besides several of Henrik Ibsen's and Chekhov's plays also Eugene O'Neill's *Mourning Becomes Electra* (1931), Bernard Shaw's *Candida* (1898, produced 1895), John Galsworthy's *Strife* (1909), Henri-René Lenormand's *Time Is a Dream* (1918, produced 1919), Lillian Hellman's *The Children's Hour* (1934) and John Steinbeck's *Of Mice and Men* (1937).[107] Nabokov's general background reading included William Archer's *Play-Making: A Manual of Craftsmanship* (1912), Brander Matthews' *The Principles of Playmaking and Other Discussions of the Drama* (1919), Basil Hogarth's *How to Write Plays* (1933) and several articles on contemporary theatre.[108] The lectures

---

[105] See Boyd, *Russian Years*, 494; see *P'esy*, 608.

[106] 'The Waltz Invention', typescript of early translation of play, VN Berg. That Nabokov did not translate the play himself becomes clear in a letter to Edmund Wilson in March 1943: 'The other day I found an old play of mine, which was translated in England some years ago. Will you read it please. Perhaps something may be done with it. The English is very stilted – it is not mine' (*NWL*, 106). That the play in question is indeed *The Waltz Invention* is indicated by Wilson's later reference to Nabokov's 'play about the dictator' (*NWL*, 210).

[107] Many years later, Nabokov still remembered Lenormand fondly: 'I greatly liked Lenormand's plays when I was young.' He described them as 'so pretty, so poetic' ('The Good Mr. Nabokov').

[108] See Nabokov, 'Notebook for lectures (1940–1941)', VN Berg.

which Nabokov gave especially for the Dramatists' Alliance, an association of academics and students in the School of Letters and in Drama at Stanford University, were part of a series of lectures and performances in the history of tragedy and 'attracted unusually large audiences', as the Slavic department reported.[109] Nabokov 'spoke with wit and point upon the deadening effect of convention upon tragic drama'.[110]

Inspired by his research for these lectures at the New York Public Library, Nabokov contemplated two more dramatic projects. His notes for his lecture 'Playwriting' contain an idea for another drama which seems to have been modelled on the meta-theatrical nature of *The Event*:

write a play: laborious explanations at beginning and all other tricks noted here [dramatic stock situations Nabokov identified in his lecture notes to introduce characters and the situation at the beginning of a play]. A detective longing for the live (or real) passion who has trespassed on the stage – this is the idea of a self-conscious play ... attempts of one [character] to explain that or that [*sic*] relationship and the other criticising such an approach and at last telling the audience who it is. A man ill on stage and a doctor from the audience.[111]

During the same time he also considered making a play out of 'Ultima Thule' (1942), a chapter of an abandoned novel, which later became a short story: 'Oh to write my play about "Falter"!'[112]

Nabokov's interest not only in drama but also in theatre during this time is reflected in his approach to Mikhail Chekhov, suggesting an adaptation of *Don Quixote* for Chekhov's theatre studio in Connecticut. Nabokov envisioned the play being 'carried out in a manner akin to that of his own plays, *The Event* and *The Waltz Invention*'.[113] Nabokov was particularly interested in the practical conditions of staging during his preparation of the adaptation.[114] His sketch which was finished in January 1941, was, however, not well received, as the letter of the administrator of Chekhov's theatre studio indicates:

I understand that you have sent the first draft of this sketch to Mr Chekhov, and, as he remarked to me, it evokes a great many questions and suggestions which must be answered before it can be considered as a skeleton of a future play. Mr Chekhov is now preparing his answer to you with all the remarks,

[109] 'Annual Report of the President of Stanford University for the Fiftieth Academic Year Ending August 31, 1941', December 1941, 300. Stanford University Archives.
[110] *Ibid.*
[111] Nabokov, 'Notebook', VN Berg.
[112] See Boyd, *American Years*, 23.   [113] *Ibid.*
[114] See Mikhail Chekhov to Vladimir Nabokov, 12 December 1940, VN Berg.

suggestions and questions which he has in mind. I hope that upon receipt of his questions and commentary you will be in a position to revise your script.[115]

At the end of March, Nabokov and Chekhov realised that their concepts and ideas for the adaptation did not coincide.[116] No doubt because of Chekhov's deep admiration for Nabokov's work in general, the final rejection of Nabokov's sketch arrived in the guise of a postponement, allegedly due to war-related financial and organisational difficulties. The promise to approach Nabokov again at the end of 1941 was never fulfilled,[117] although Chekhov continued to develop his plans for a staging of *Don Quixote*.[118] This failed theatrical project might have contributed to Nabokov's negative views on any form of artistic collaboration, against which he would rail a few months later in his lectures.[119]

It is important to note that after his work on the adaptation of *Don Quixote*, Nabokov would never again write drama for the theatre, but he retained a loose connection with the dramatic art through other writers who adapted his work for the stage or were interested in staging his plays. In 1955, for instance, he corresponded with Evan Jones about the latter's adaptation of *Bend Sinister* for the stage.[120] Nabokov even tried to use his contacts for a production of it, sending it to the stage and film director Elia Kazan, whom he had met briefly in the spring of 1952.[121] Two years later Zinaida Shakhovskoy was contemplating staging one or two of Nabokov's plays in Paris, an idea which the Nabokovs warmly welcomed.[122] In 1957, he responded to a letter from Patricia Kip Millstein who had adapted *Invitation to a Beheading*, giving detailed criticism of Millstein's reading of the novel and his suggestions as to how to transform the novel into a drama.[123] The final instance of a clear engagement

---

[115] E[ugene] Somoff to Vladimir Nabokov, 13 January 1941, VN Berg.
[116] See Boyd, *American Years*, 26.
[117] See E. Somoff to Vladimir Nabokov, 13 May 1941, VN Berg.
[118] See Liisa Biukling, *Mikhail Chekhov v zapadnom teatre i kino* (St Petersburg: Akademicheskii proekt, 2000), 350.
[119] Early in 1941, Nabokov and Wilson had worked together closely on an English translation of Pushkin's 'Mozart and Salieri' (Boyd, *American Years*, 26). However, this unusually productive experience of collaboration for Nabokov does not seem to have left any impact on his attitude towards artistic team efforts. Nabokov appeared as the sole translator when the play was published in English (Alexander Pushkin, 'Mozart and Salieri', trans. Vladimir Nabokov, *The New Republic*, 104 (21 April 1941), 559–65).
[120] See Vladimir Nabokov to Evan Jones, 6 February 1955, VN Berg.
[121] See Vladimir Nabokov to Elia Kazan, 6 February 1955; 6 June 1955, VN Berg. Despite Nabokov's efforts the play was rejected (see Elia Kazan to Vladimir Nabokov, 10 August 1955, VN Berg).
[122] Véra Nabokov to Zinaida Shakhovskoy, 5 August 1954, VNLOC, Box 22, Folder 3.
[123] See Brian Boyd, '"Welcome to the Block": *Priglashenie na kazn'* / *Invitation to a Beheading*: A Documentary Record', in Julian W. Connolly (ed.), *Nabokov's* Invitation to a Beheading: *A Critical Companion* (Evanston, IL: Northwestern University Press, 1997), 141–79 [165–8].

with a theatrical production comes in 1968 when Nabokov showed some interest in the staging of *The Waltz Invention* by the Oxford University Russian Club under the direction of David Bellos. Véra Nabokov volunteered, with her husband's approval, to translate into Russian the passages added to the English translation of the play, as well as the list of dramatis personae. Nabokov himself took sufficient interest in the project to suggest 'that you [Bellos] reprint in your programmes his Foreword to the English edition (if you wish to do this)'.[124] A translation of the foreword into Russian was revised by Nabokov himself as the annotated typescript shows.[125] It is not clear whether Nabokov thought that the foreword in Russian would be more suitable for a performance of the Oxford Russian Club or whether this Russian translation of the foreword was already part of another project, perhaps a Russian edition of his plays, as Babikov suggests.[126] In any case, the programme for the performance at Oxford contained Nabokov's foreword in the original English.[127] According to Bellos, the production itself was anything but professional:

All that I recall of this youthful adventure is the difficulty (given our means and tiny talents) of making a mountain explode. In the end it was a silly plywood structure with a spring-loaded hinge. It took thousands of hours to invent (we were all language and lit people, not set designers!) and raised a laugh more for its amateurishness than for its effect.[128]

Perhaps it was more than just polite encouragement for the young producer when Véra Nabokov expressed her regret that 'we could not attend. It would have been so much fun to attend your premiere of the play in Russian.'[129]

The small numbers of plays Nabokov wrote is not necessarily an indication of his general indifference towards drama or theatre, but rather a reflection of the difficult situation in which Russian émigré theatres in Berlin and Paris had to operate. In particular Nabokov's last two plays were written in an attempt to ease his financial difficulties, capitalising on a relatively successful phase of the Russian émigré theatre in Paris. Both *The Event* and *The Waltz Invention* might never have been written had not his economic hardship been so acute. That his incentives for playwriting

---

[124] Véra Nabokov to David Bellos, 23 February 1968, VN Berg.

[125] See Vladimir Nabokov, 'Izobretenie Val'sa' [Russian], foreword, VN Berg.

[126] See *P'esy*, 608.

[127] 'Programme: "Izobretenie Val'sa" at the Oxford University Russian Club', Personal Archive David Bellos, Princeton.

[128] Author's personal correspondence with David Bellos, 27 March 2002.

[129] Véra Nabokov to David Bellos, 14 April 1968, VN Berg.

were very practical financial considerations rather than lofty artistic ideals only confirms Nabokov's interest in the performance side of theatre in the first half of his writing career. For the same reason, Nabokov wrote his plays specifically for his fellow Russian émigrés who made up the major and only potential audience for the plays of a Russian émigré writer at the time. This explains to some extent why Nabokov's plays seem to lack the transnational appeal of his other works. Instead, they are inextricably linked to specific cultural traditions of the Russian stage. Later attempts to translate the plays into English (and French) appear more as an afterthought. This together with their inward-looking orientation towards Russian émigré culture explain at least partly why Nabokov's plays have with few exceptions not reached the stages of theatres outside a Russian cultural context.

2

Theatre on trial: Nabokov's dramaturgy

Initially, Nabokov's interest in the performance side of theatre was contingent on the economic and cultural conditions for staging his plays. In other words, the opportunities for theatrical performances fed Nabokov's imagination in writing his dramas with projected theatrical performances in mind. This acceptance of the performance as an integral part of the theatrical process has disappeared in his lectures on the dramatic art which he gave shortly after his arrival in the United States. Here he expresses what Jonas Barish calls the 'antitheatrical prejudice',[1] which condemns the theatrical performance *per se* and informs his polemical approach to dramatic and theatrical art. Instead of a performance-centred approach, Nabokov insists on a drama-centred model of theatre. His later concern with literal, faithful translations is already foreshadowed in these lectures which stipulate 'word-for-word' productions of dramas.

One of Nabokov's first teaching assignments in the United States was at Stanford, where he taught two courses over the summer of 1941, 'Modern Russian Literature' and 'The Art of Writing'. With regard to the latter, Nabokov was asked by Professor Lanz of the Slavic department at Stanford University to place a strong emphasis on playwriting:

In all my advertising notes and pamphlets I strongly emphasize your qualifications as a Russian playwright, for – as you have probably discovered yourself – playwriting in America is the most popular and practical form of literature, and if you will have any number of students in the course they will be from the play-writing class.[2]

In addition, Nabokov gave two public lectures for the Dramatists' Alliance, 'The Technique of Modern Tragedy' and 'Life and Fiction: A Demonstration'.[3] In preparation for these teaching commitments,

---

[1] See Jonas Barish, *The Antitheatrical Prejudice* (Berkeley: University of California Press, 1981).
[2] Quoted in Boyd, *American Years*, 22.
[3] See 'Report of the President of Stanford University', December 1941, 315.

Nabokov filled a whole notebook with notes and lecture drafts on drama.[4] Two lectures were posthumously published in essay form under the title 'Playwriting' and 'The Tragedy of Tragedy',[5] while his notes for an analysis of Chekhov's *The Seagull* (*Chaika*, 1896) went into the posthumously edited collection of Nabokov's lectures on Russian literature.[6]

Although Nabokov briefly considered writing a book on the art of drama,[7] and later thought of publishing at least his lectures on literature, these plans were not realised during his lifetime.[8] As such, the majority of unpublished and posthumously published material which focuses on the theatrical art (with the exception of the chapter on *The Government Inspector* in his *Nikolai Gogol* (1944)) was never authorised by Nabokov for a public readership. It is, therefore, problematic to regard these lectures as a coherent manifesto of his aesthetics, the more so as they were intended for a specific audience of budding playwrights. Although Nabokov would return to some of his ideas laid down in his Stanford lectures in subsequent correspondence and various remarks intended for the public, Dmitri Nabokov is surely justified in pointing out that 'later in life, Father might have expressed certain thoughts differently'.[9] The Stanford lectures together with Nabokov's notebooks are, however, essential in marking a turning point in Nabokov's thinking on theatre, defining the shift from a performance-orientated to a text-based approach at a particular juncture in Nabokov's personal and artistic life.

THE PAGE AND THE STAGE: DRAMA AND
THEATRICAL PERFORMANCE

The alternative reception modes of drama as a printed text or as a performance give it an uncertain status as both a literary and a theatrical product. In the century-long discussion over which side is to be prioritised,[10] Nabokov is clearly on the side of the antitheatricalists, with a generally negative attitude towards theatrical performance which emerges in the Stanford lectures. Nabokov's antitheatrical bias has to be viewed in the context of the modern antitheatrical strand which is closely connected

---

[4] See Nabokov, 'Notebook', VN Berg.   [5] See *Plays*.
[6] See Nabokov, *Lectures on Russian Literature*, 282–95.
[7] See Boyd, *American Years*, 23.   [8] See *SO*, 103.
[9] Dmitri Nabokov, 'Introduction [to Nabokov's lectures on drama]', in *Plays*, 311–13 [311].
[10] See Barish, *Antitheatrical Prejudice*. In his book, Barish traces the tradition of the 'antitheatrical prejudice' from Plato to the 1970s.

with questions of authorial control and property.[11] For Ben Jonson, for instance, the stage remained an untrustworthy medium which subverted his control over his texts. The careful supervision of the printing of his dramas is telling in this context.[12] A similar attitude led to a far more extreme reaction in a writer like Byron who tried to preclude potential stagings of his plays in the actual drama texts.[13]

This discussion about the different reception modes of theatre was taken up at the turn of the century in Russia. Significantly, it coincides with the rise of the director in the Russian theatre, in particular Stanislavsky, but also Meyerhold, Evreinov and Alexander Tairov, which raised questions about the rivalry of playwright and director over control of the play. Fyodor Sologub, for instance, stipulated a 'theatre of one will' (*teatr odnoi voli*), in which he 'advocated the replacement of theatrical performance with a "theatricalised" reading of a play, so that the subtleties of the author's words might be better appreciated, and any distortions introduced to the interpretation of the work by the actor were precluded'.[14] This anti-theatrical bias was taken to its extreme by the literary critic Iulii Aikhenvald, to whom Nabokov would grow quite close during his time in Berlin as a like-minded friend and critic. Aikhenvald denied the very legitimacy of theatre as an art, 'as its physical nature rendered it incapable of communicating the abstractions that were more properly the sphere of literature'.[15] Aikhenvald's stance has to be seen within the context of a wider Modernist mistrust of the human actor which is also manifest, for

---

[11] For a discussion of the relationship between intellectual property and printing privileges of a play and the possible ownership of drama by different parties, such as the publisher, the theatre company and the author in seventeenth-century England, see Julie Stone Peters, *Theatre of the Book, 1480–1880: Print, Text, and Performance in Europe* (Oxford University Press, 2000), 219–36. Robert Weimann also points to the link between the antitheatrical prejudice and questions of individual authorship: 'It should not come as a surprise, then, that "author's pen" finds itself at a critical conjuncture wherever, in the wake of the recent upheaval in editorial and textual theory and practice, a highly personalized conception of the individual creative consciousness is discarded as providing an authoritative source of textually inscribed intentions and meanings' (*Author's Pen and Actor's Voice: Playing and Writing in Shakespeare's Theatre* (Cambridge University Press, 2000), 16).
[12] See Barish, *Antitheatrical Prejudice*, 139–40.
[13] See *ibid.*, 332–3.
[14] Barbara Henry, 'Theatricality, Anti-theatricality and Cabaret in Russian Modernism', in Catriona Kelly and Stephen Lovell (eds.), *Russian Literature, Modernism, and the Visual Arts* (Cambridge University Press, 2000), 149–71 [151].
[15] Henry, 'Theatricality in Russian Modernism', 152. For a detailed analysis of Aikhenvald's rejection of theatre, see J. B. Woodward, 'From Brjusov to Ajkhenvald: Attitudes to the Russian Theatre, 1902–1914', *Canadian Slavonic Papers*, 1 (1965), 173–88. Babikov identifies Aikhenvald as a direct influence on Nabokov's theory of drama ('Izobretenie teatra', 15–16).

instance, in Edward Gordon Craig's ideal of the actor as marionette and Meyerhold's vision of the actor as machine.[16]

Barish identifies two opposed impulses that lie at the heart of the discussion over theatricality. He aligns the antitheatrical prejudice with the desire for 'order, stability, constancy, and integrity', while the tolerance of theatricality is linked to an emphasis on 'growth, process, exploration, flexibility, variety and versatility of response'.[17] Irrespective of the ideological underpinnings which inform Barish's argument, the theatrical performance confronts the viewer with an ever-changing medium which subverts stability and constancy. The unique context in which each theatrical performance takes place conditions the actual theatrical production and facilitates its inimitable quality. Together with music and dance performances, theatre is therefore defined by Nelson Goodman as 'allographic', an art which is realised in innumerable concrete instances or tokens (i.e. the performances) of a universal abstract type (the written drama text). Literature and painting, in contrast, are termed 'autographic' arts, defined by the impossibility of producing genuine copies or instances of the original art work.[18] Goodman's distinction between abstract type and individual instance works in analogy with Saussure's distinction between *langue*, the abstract potential of language and *parole*, the individual utterance as a concrete realisation of the potential, which was later adapted by Noam Chomsky as 'generative grammar competence' and 'performance', the actual speech act. With some modification, Roland Barthes' distinction between the Work and the Text develops along similar lines: 'the work can be seen (in bookshops, in catalogues, in exam syllabuses), the text is a process of demonstration … the work can be held in the hand, the text is held in language, only exists in the movement of a discourse'.[19] Applied to theatrical performance, the universal (assumed to be stable and pre-existing) type and the concrete instance become analogous to the written drama and the performance.

The ephemeral nature of the theatrical performance with its infinite number of possible manifestations of the text is opposed to the (perceived) stability of the printed text. Nabokov takes up this opposition in his argument for the permanence of the printed text: 'What the theatre adds is a

[16] See Martin Puchner, *Stage Fright: Modernism, Anti-Theatricality, and Drama* (Baltimore and London: Johns Hopkins University Press, 2002), 4–6.

[17] Barish, *Antitheatrical Prejudice*, 117.

[18] Nelson Goodman, *Languages of Art: An Approach to a Theory of Symbols* (London: Oxford University Press, 1969), 112–22.

[19] Roland Barthes, 'From Work to Text', in Vincent B. Leitch (ed.), *The Norton Anthology of Theory and Criticism* (New York and London: W. W. Norton and Company, 2001), 1470–75 [1471].

lot but it varies with the age, whereas the artist's writing is constant.'[20] Elsewhere he remarks that

[there] is also this important point that even an actor of genius may now and then in his 'addition' to the dramatist, display a certain colourful vulgarity that is better appreciated by his fans than by the reader. The indefinite and infinite number of such possible gestures and dramatic effects 'added' to the play is a very telling contrast with the constant of the immortal written drama. Histrionic accretions cannot save a bad play from oblivion just as they cannot improve a good one. They change, the play remains.[21]

It is theatre's inability to reproduce itself, which emerges as the main problem in Nabokov's thinking:

until science has given us all magic boxes in which the best plays can be seen and heard in the best interpretation they ever were blessed with, until then we must be content with the written page for forming our judgement on a play, though I admit it would [be] a great pleasure to slip a slide into a slit and see a Chekhov play as had been staged by the Moscow Art Theatre forty years ago.[22]

The permanence of these hypothetical slides would transform theatre effectively into cinema (which produces a fixed text on celluloid), removing the immediacy and the flexibility of the theatrical performance.

The unpredictability of the actual performance raises questions of artistic control. The imagined performance implied in the drama text by the playwright competes with the actual performance which is determined 'by the very different authorship of production, the collaborative effort of director, designer, technician, and actor'.[23] In the theatrical production, the written drama text is transformed into the physical presence of the stage, into space, objects and people that exist on their own terms. This autonomy, or in Stanton B. Garner's words, theatre's 'material independence', removes the playwright as an influencing or controlling entity from the stage.[24] Nabokov eliminates the potential tension between text and performance, single author and theatrical collaboration, by reducing the theatrical production to a faithful translation of the dramatist's text: '[the theatre performance] may clarify and bring to life [the dramatist's] suggestions, it can even make a bad play look – and only look – like a good one; but the merits of the plays as disclosed by the printed word are what they are, not more, not less' ('Playwriting', 320). In his view, the playwright's imagined production is to be identical with the actual staging

[20] Nabokov, 'Notebook', VN Berg.   [21] *Ibid.*   [22] *Ibid.*
[23] Garner, *Absent Voice*, xii.   [24] *Ibid.*

of the drama. Therefore Nabokov demands a 'verbatim' translation of Shakespeare's dramas into a theatrical production:

Incidentally, I want to stress the point that the way Shakespeare is produced in all countries is not Shakespeare at all, but a garbled version flavoured with this or that fad which is sometimes amusing as in the Russian theatre and sometimes nauseating as, for instance, in Piscator's trashy concoctions. There is something I am very positive about and that is that Shakespeare must be produced in toto, without a single syllable missing, or not at all. ('Tragedy', 327)

That Nabokov fails to explain how exactly this production of Shakespeare is to be determined (a particularly intriguing question in regard to a playwright who never authorised any of the drama texts that were left behind in his name) is here less important than Nabokov's implicit position that the actual production relies entirely on the dramatic text. In this thinking, the performance becomes a mere illustration of the drama text, rather than an independent artistic product.

Just like Aikhenvald, Nabokov finally rejects theatre not only in relation to the dramatic text, but also in its own right as an artistic form, albeit for different reasons. The inherently collaborative nature of a theatrical performance, including the joining of the different artistic impulses of a director, actors, costume and stage designers, lighting technicians and others, automatically discredits theatrical art, in Nabokov's opinion:

a play will be created by the management, the actors, the stagehands – and a couple of meek scriptwriters whom nobody heeds; it will be based on collaboration, and collaboration will certainly never produce anything as permanent as can be the work of one man because however much talent the collaborators may individually possess the final result will unavoidably be a compromise between talents, a certain average, a trimming and clipping, a rational number distilled out of the fusion of irrational ones. ('Tragedy', 323)

Much later, in the foreword to *Lolita: A Screenplay* (1974), Nabokov reiterates his contempt for theatre yet implies that hypothetically an omnipotent auteur-director would be able to overcome theatre's artistic inferiority, which is inherent in its artistic collaboration:

if I had given as much of myself to the stage or the screen as I have to the kind of writing which serves a triumphant life sentence between the covers of a book, I would have advocated and applied a system of total tyranny, directing the play or the picture myself, choosing settings and costumes, terrorizing the actors, mingling with them in the bit part of guest, or ghost, prompting them, and, in a word, pervading the entire show with the will and art of one individual – for there is nothing in the world that I loathe more than group activity.[25]

It is only Stanislavsky who, for Nabokov, comes close to his ideal of a despotic director. Nabokov might have seen some of his productions in the autumn of 1922 when Stanislavsky toured Germany where Nabokov was living with his mother after having returned from Cambridge. Nabokov ascribes the Moscow Art Theatre productions to the sole authorship of Stanislavsky, the theatre's 'dictatorial head'.[26] He thus cancels the collaborative nature of the theatrical performance and legitimates the Moscow Art Theatre productions by assigning them the status of a single-authored text. Although a common assumption, the notion of an auteur-director is riddled with conceptual problems, as John Rouse points out:

we all know, and usually murmur in passing, that this text is 'written' through a collaboration between those who control its various signifying systems (actors, designers, composers, etc.), but we 'legitimize' the text's authority by attributing it to the director. And the authority we usually legitimize in this way is not that over the internal constitution of the systems within the performance text but, instead, the relationship between the performance text and the dramatic text, defined as interpretation. /Director/ has become that sign we use to inscribe that connotational consistency and interpretational purpose we propose to glimpse within and behind a 'weaving together' of the strands of the dramatic with those of the performance text.[27]

In some way, Nabokov's idea of Stanislavsky as auteur-director is a vivid illustration of Barthes' confession, 'I desire the author', rather than a realistic assessment of Stanislavsky's professional capability as a director. It is presumably again Stanislavsky who channels the different collaborative forces of his ensemble into one organic whole in Nabokov's uncharacteristically sentimental account of the Moscow Art Theatre:

Carried away by the profound artistic enthusiasm of its founders [Stanislavsky and Nemirovich-Danchenko], living like one big family, the actors worked away at every one of the productions as if this were to be the one and only production in their lives. There was religious awe in their approach; there was moving self-sacrifice. And there also was amazing teamwork. For no actor was supposed to

---

[25] Nabokov, *Novels 1955–1962*, 673. This statement clearly echoes Bernard Shaw's idea of the playwright's limited influence on the performance: 'since he [the dramatist] could not act the play singlehanded even if he were a trained actor, he must fall back on his powers of literary expression, as other poets and fictionalists do' (quoted in Garner, *Absent Voice*, xii).
[26] Nabokov, *Lectures on Russian Literature*, 302.
[27] John Rouse, 'Textuality and Authority in Theater and Drama: Some Contemporary Possibilities', in Janelle G. Reinelt and Joseph R. Roach (eds.), *Critical Theory and Performance* (Ann Arbor: University of Michigan Press, 1992), 146–57 [147]).

care more for his personal performance or success than for the general performance of the troupe, for the general success of the performance.[28]

This idealised interpretation of artistic collaboration is, however, an isolated instance in Nabokov's writings.

The charges Nabokov levels against artistic collaboration remain
rather one-sided and do not extend (here or elsewhere) beyond the
theatre to other art forms. For instance, Nabokov's criticism does not
even touch on the whole area of music production, another artistic form
which tends to rely on collaboration. Indeed, music is not dismissed
either in its production by an orchestra or as an operatic performance.[29]
The cinema, an equally collaborative art form, is initially in Nabokov's
Stanford lectures also completely left out of his condemnation of artistic cooperation. Only later in his foreword to the screenplay of *Lolita*
does he briefly mention cinema – yet in an explicitly theatrical context ('if I had given as much of myself to the stage or the screen'). This
slight admonition might have been provoked by the rather unsuccessful
collaboration with Kubrick for the film adaptation of *Lolita*. Although
Nabokov was named as the sole author of the film script, Kubrick's version differs considerably from Nabokov's screenplay.[30] Nabokov's delight
at the prospect of reclaiming his original screenplay in print is revealing
in this context:

Another project I have been nursing for some time is the publication of the
complete screenplay of *Lolita* that I made for Kubrick. Although there are just
enough borrowings from it in his version to justify my legal position as author
of the script, the film is only a blurred skimpy glimpse of the marvelous picture
I imagined and set down scene by scene during the six months I worked in a Los
Angeles villa … It is a great pity: but at least I shall be able to have people read
my *Lolita* play in its original form. (*SO*, 105–6)

The premise that by its inherently collaborative nature, the theatrical performance is condemned to artistic mediocrity, validates Nabokov's stipulation that a drama could and should be read in print instead of being
seen on stage. Clearly echoing Samuel Johnson's dictum that 'A play read
affects the mind like a play acted', Nabokov declares that 'a fine play … is

[28] Nabokov, *Lectures on Russian Literature*, 302.
[29] Cf. Barish on this point: 'No musician, however persuaded of the inability of human pianists
to do justice to Beethoven's last sonatas would ever choose to content himself with simply reading the score, or could ever be imagined as saying, "We do not like to hear our master's sonatas
played, and least of all Opus 106"' (*Antitheatrical Prejudice*, 331–2).
[30] Nabokov received $35,000 for being named as the sole author of the screenplay (see Boyd,
American Years, 404).

equally delightful on the stage and at home' ('Playwriting', 319).[31] In some way, the reading of a play becomes actually a preferable mode of reception, as the printed drama text leaves an unlimited number of possible performances to the imagination of the reader. The theatrical performance, on the other hand, restricts the reader's freedom by realising only one unique manifestation of the written text:

a certain part of footlight-pleasure is not the same as the corresponding part of reading-lamp pleasure, the one being in that part *sensual* (good show, fine acting), the other being in the corresponding part *purely imaginative* (which is compensated by the fact that any definite incarnation is always a limitation of possibilities). ('Playwriting', 320)

Nabokov's understanding of the relationship between drama and the theatrical performance is strictly hierarchical. To use Goodman's terminology again, the universal type (the written drama) constitutes, in this thinking, the stable original against which the degree of variation and aberration of the token (the actual performance) can be measured. The less the token deviates from the type, the more closely the relationship between them approximates to its ideal form, in Nabokov's mind. The drama is, therefore, clearly superior in its relationship to the theatrical performance: 'We must draw a definite line between the author's gift and the theatre's contribution. I am speaking only of the former and refer to the latter insofar as the author has *imagined* it' ('Playwriting', 320; emphasis added). All actual productions are bound to fail in comparison with this ideal performance of the mind as envisaged by the author. Here drama becomes a merely literary genre, effectively closet drama, to be read rather than performed, while the theatrical production is reduced to a superfluous by-product, as Nabokov's dismissive remark in his notebook indicates: 'drama is not a compound collaborative art. It is the art of one man. And what is solely important is to write the thing. The rest is paint and carpentry – and the actor's act.'[32] Nabokov establishes the author's ultimate control over the text and the reader, essentially transforming the dramatic text into a literary work without any need for or link to its performance.

The different modes of drama reception are given a far wider significance by Nabokov, reflecting an individual's distinct attitude towards life. In a singular reworking of the notions of 'life is a dream' and 'the world as stage', Nabokov stipulates that 'reading a play and seeing a play correspond

---

[31] Quoted in Manfred Pfister, *The Theory and Analysis of Drama* (Cambridge University Press, 1991), 13.
[32] Nabokov, 'Notebook', VN Berg.

to living one's life and dreaming of one's life' ('Playwriting', 322). Just as Nabokov's ideal reader of drama and fiction realises the author's work in his or her imagination, the alert observer constantly shapes the material from the objective world through subjective perception. The reader and the observer become thus co-creators of a reality which is based on the materials provided by fiction, drama or the outside world. In other words, the reader and observer actualise and control one specific performance (Goodman's token, Saussure's *parole*, or Barthes' Text) out of the potentially infinite number of possible interpretations, which are conditioned by an original source (Goodman's type, Saussure's *langue*, or Barthes' Work). The world is a drama text, life is one of its possible performances, an idea which is in slight variation present in Nabokov's thinking from the very beginning: '*We* are translators of God's creation, his little plagiarists and imitators, we dress up what he wrote, as a charmed commentator sometimes gives an extra grace to a line of genius.'[33] By contrast, an individual who is directly confronted with the world, is, like the spectator of a play, exposed to a fixed reality without the power to control its course. This prompts Nabokov's analogy with a dreamer who is equally powerless over the development of the dream. Underlying these analogies are two key notions in Nabokov's thinking, the dualistic notion of an objective and stable world (the original) in opposition to a subjective and unstable world (the variation), and the belief in individual agency and control which can be exerted over the surrounding world. The implicit evaluation of reading a play as a demanding and creative exercise, and seeing a theatrical performance as merely passive consumption, serves as further ammunition against theatrical art.

THE FOURTH WALL: THEATRICAL REALITIES

Theatre is unique among all art forms in that it lets two different worlds, the theatrical reality of the stage and the external reality of the auditorium, coincide in an identical space and time continuum. This parallel existence of two worlds is conditioned by the fact that the theatrical performance is created simultaneously with its reception.[34] While a written text is automatically situated in the past of the reader by virtue of its 'having been written' before being read, the theatre performance develops at the same time as the viewer perceives it. The immediacy of the theatrical

---

[33] Quoted in Boyd, *Russian Years*, 245 [Nabokov to Elena Nabokov, 13 October 1925].
[34] See Pfister, *Theory and Analysis of Drama*, 5.

performance is further engendered by the inherent self-reflexivity of theatre, as Garner points out: 'the materials of performance constitute the materials of [the stage's] fictional world ... the objects, actors, sounds, and lights of the theater evoke the imaginative realm of fiction by pointing at themselves in an inescapable self-focus'.[35] In contrast to reading a book or seeing a film where the fictional world overcomes and replaces the experience and perception of the actual world, the illusion in theatre can never be all-encompassing. It is in this sense that theatre creates a twofold reality. In other words, while literature creates imaginary presence from absence, theatre deals essentially with double presences, transforming one presence into another presence. In this sense, the illusionist theatre denies its own theatricality. The theatrical gap between two different realities, between an object and its representation is, as it were, filled by the attempt to replace the audience's reality with the world of the stage.

The extra-fictional reality of the auditorium and the dramatic reality on stage are separated by the so-called Fourth Wall convention, which in modern theatre is realised in the proscenium arch between the auditorium and the stage. 'The audience looks into a room, one of whose walls is missing – apparently without the actors within that room being aware of this. All forms of addressing the audience directly are thus ruled out since, in its capacity as an inviolable dividing-line, the front of the stage is the scenic manifestation of the absence of a mediating communication system [between auditorium and stage].'[36] The concept of the illusionist theatre is based on this model which assumes the existence of one stable and objective world as the cornerstone against which the reality of other worlds and fictions can be measured. The shattering of the Fourth Wall as an artistic device seeks to challenge these conventional assumptions about the hierarchically ordered relationship between the different worlds of the stage and the auditorium, making unsettling suggestions about the stability of the spectators' reality.

Once more in close affinity with Stanislavsky's theatre, Nabokov defines the nature of theatrical reality based on the fundamental premise of the illusionist theatre ('one inescapable law ... laid down by that genius of the stage, Stanislavsky' ('Playwriting', 316)) as the non-violation of the Fourth Wall convention: 'The one and only stage convention that I accept may be formulated in the following way: the people you see or hear can under no circumstances see or hear you' ('Playwriting', 315). Accordingly, Nabokov assigns to the spectator the role of a 'most secret watcher or eavesdropper',

---

[35] Garner, *Absent Voice*, xi. [36] Pfister, *Theory of Drama*, 22.

without the risk of being found out ('Playwriting', 315).[37] He, therefore, concludes that '[a] play is an ideal conspiracy, because, even though it is absolutely exposed to our view, we are as powerless to influence the course of action as the stage inhabitants are to see us, while influencing our inner selves with almost superhuman ease' ('Playwriting', 315).[38] For the same reason, Nabokov argues that the person on stage as a dramatic character cannot become aware of the spectator in the auditorium. The direct addressing of the actual audience is therefore, in Nabokov's view, a paradoxical device:

> when the player stalks up to the footlights and addresses himself to the audience with a supposed explanation or an ardent plea, this audience is not the actual audience before him, but an audience imagined by the playwright, that is, something which is still *on the stage*, a theatrical illusion which is the more intensified the more naturally and casually such an appeal is made. In other words, the line that a character cannot cross without interrupting the play is this abstract conception that the author has of an audience. ('Playwriting', 317–18)

The dramatic character can only address an audience which is part of the same world, that is a fictional audience ('an audience imagined by the playwright'), which in Nabokov's thinking is identical with the implied audience ('the abstract conception that the author has of an audience'). Consequently, the dramatic reality is destroyed, as Nabokov states: 'as soon as [the actor] sees [the audience] as a pink collection of familiar faces the play stops being a play' ('Playwriting', 318). The actor's distance from his role as a fictional character is here diminished to the point where the actor actually *becomes* his role for the duration of the play without the ability to perceive a world beyond the stage. Nabokov's view implies therefore that the actor's art lies in his skill to transform himself into a fictional character, removing the gap between the actor and his role, and between the physical reality and the imaginary one. Nabokov sums up his stance poignantly: 'when there is any freakish attempt to break it [the Fourth Wall convention], then either the breaking is only a delusion, or the play stops being a play' ('Playwriting', 316).

---

[37] The very idea of the 'eavesdropping' spectator might have been inspired by Clayton Hamilton's book *Studies in Stagecraft* which Nabokov used for the preparation of his lectures. Hamilton suggests we 'call our present convention the eavesdropping convention – the convention which charges playgoers half-a-crown or half-a-guinea for pretending to remove the fourth wall, and pretending to give them an opportunity of spying upon actual life' (*Studies in Stagecraft* (London, 1914), 72).

[38] The idea of a 'conspiracy' is a somewhat unfortunate metaphor as it remains unclear against whom the two parties are conspiring. It refers presumably to the contract between spectator and actor not to violate this convention.

The Fourth Wall becomes in Nabokov's thinking more than just a theatrical convention, providing an analogy to the relationship between the individual and the world:

the first [the spectator in the auditorium] is aware of the second [theatrical reality on stage] but has no power over it; the second is unaware of the first, but has the power of moving it. Broadly speaking, this is very near to what happens in the mutual relations between myself and the world I see, and this too is not merely a formula of existence, but also a necessary convention without which neither I nor the world could exist. ('Playwriting', 321)

This idea recurs in a more extreme form in *Pnin* where the removal of borders is explicitly equated with death: 'Man exists only insofar as he is separated from his surroundings. The cranium is a space-traveller's helmet. Stay inside or you perish. Death is divestment, death is communion. It may be wonderful to mix with the landscape, but to do so is the end of the tender ego.'[39] Nabokov distinguishes here between a stable and objective external world (elsewhere called 'non-ego') and a subjectively perceived inner world (which he calls 'ego'). Applying this notion to the dualistic world of theatre, Nabokov equates the world of the auditorium with the subjective, and the theatrical reality with the objective world. This juxtaposition of the world with theatre takes up the topos, famously expressed by Shakespeare's Jacques, of 'all the world's a stage' – a notion which Nabokov also expressed elsewhere:

How many times, in a city street, I have suddenly been dazzled by this miniature theatre that unpredictably materializes and then vanishes … I have watched comedies staged by some invisible genius, such as the day when, at a very early hour, I saw a massive Berlin postman dozing on a bench, and two other postmen tiptoeing with grotesque roguishness from behind a thicket of jasmine to stick some tobacco up his nose. I have seen dramas: a dressmaker's dummy with its torso still intact but with a lacerated shoulder, sprawling sadly in the mud amid dead leaves. Not a day goes by that this force, this itinerant inspiration, does not create here or there some instantaneous performance.[40]

By establishing the Fourth Wall convention as the fundamental feature of theatre, Nabokov stipulates an uninterrupted, perfect illusion – the closing of the theatrical gap – as the ideal stage reality, positing his theatrical ideal once more close to fiction. Through the clear-cut separation of the

---

[39] Nabokov, *Pnin*, 17.
[40] Vladimir Nabokov, 'Pushkin, or the Real and the Plausible', trans. Dmitri Nabokov, *New York Review of Books*, 35/5 (1988), 38–42 [42]. Originally published in French as 'Pouchkine ou le vrai et le vraisemblable', *La Nouvelle Revue Française*, 25/282 (1 March 1937), 362–78.

stage from the auditorium, Nabokov creates two isolated spaces in which no alternative, no 'Other' can facilitate the intrinsically twofold reality of theatrical performance. Nabokov thus puts the stage and the auditorium into a relationship which is governed by a diachronic 'either–or' opposition rather than a synchronical 'as-well-as' relation, facilitating a chronological rather than a simultaneous perception of theatrical reality.

A MIRROR TO NATURE: DRAMATIC REALITIES

Nabokov's preference for an essentially Realist drama in a manner akin to Stanislavsky comes to the fore also in his criticism of theatrical conventions, which in his opinion have replaced dramatic innovation. His criteria for determining the value of a play, surprise, realistic depiction and unconventionality, are essentially the same as those he uses for the judgement of fiction. This is entirely in tune with his text-based approach to the theatrical art. In his Stanford lectures Nabokov gives a damning verdict of both historical and contemporary dramas: 'The most popular plays of yesterday are on the level of the worst novels of yesterday. The best plays of today are on the level of magazine stories and fat best-sellers. And the highest form of dramatic art – tragedy – is at its best a clockwork toy made in Greece that little children wind up on the carpet and then follow on all fours' ('Tragedy', 327). Shortly after his Stanford lectures in his book on Nikolai Gogol, he comments that

[a] bad play is more apt to be good comedy or good tragedy than the incredibly complicated creations of such men as Shakespeare or Gogol. In this sense Molière's stuff (for what it is worth) is 'comedy', i.e. something as readily assimilated as a hot dog at a football game, something of one dimension and absolutely devoid of the huge, seething, prodigiously poetic background that makes true drama. In the same sense O'Neill's *Mourning Becomes Electra* (for what *that* is worth) is, I suppose, a 'tragedy'.[41]

In public, he singled out as exceptional masterpieces only Shakespeare's *King Lear* and *Hamlet* and Gogol's *The Government Inspector* ('Tragedy', 326). In his private notes, however, he went further and concluded that even Shakespeare's dramatic work was deficient: 'My fundamental standpoint: … drama exists, all the ingredients of a perfect play exist, but this perfect play (though there exist perfect novels, short stories, poems, essays) has not been produced yet neither by Shakespeare nor by Chekhov. It can be imagined and one day it will be written – either by an Anglo-Saxon or a Russian.[42] In regard to Chekhov, he reiterated this iconoclastic

---

41 Nabokov, *Nikolai Gogol*, 55.   42 Quoted in Boyd, *American Years*, 30.

opinion in his lecture on *The Seagull*, noting that 'with all my fondness for Chekhov, I cannot hide the fact that in spite of his authentic genius he did not create the perfect masterpiece'.[43]

Nabokov's principal criticism of drama, and of tragedy in particular, is that aesthetic conventions have come to replace a realistic depiction of the external world. Nabokov summarises the 'conventional tricks which are used in the conventional expositions of a play' as:

1) trustworthy characters telling the audience about the people and atmosphere of the play 2) reference to somebody or other coming soon, which is promising the audience a visit to look forward to 3) this promised person appearing promptly 4) the Leap Frog trick – when another character is used to divert the audience's [attention] from unlikely promptitude 5) the suggestion of an antithesis, negation of a coming arrival or event – to enhance the spectator's pleasure by mingling the element of surprise to that of expectation and 6) the conventional devices employed in getting the audience to understand as quickly as possible the relations between the characters.[44]

In his notebook he approves of Shakespeare's strategy of subverting the audience's expectations in the character depiction of Polonius:

Polonius is an elderly experienced statesman; and he is called upon to speak the wisest lines in the entire play, yet on the other hand, Hamlet makes fun of him, toys [with him] and teases him into easily appreciable muddles of senile bewilderment, and dismisses him airily as a 'tedious old fool'. The audience, taking its cue from Hamlet, persists in the intention of regarding Polonius as a ridiculous character. Yet, on the other hand, his speech of parting to his son Laertes is compacted of wise saws that have sustained the centuries. (Shakespeare was right!) (A very important point: The audience must learn that the hero may be wrong, and it [is] up to the dramatist to destroy the old fallacy of implying that the audience is meant to see the characters in the play as the 'good' (or positive hero or heroine) sees them. For instance it would be great fun if a really good minor character was for some odd reason (as happens in real life) disliked by the 'good' hero.[45]

To describe the predictability of the dramatic plot development through aesthetic conventions, Nabokov coins the term 'dramatic determinism'. In his lecture on tragedy, he illustrates his idea by developing the example of a hypothetical tragic character, from which he concludes that

[g]ossiping around a man's fate has automatically led us to construct a stage tragedy, partly because we have seen so many of them at the theatre or at the other place of entertainment [presumably cinema], but mainly because we cling to the

---

[43] Nabokov, *Lectures on Russian Literature*, 285.
[44] Nabokov, 'Notebook', VN Berg.   [45] *Ibid.*

same old iron bars of determinism which have imprisoned the spirit of playwriting for years and years. ('Tragedy', 326)

This essentially 'closed form drama' is the result of 'this sound logic of ours [which] is so hypnotized by the conventionally accepted rules of cause and effect that it will invent a cause and modify an effect rather than have none at all' ('Tragedy', 326).[46] The structure of a closed form drama with its implicit assumption of the inevitable force of fate as the guiding principle of life runs contrary to Nabokov's belief in chance and surprise: 'Most of the worst and deepest human tragedies, far from following the marble rules of tragic conflict, are tossed on the stormy element of chance' ('Tragedy', 340).

Nabokov criticises firstly the artificiality and lack of verisimilitude in conventional dramas: 'In what we call "real life" every effect is at the same time the cause of some other effect, so that the classification itself of causality is merely a matter of standpoint' ('Tragedy', 330). In a second step, he examines how this norm shapes the spectator's aesthetic expectations and the consequent predictability of the dramatic plot. In regard to dramaturgy, Nabokov sees this dramatic determinism realised in the *scène à faire*, or obligatory scene, which, in Nabokov's discussion of drama, refers to a scene which can be predicted based on aesthetic preconceptions of the closed form of drama.[47] Nabokov gives as an example 'the promise of somebody's arrival', explaining that

So-and-so is expected. We know that so-and-so will unavoidably come. He or she will come very soon. In fact he or she comes a minute after it has been said that the arrival will occur perhaps after dinner, perhaps tomorrow morning (which is meant to divert the audience's attention from the rapidity of the apparition: 'Oh, I took an earlier train' is the usual explanation). ('Tragedy', 335)

Nabokov returns to this idea in his discussion of Gogol's *The Government Inspector*. Noting that Gogol undermines the closed form by introducing characters who have no function in the subsequent development of the plot, he states that: 'The beauty of the thing is that these secondary

---

[46] The closed drama is closely associated with the principles of sound craftsmanship by the French playwright Eugène Scribe (1791–1861), who wrote a vast amount of mainly vaudevilles and comedies of manners. His dramaturgy was based on a direct cause and effect logic and relied heavily on the audience's knowledge of dramatic conventions.

[47] William Archer, whose *Play-Making* Nabokov read in preparation for his lectures, gives a similar definition, though the predictability of this scene has a far more positive effect in his view: '[the *scène à faire*] is a scene which, for one reason or another, an audience expects and ardently desires'. It causes 'expectation mingled with uncertainty [which] is one of the charms of the theatre' (*Play-Making: A Manual of Craftsmanship* (London, 1913), 173).

characters will not appear on the stage later on.[48] Paraphrasing Chekhov's famous maxim not to introduce a loaded gun onto the stage unless it is to be fired at some point, Nabokov concludes that: 'Gogol's guns hang in midair and do not go off.'[49] In similar vein, he admires Chekhov's rejection of the unity of plot: 'There has been no definite line of conflict. Or rather there have been several vague lines and a futility of conflict … and the romances of the other characters are blind alleys. Finishing the [first] act [of *The Seagull*] with an obvious dead end seemed an insult to people eager for a good tussle.'[50]

Closely related to the *scène à faire* is what Nabokov calls the 'positive finality of effect', which refers to the unambiguous ending in closed forms of drama. His ironic analysis of the techniques to achieve a closed ending through the death of the protagonist demonstrates the implausibility and artificiality of such a self-contained ending. Yet, in Nabokov's view, the playwright cannot violate the rules of the closed dramatic forms because of the audience's aesthetic expectations:

This element of chance playwrights have so completely excluded from their dramas that any denouement due to an earthquake or to an automobile accident strikes the audience as incongruous if, naturally, the earthquake has not been expected all along or the automobile has not been a dramatic investment from the very start. ('Tragedy', 340)

The very idea of a self-contained ending is, according to Nabokov, artificial: '[Drama] is always the same: conflict between this and that, and then the same iron rules of conflict leading either to a happy or miserable end, but always to *some* end which is unavoidably *contained* in the cause. Nothing ever fizzles out in a tragedy, though perhaps one of the tragedies of life is that even the most tragic situations just fizzle out' ('Tragedy', 337–8).

Nabokov's negative assessment of modern drama is based on a selective choice of examples. He illustrates his ideas in another long lecture, which has remained unpublished, on contemporary Soviet drama, looking at two propaganda plays, Nikolai Pogodin's *Aristocrats* (*Aristokraty*,

---

[48] Nabokov, *Nikolai Gogol*, 43. One of the reviewers of *The Event* criticised Nabokov's play precisely for the introduction of these Gogolian secondary characters without a main function: 'There are too many passing characters in the play, who appear only briefly in one of the acts and then do not appear again' (Zheleznov, '"Sobytie" V. V. Sirina', 4).

[49] See Anton Chekhov to A. S. Lazarev-Gruzinskii, 1 November 1889, in *Sobranie sochinenii v dvenadtsati tomakh* (Moscow: Gosudarstvennoe izdatel'stvo khudozhestvennoi literatury, 1960–4), vol. XI, 380–1 [380], item 187; Nabokov, *Nikolai Gogol*, 44.

[50] Nabokov, *Lectures on Russian Literature*, 285.

1934) and Vsevolod Vishnevsky's *Optimistic Tragedy* (*Optimisticheskaia tragediia*, 1933).[51] In this rather pedestrian lecture, which devotes a large part to detailed summaries of the plays' plots, he suggests that the concept of fate in bourgeois drama has been replaced by political ideology in Soviet plays: 'good and its political form is quite sure to triumph over evil and that before our eyes in the last act [,] and we know that it must happen, because otherwise the government would not have sanctioned the play'.[52] Soviet plays, therefore, still adhere to the conventional 'deterministic' forms of drama: 'the structure and the atmosphere, the implication of these plays may be proved to be essentially the same as in a certain type of European and American plays cropping up on the stage since the seventies or so'.[53] He does not, however, mention Mikhail Bulgakov's *The Days of the Turbins* (*Dni Turbinykh*, produced 1926 in Moscow), which in one article on Soviet theatre was called '[a] distinguished realistic drama in any man's language'.[54] In the margin next to this, a brief note in Nabokov's handwriting approves of this judgement: 'accepted!'[55] Almost like an afterthought to his lectures, Nabokov lists also a whole number of modern playwrights who, in his opinion, have created plays which include 'magnificent bits, artistically rendered emotions and, most important, that special atmosphere which is the sign that the author has freely created a world of his own' ('Tragedy', 340). Among them are Strindberg, Chekhov, Shaw, Galsworthy and Steinbeck.

---

[51] Nabokov probably read these plays in English translation in an anthology of Soviet dramas as a reference to *Four Soviet Plays* in his notebook indicates. The New York Public Library where Nabokov prepared a large part of his lectures on dramas holds a copy of *Four Soviet Plays*, ed. Ben Blake (Moscow: Co-operative Publishing Society of Foreign Works in the USSR, 1937), which includes Pogodin's *Aristocrats* and Vishnevsky's *Optimistic Tragedy*. There is also an American edition of *Four Soviet Plays* (New York: International Publishers, 1937). The lecture 'The Soviet Drama' was given during another short assignment at Wellesley College in March 1941 (see Boyd, *American Years*, 25). The material for this lecture had been initially gathered for an article on Soviet literature which was never published, but 'fit[ted] in with his preparations for Stanford' (Boyd, *American Years*, 24).

[52] Nabokov, 'Notebook', VN Berg.   [53] *Ibid*.

[54] John Gassner, 'Broadway 1941: Europe and the American Theatre', *The Atlantic Monthly*, March 1941, 329–37 [330].

[55] See clipping of Gassner's article in Nabokov's notebook ('Notebook', VN Berg). Bulgakov's play was staged several times in Russian émigré theatres in Paris under the title of the novel on which it is based, *The White Guard* (*Belaia Gvardiia*). In December 1927, the play was staged by a Russian émigré troupe (Litavrina, *Russkii teatral'nyi Parizh*, 36–7). There also seems to have been a performance in 1936 at the Russian Theatre in Paris (Litavrina, *Russkii teatral'nyi Parizh*, 135; 138). Khodasevich stated that 'the success of *The Days of the Turbins* was not theatrical but political' ('"Sobytie" V. Sirina', 423). Nabokov read the play probably in English translation in *Six Soviet Plays*, ed. and trans. Eugene Lyons (Boston: Houghton Mifflin, 1934). *The Days of the Turbins* was published in Russian only in 1955 (Mikhail Bulgakov, *Dni Turbinykh. Poslednie dni (A. S. Pushkin)* (Moscow: Iskusstvo, 1955).

Against the conventional predictability in drama, Nabokov sets the element of surprise, 'the irrational and illogical … that spirit of free will that snaps its rainbow fingers in the face of smug causality' ('Tragedy', 326). The few dramas which fulfil this stipulation are associated with dreams. 'What masterpieces can we name except a few dream-tragedies resplendent with genius, such as *King Lear* or *Hamlet*, Gogol's *Inspector*, and perhaps one or two Ibsen plays (these last with reservations)' ('Tragedy', 326). He goes on to explain that '*King Lear* or *Hamlet* [are] dream-tragedies because dream-logic, or perhaps better say nightmare-logic, replaces here the elements of dramatic determinism' ('Tragedy', 327). In his notebooks this idea is taken further in Nabokov's interpretation of *Hamlet* as the protagonist's dream:

we who read the play, we who refuse to see any stage melodrama in a farci[cal] King and his coarse wife clowning their way to doom, we who refuse to be moved by these actions in the same sentimenta[l] way as we are moved by third rate literature – 'Uncle Tom's Cabin' or 'For Whom the Bell Tolls' – we are free to be moved by the prodigious dream beauty of 'Hamlet'. Indeed the whole thing seems to be the dream Hamlet dreams *before* landing while still on board ship during his vacation trip home from his German university, – and then all the irregularities of the play turn out to be the logic of dreams, which logic in its turn lurks behind the logic of life. The prodigious beauty of 'Hamlet' which is probably the greatest miracle in all literature consists not in any of its faked ethical implications, not in the melodrama which the stage lends it, but in the dramatic spirit of every dream detail, every word being a source of wonder and joy, – and alas we never shall know what was that queer liquor which Hamlet refers to in his competitions with Laertes.[56]

Gogol's *The Government Inspector* is also seen as a dream-like, irrational work and is juxtaposed with a nightmare: 'The characters are nightmare people in one of those dreams when you think you have waked up while all you have done is to enter the most dreadful (most dreadful in its sham reality) region of dream.'[57] This might be the reason why Nabokov found something akin to his own vision of Gogol in Meyerhold's staging of *The Government Inspector* as a grotesque nightmare.[58] Nabokov's demand for

---

[56] 'The tragedy of tragedy'. Typescript draft. With Nabokov's holograph draft (fragment). VN Berg.

[57] Nabokov, *Nikolai Gogol*, 42.

[58] *Ibid.*, 38. Nabokov also recalled seeing an English production of Gogol's *The Government Inspector*, dismissing it as 'not a memory I care to evoke' (*Nikolai Gogol*, 38). This might have been Fyodor Komissarzhevsky's production of *The Government Inspector* at the Duke of York Theatre in April 1920. Komissarzhevsky staged the play in a realistic manner, which would explain Nabokov's dismissal of this production (see Victor Borovsky, *A Triptych from the Russian Theatre: The Komissarzhevskys* (London: Hurst and Company, 2001), 326–7).

an authentic depiction of life in drama reveals a particular view of life and reality as dream-like concoctions, essentially creative endeavours. While in his lecture 'Playwriting', dreams came to stand for external control and determinism of the individual, in the context of drama conventions, dreams receive a far more positive connotation which runs counter to conventional notions of Realism and defines reality as an illogical, startling and stunning dream.

In the three years between his last two plays and the Stanford lectures, Nabokov seems to have switched from a performance-oriented playwright to an antitheatrical drama critic. His unease at having to give up his position of authoritative control over the written text for it to be realised in performance is consistent with his general aesthetics of an autocratic author as God in his fictional universe. The insistence on the 'translating' function of theatre highlights Nabokov's concerns as an émigré writer who experienced the loss of his native Russian as a personal tragedy. The anxiety of losing control over an original, fixed and stable text informs his stipulation that theatre should faithfully translate the fixed drama text. The text itself is to provide an accurate copy or translation of the objective and stable, external world (even though Nabokov's view of this external world as a dream-like concoction has little to do with conventional Realism). Nabokov favours an imaginary theatre production staged in the reader's mind, which essentially transforms drama into the literary genre of closet drama, a stable entity which resists an artistically fickle and capricious medium with an extreme vulnerability to economic decline. In his last clear engagement with theatre in these lectures, in a sense, Nabokov moves back to the closet dramas of his early career.

Nabokov's dramatic principles sound singularly old-fashioned for the 1940s, especially when seen in the context of his formally and stylistically innovative novels. His advocacy of a Realist stage in the manner of Stanislavsky favours a theatrical tradition which had already come of age during Russia's Silver Age several decades earlier. Although the Realist theatre was still dominant in the traditional and commercial theatres in the 1940s, artistically it had been superseded by avant-garde theatrical forms and experiments more than thirty years earlier. The performance of Nabokov's own play, *The Event*, only two years before the Stanford lectures, had severely challenged the conservative tastes of Russian émigré audiences. Yet the views Nabokov develops in the Stanford lectures position him much closer to the widespread suspicion among émigrés against avant-garde art and its perceived association with the Soviet government.

3

Thresholds and transgressions: The Man from the USSR, The Event *and* Invitation to a Beheading

As a concrete performance space, the conventional proscenium stage with its clear division into the stage and the auditorium shapes and moulds Nabokov's dramas, which take up and rework the metafictional concerns of his novels and short stories. Despite their different tone and subject matter, all of his plays explore the instability of reality and its precarious, illusory nature within the theatrical world of illusions and make-believe. Competing realities challenge and subvert each other, drawing attention to the different realities of the stage and the auditorium. The plays thus probe the very medium through which they are enacted, creating a series of reflections in which the play and the theatrical space both enhance and destabilise each other. In this way, the theatrical performance is inscribed into Nabokov's dramas, albeit with different degrees of depth and intensity. While *The Tragedy of Mr Morn* only intimates the presence of the stage, the later *The Man from the USSR*, *The Event* and *The Waltz Invention* play more boldly with the realities of the stage on which they are performed. Nabokov examines similar questions in his fiction, most obviously in *Invitation to a Beheading* but also in the related short stories 'The Leonardo' and 'Lik', where the reader is invited to witness crude and cruel performances. The theatrical space in *Invitation to a Beheading* is purely imaginative, yet the reader becomes an integral part of the performance which gradually blurs the boundaries between the book and the reader just as Nabokov's meta-theatre confuses the realities of stage and auditorium.

Two themes which are inextricably linked pervade Nabokov's plays: theatre as disillusionment and theatre as a dream. In *The Man from the USSR* and *The Event*, the stage becomes visible and deliberately reveals its own theatrical illusion, while in *The Tragedy of Mr Morn* and *The Waltz Invention*, the theatrical performance overlaps with a dream, a powerful yet fragile enchantment, which arrests the dreamer for the duration of the theatre performance. This thematic link does not correspond with the plays' chronological development. The plays of theatrical disillusionment, *The Man from the USSR* and *The Event*, are separated by almost twelve years and almost two decades lie between Nabokov's two dream plays *The Tragedy of Mr Morn* and *The Waltz Invention*. Therefore, one cannot find a clear development, for instance, from the dream play *The Tragedy of Mr Morn* to the disintegrating theatrical realities of *The Event*. Rather these different properties of the intrinsically twofold theatrical reality, its enchantment and its inherently flawed illusion, are from the very beginning closely interwoven in Nabokov's dramatic work as a whole. All four plays contain elements of both theatrical enchantment and disenchantment. It is a question of emphasis rather than a clear-cut distinction which justifies the thematic division into dream plays and plays of theatrical disillusionment in the following two chapters.

This chapter will look at instances where Nabokov exposes the fictionality of his worlds in explicitly theatrical contexts, in his plays *The Man from the USSR* and *The Event*, and in his novel *Invitation to a Beheading*. Although *The Man from the USSR* is thematically related to *The Event*, one cannot see the latter as a direct continuation of the dramatic work of Nabokov's younger self. Nabokov had undergone in the meantime a distinct artistic development, reworking and defining themes which are pivotal to his art. The setting in a closed émigré community and the preoccupation with the instability of reality, which both plays share, had become essential motifs of Nabokov's wider fiction. The juxtaposition of the real and the unreal in particular appears also in *Invitation to a Beheading* which marks a mid-point between these two plays. It is therefore not so much the themes themselves as their meta-theatrical treatment which provides a bridge between *The Man from the USSR*, *The Event* and *Invitation to a Beheading*. Although they commence as conventional Realist dramas, the reality of both plays is destabilised during the course of the performance in parallel with the psychological disillusionment that the protagonists experience. A similar process takes place in *Invitation to a Beheading* where the stability of the theatrical world depends on Cincinnatus's participation in the creation of reality.

DISINTEGRATING REALITIES: *THE MAN FROM THE USSR*

The Man from the USSR retains the theme of exile from Nabokov's first play *The Tragedy of Mr Morn*, but it has abandoned the Romantic dreaminess and escapist fantasy world for a dreary realistic setting in the Russian émigré community in Berlin. In this sense it is much closer to Nabokov's first novel *Mary*, written a year before his work on *The Man from the USSR*. Yet while the novel's hero, Ganin, is granted the luxury of lingering in the past and wholly reconstructing the story of his first romance, in the play this freedom of a creative memory is gradually limited by an oppressive present reality which takes over increasingly more mental and physical space during the course of the play.

This contemporary theme, which Nabokov was the first to take up in a drama, struck a chord in the Russian émigré community in Berlin. By the second half of the 1920s, Berlin had lost out to Paris as the capital of the Russian emigration and the exile community in Germany was disintegrating. Following the official recognition of the Soviet Union by major European countries like Great Britain, Italy and France in 1924 and the increasing consolidation and stabilisation of power within the Soviet Union in the latter part of the 1920s, the émigrés' displacement could no longer be discounted as a merely transitional stage but had to be accepted as a permanent state of being. The play's balanced depiction of the different reactions to this perception and experience of exile was praised in a contemporary review: 'On one side, lack of willpower, confusion and garrulous neurasthenia with a naïve faith in miracles. On the other – clenched teeth, no sentimentalities and intelligent reserve.'[1] The resignation to the émigré fate is reflected in the melancholy tone of the play, the review detected: 'The author neither mocks nor curses [the émigré life], but he smiles sadly.'[2]

Only the first act ever appeared in Russian, in *Rul'*,[3] while the entire play was published posthumously in Dmitri Nabokov's English translation from a copy of the drama's Russian manuscript in Elena Nabokov's album.[4] The complete Russian text has been preserved in this album copy, which was posthumously transcribed,[5] in preparation for a planned publication of Nabokov's plays in Russian by Ardis at the end of the eighties.[6] The entire play was published recently for the first time in Russian in the Azbuka edition of Nabokov's plays.

The Man from the USSR follows the lives of a loosely connected group of émigrés over the course of nearly two weeks. Like the later *The Event*, this is a strangely eventless play revolving around the return of

---

[1] Brodskii, 'Chelovek iz SSSR', 5.   [2] *Ibid.*
[3] See 'Chelovek iz SSSR' [Act One], *Rul'*, 1 January 1927, 2–3.
[4] See Dmitri Nabokov, 'Introductory Note [to *The Man from the USSR*]', in *Plays*, 33.
[5] See 'Chelovek iz SSSR'. Typescript of play, unsigned and undated, VN Berg.
[6] See Dmitri Nabokov, 'Nabokov and the Theater', 26.

the double-agent Kuznetsov from the Soviet Union. Although there is the illusion of frantic action evoked by frequent entries and exits and five scene changes, there is no clear plot development. Kuznetsov arrives, starts an affair with the film actress Marianna, splits up with her after a week and, finally, in the last act, admits that he still loves his wife Olga from whom he is separated. Minor characters, like the former White Army officer Taubendorf who has been reduced to earning his money as a waiter and film extra and the old impoverished tavern owner Oshivensky, anchor the play firmly in the milieu of Russian émigré life. The reviewer of *The Man from the USSR* saw the lack of plot development as the play's major deficiency: 'A serious fault of the play is the lack of action.'[7] Dmitri Nabokov offers a more subtle reading of the play: 'the real action is taking place elsewhere. This is true in a general sense: one has the feeling that the interpersonal relations around which the play itself revolves are over-shadowed by much larger events occurring outside the stage, outside the theatre, outside the country.'[8]

In *The Man from the USSR*, Nabokov stages the different, sometimes competing realities which condition the émigré existence. The Russian émigrés of the play live inside a mesh of parallel realities which are set off against each other. The external world of 'German' Berlin is contrasted with the inner reality of the émigré community, 'Russian' Berlin, while Soviet Russia provides the foil for the memory of a bygone era, pre-revolutionary Russia. Amongst Nabokov's dramas, *The Man from the USSR* gives the most exact and detailed stage directions which create a clear picture of the space in which the action is to take place. Contrary to English dramatic conventions, the space on stage is described in 'the reverse of stage left and stage right', as Dmitri Nabokov points out (*Plays*, 35). In the third act, for instance, the stage directions are clearly given in relation to the position of a spectator: 'Against the wall, *facing the audience*, stands a small red velour settee' (*Plays*, 79; emphasis added) ['У стены, против зрителя, красный плюшевый диванчик' (*P'esy*, 335)]. This break with convention might be partly explained by the inexperience of a new playwright, but more importantly it indicates a clear focus on the actual effect of the stage space on the audience. The physical presence of the stage is used to let the different realities of exile coincide, challenge and resist each other. The complex relationships between the nostalgic-ally perceived past, the present reality in the enclosed world of an émigré

---

[7] Brodskii, 'Chelovek iz SSSR', 5.
[8] Dmitri Nabokov, 'Nabokov and the Theatre', 7.

community almost hermetically sealed against the external reality of the host country and the present state of the home country are all ingrained in the changing space of the stage.

Most of the émigrés in the play linger in the past, avoiding any confrontation with the present reality of their existence. In an accurate depiction of the Russian émigré mentality of the 1920s, all of them, with the notable exception of Kuznetsov, refer to the Soviet Union as 'Russia'. This 'Russia' is manifest in Olga's dream of a remote idyll, some place close to the fictional provinces from Gogol's stories. The longing for a place that no longer exists comes also to the fore in Taubendorf's homesickness and in Oshivensky's unrealistic plans to return to Russia, albeit as a place of last rest. This flight into fancy, devoid of any realistic evaluation of the current Soviet Union, marks the émigrés' 'Russia' as an overtly imaginary space. The unreality of a past Russia is also mirrored in the film about the revolution, where Russia itself is reduced to clichéd props and stylised maps – a mere fiction on celluloid.

The world of German Berlin outside the closed émigré community is initially a remote entity which is barely acknowledged in the émigrés' minds or the space of the stage. German Berlin exists only beyond the stage in the form of the legs of passers-by seen through a pavement window, the sound of a violin or a few German words spoken by a maidservant offstage. As Dmitri Nabokov points out, the juxtaposition of the inside and the outside reality 'make[s] the spectator's, or reader's, attention rebound from somewhat dubious offstage matters, *travel* back, and focus with increased intensity on the *visible* microcosm of the play, causing him to perceive it in a relief that would not otherwise be so vivid'.[9] Nabokov would later recall his impressions of the lack of interaction between the émigré communities and the external reality of the outside world:

As I look back at those years of exile, I see myself, and thousands of other Russians, leading an odd but by no means unpleasant existence … among perfectly unimportant strangers, spectral Germans and Frenchmen in whose more or less illusory cities we, émigrés, happened to dwell. These aborigines were to the mind's eye as flat and transparent as figures cut out of cellophane. (*SM*, 211)

This perception of the Germans or Frenchmen as unreal, two-dimensional characters is rendered visually in the first act of *The Man from the USSR*, where the legs seen through the window are described in the stage

---

[9] *Ibid.*, 8.

directions as silhouette-like shadows reminiscent of a black and white film:

From time to time legs pass from left to right and from right to left in the strip of window. They stand out against the yellowish background of evening with a two-dimensional clarity, as if cut out of black cardboard. (*Plays*, 36)

Изредка в полосе окна слева направо, справа налево проходят ноги. На желтоватом фоне вечера они выделяются с плоской четкостью, словно вырезанные из черного картона.[10] (*P'esy*, 315)

The window itself is reminiscent of a shadow theatre or a cinema screen: 'a narrow horizontal window – a strip of glass spanning almost the entire length of the room' (*Plays*, 35) ['узкое продольное окно, полоса стекла, почти во всю длину помещения' (*P'esy*, 315)] – a flat two-dimensional reality separated from the present. Later in the first act, this outside reality is literally shut out when the blinds are closed. What seems to protect the émigrés also closes them in. The clearly delineated space of the stage comes thus to actualise the confined space of the émigrés' existence inside their small community without any opening on to the external world.

The artificiality and sense of unreality of this insular existence is brought to the fore by the distinctly theatrical settings of the first two acts. Oshivensky's tavern, a poor imitation of a pre-revolutionary restaurant, creates out of tired stereotypes a Russia which no longer exists:

The proprietor has evidently attempted to give the tavern a Russian atmosphere by means of blue babas and peacocks painted on the rear wall above the strip of window, but his imagination has stopped there. (*Plays*, 35)

Хозяин, видимо, постарался придать кабачку русский жанр, который выражается в синих бабах и павлинах, намалеванных на задней стене, над полосой окна, но дальше этого его фантазия не пошла. (*P'esy*, 315)

Kuznetsov later dismisses the entire décor as '[theatrical] props [*butaforiia*]' (*Plays*, 41). This markedly theatrical setting is accentuated by the entry of Taubendorf, who still wears make-up from his work as a film extra. In a similar vein, Marianna's tasteless room, decorated in a bad imitation of middle-class living 'with aspirations to bourgeois comforts' (*Plays*, 58) [с потугами на буржуазное благополучие (*P'esy*, 325)] seeks to be something it is not.[11] The distinct theatricality of the actual settings

[10] Diment also notes the 'cinematographic elements' in the play, including the screen-like window and the '"script-like"' stage directions in the first act ('Plays', 591).

[11] The rented room itself is for Nabokov an image which crystallises the temporary and shabby nature of émigré life, as he noted in his obituary of Gessen: 'The Russian Berlin of the Twenties was all in all nothing more than a furnished room which was let by a rude and ill-smelling

exposes the sham reality of self-delusions and pretences which the Russian émigrés have created around them.

The play-acting by the main characters who perpetually hide their true feelings and intentions behind shifting masks and fake identities further enhances the sense of the play's theatricality. Kuznetsov leads a double life, simultaneously fulfilling several roles which obscure each other. His part as businessman conceals his role as Soviet agent, which in turn disguises his actual mission for the White cause.[12] He performs a role as Marianna's lover in order to protect his wife against possible repercussions from the Soviets should he ever be found out, as Boyd suggests.[13] His wife plays along with this, in her turn pretending not to love him anymore. In the developing love triangle, Marianna inadvertently re-enacts her film part as the 'other woman'. Allusions to theatrical performance abound. Refusing to act the part of the romantic lover, Kuznetsov ironically intimates the limits of his play-acting: 'Forgot my lines' (*Plays*, 72) ['Забыл реплику' (*P'esy*, 332)]. Marianna also refers to their relationship in theatrical terms, claiming that it 'was all playacting. I was just doing a part' (*Plays*, 99) ['[c] моей стороны это все было комедией. Я только играла роль' (*P'esy*, 345)]. That most of the play's characters are involved in the making of the film either as actors or as extras (ironically in the role of Russian revolutionaries) and frequently appear in costumes and make-up further underscores the sense of artificiality and pretence. Playing with theatre's eternal dichotomy of seeming and being, the drama presents the life of the émigré community as a theatre-within-the-theatre where the borders between authentic and acted behaviour become blurred.

The subsequent disintegration of this illusory world is accompanied by a distinct change in the appearance of the stage. The overt theatrical settings of the first two acts correspond with the main characters donning their masks. In both acts the whole space of the stage is still available to act out their illusions, self-delusions and deceptions. In the third act, however, the action shifts to a bare foyer, dominated by a grey wall which

---

German woman (the foul sweat of that unsuccessful people is unforgettable)' ('Pamiati I. V. Gessena', *Novoe russkoe slovo*, 31 March 1943, 2. Reprinted in *Sobr. soch.*, V, 594–96 [594]).

[12] Kuznetsov's different roles as a double agent echo closely the exile situation, as Nabokov would point out in regard to his own émigré situation in New England: 'what am I doing in this stereoscopic dreamland? How did I get here? Somehow, the two sleighs have slipped away, leaving behind a passportless spy standing on the blue-white road in his New England snowboots and stormcoat' (*SM*, 78). He had used a similar image in 'A Visit to the Museum' (1938), where a Russian émigré after some phantasmagorical trip through a museum finds himself suddenly in Soviet Russia, where he immediately destroys his identity papers.

[13] See Boyd, *American Years*, 264.

takes up a quarter of the stage. The props have been reduced to a table, a chair and a sofa. It is in this act that the carefully constructed façade begins to crack when Olga admits to Taubendorf that she still loves her husband. Just as the stage seems to give up its illusionist character, Olga is the first to allow a glimpse behind her mask. In the subsequent act the same wall has moved to the front of the stage, claiming half of the available space. The remaining part of the stage is cluttered with the props of a film production, which strips the stage of any illusionist devices, emphasising the fictionality of the space. In the stage directions, the stage is explicitly compared to a *balagan*, the Russian paradigm of sham reality:

> a wide passageway crowded with movie props, creating an effect reminiscent simultaneously of a photographer's waiting room, the jumble of an amusement-park booth [*balagannye budki*], and the motley corner of a futurist's canvas.[14] (*Plays*, 89)

> широкий проход, заставленный кинематографическими декорациями, что напоминает одновременно и приемную фотографа, и балаганные [будки], и пестрые углы футуриста.[15] (*P'esy*, 340)

The shattering of the illusion is stressed in the fragmentation of the settings:

> These props have uneven gaps and apertures ... All of it reminds the viewer of a many-colored jigsaw puzzle, carelessly and only partially assembled. (*Plays*, 89)

> В этих декорациях неровные лазейки и просветы ... Всеэ то напоминает зрителю разноцветную складную картину, небрежно и не до конца составленную. (*P'esy*, 340)

As if responding to the fracturing of the illusion, Kuznetsov drops his role and leaves Marianna. In the same act, his true political conviction as an anti-Bolshevik becomes apparent in his conversation with Taubendorf. The outside reality intrudes on to the stage with increasing force, reducing the available space where the life of the internal world can be acted out, until in the last act the stage itself dissolves in the chaos

---

[14] The Russian word *balagan* has several related meanings. Dmitri Nabokov translates 'balagannye budki' as 'amusement-park booth[s]'. *Balagan* has also the meaning of a theatre farce or a puppet play, as well as the booth in which puppet plays would usually be presented at fairs. For a detailed discussion of the concept of *balagan* in Nabokov's work, see Savely Senderovich and Yelena Shvarts, 'Balagan smerti: Zametki o romane V. Nabokova "Bend Sinister"', *Kul'tura russkoi diaspory: Vladimir Nabokov – 100. Materialy nauchnoi konferentsii (Tallinn – Tartu, 14–17 ianvaria 1999)* (Tallinn: TPÜ Kirjastus, 2000), 356–70. See also Senderovich and Shvarts, 'The Juice of Three Oranges'.

[15] The Azbuka edition faithfully reproduces what must surely be a typing mistake in the original manuscript: 'balagannye budni' instead of 'balagannye budki'.

of the Oshivenskys' moving. The few remaining belongings are scattered around the room, giving it a dishevelled, fractured appearance, and it is here that all illusions are finally shattered. While Marianna confronts her lack of talent as an actress and her unreciprocated love for Kuznetsov, Oshivensky understands that a return to Russia has become impossible.[16] It is in the same scene that Kuznetsov and Olga finally admit to still loving each other. While the characters' masks are crumbling, the setting is collapsing. The parallel disintegration of the stage and the émigrés' illusions and pretences establishes thus a close association between the theatre and the émigrés' world.

The off-stage reality continuously comments on the internal reality of the play. The legs seen in the back window of the tavern, for instance, provide both a close analogy and a strong contrast to the reality of the first act. The two-dimensional shadow theatre performed by the legs serves as a fitting background to the unreality of the tavern's contrived Russianness. At the same time, the continuous movement outside throws into relief the émigrés' situation inside where time is standing still despite the superficial bustle of hectic entries and exits in the first act. Initially, in the manuscript, Nabokov had created an even closer link between the reality on the outside and that on the inside: 'If one compared the action onstage to music, these silhouettes [of legs in the window in Oshivensky's tavern] would serve as black quavers and semiquavers' (*Plays*, 36) ['Если сравнить действие на сцене с музыкой, то эти силуэты ног служат как бы черными музыкальными нотами' (*P'esy*, 581)].[17] The musical notes are the fixed, written-down signs, which are more enduring and stable yet also mute and less real than the émigrés' inside reality. The ephemeral exile existence is initially more audible than the legs or musical quavers on the outside, but like a musical performance, it is bound to vanish and be lost forever. Interestingly, the musical motif recurs in the subsequent act when a violin is audible from outside the window where Olga is sitting (as if the legs previously confined to the external reality, were now walking as musical sounds into the space of the stage). Olga pretends not to notice the sound of the music just as she pretends not to love Kuznetsov anymore. In the final act, the outside world makes itself once more heard in the sound of a violin playing the same tune as in the second act. This time it is acknowledged by

---

[16] Marianna's disappointment in her screen appearance foreshadows Magda's shock at seeing herself on screen in the later *Kamera obskura* (1932–3).

[17] This sentence was omitted in the published first act which appeared in *Rul'* but has been retained in Dmitri Nabokov's English translation. The recurrence of the musical theme in subsequent acts suggests that the omission was a printer's mistake rather than Nabokov's decision.

Kuznetsov, which by analogy suggests that the music is now as real as his
love for Olga. In the third act, Olga's resolve to drop her role as the indifferent separated wife is accompanied by roaring applause from the lecture
room behind the wall, as if to encourage her. In the fourth act the sounds
of making a film illustrate the process of fiction-making, which forms a
contrapuntal theme to accompany Kuznetsov's revelation that he is neither
Marianna's lover nor a Bolshevik. Throughout the play, the implied reality
of the outside world encroaches ever more audibly upon the internal space
of the émigrés and gradually reduces the available space in which they are
allowed to create their illusionary worlds.

The dissolution of this world in the last act is reminiscent of Chekhov's
The Cherry Orchard where the final act is marked by the general mood of
departure. The dishevelled state of the stage left bare by the inhabitants'
moving out as well as the constant anxiety about missing the train in *The
Cherry Orchard* recur in *The Man from the USSR*. The thematic significance of Chekhov's play as a Russian literary paradigm of a vanishing
old world could not have been lost on the contemporary audience.[18] The
play ends with a gloomy outlook on the future of the Russian emigration,
setting up a whole series of images and allusions pointing to imminent
death. Dmitri Nabokov also suggests that '[the] real backdrop for the
shabby, bittersweet, temporary existence of the characters is one of terror
and of doom … we must return perforce to the tragic realization that the
destiny of these people, with all their dreams, their quirks, their foibles, is
sealed.'[19] Oshivensky declares that 'We'll move straight into the Kingdom
of Heaven. At least there you don't have to pay the rent in advance' (*Plays*,
102) ['Прямо в царство небесное переедем. Там, по крайней мере, не
нужно платить вперед за квартиру' (*P'esy*, 346)].[20] Shortly afterwards he

---

[18] This melancholy act is only briefly lit up by Fedor's enthusiasm about the future: 'I like variety.
I'm grateful to Communism – it made us discover the whole wide world. Now I'm going to see
Paris – new city, new impressions, the Eiffel Tower. It's a great feeling …' (*Plays*, 113) ['Я люблю
разнообразие. Спасибо коммунизму – показал нам белый свет. Увижу теперь Париж, новый
город, новые впечатления, Эйфелеву башню. Прямо так легко на душе…' (*P'esy*, 351)]. This opti-
mism about his move to Paris echoes the delight of Iasha about the prospect of going to Paris at
the end of *The Cherry Orchard*. A year later Nabokov would express similar sentiments, although
his notion of the freedom of emigration goes beyond the opportunity to travel to include creative
and intellectual freedom (see Vladimir Nabokov, 'Iubilei', *Rul'*, 18 November 1927, 2. Reprinted
in *Sobr. soch.*, II, 645–7).

[19] Dmitri Nabokov, 'Nabokov and the Theatre', 21–2.

[20] Stephen H. Blackwell suggests an interesting analogy between the émigré community and the
'otherworld' in a metaphorical reading which is easily applicable to *The Man from the USSR* :
'Émigré society was already a kind of *потусторонность* (beyond, otherworld), a cultural existence beyond the world of Russia. (This metaphor is especially apt, because the old Russia was in
fact dead, and its living remains were there, in the European emigration.)' (*Zina's Paradox: The
Figured Reader in Nabokov's* Gift (New York: Peter Lang, 2000), 147).

and his wife find a new room in Paradise Street with a landlord called Engel.[21] Kuznetsov has earlier stayed at the hotel Elysium, the otherworld for courageous heroes in Greek mythology. The closing lines of the play, Kuznetsov's beginning of a story about Napoleon, the artillery officer in Toulon, receive ultimately negative implications.[22] Although Napoleon led a powerful military advance against Russia, the attack on Russia was also a military catastrophe from which his Grand Army never recovered. And although Napoleon successfully escaped from his first place of exile on Elba back to France, he was soon exiled again to St Helena, a place whence he would never return. The play ends thus on a melancholy note, suggesting the failure of Kuznetsov's secret battle against the Soviet Union, his death and the dispersal and disintegration of the émigré community. While on the outside nothing ever seems to happen in the lives of the émigrés, the real drama takes place underneath the surface of this bleak émigré existence. It is the dissolution of the internal reality of a closed émigré community that constitutes the actual development of the play. Not only the shattering of their illusions but also the gradual disappearance of the émigré world itself, which is replaced by an intruding external world, emerge as Nabokov's main concerns in this play. The end of the play, giving way to the outside reality of the auditorium, coincides with the émigré world yielding to an external reality.

This apparently Realist play subverts the conventions of the illusionist theatre by introducing subtle meta-theatrical devices. Throughout the play, the émigrés' internal world is associated with play-acting, masks and props. This network of theatrical references becomes a metaphor for the artificiality of the exile existence and the characters' lives, which seem to be merely acted out in the hastily assembled reality of a second-rate theatre. At another level, this metaphor is, of course, neatly realised and replicated in the actual staging of Nabokov's play by Russian émigré actors in 1920s Berlin. In a similar vein, the theatre's strict separation of audience and stage, or external and internal reality, becomes the backdrop for the émigré world closed off against the outside world. *The Man from the USSR* is still a cautious experiment with the nature of theatre and has at first sight not much in common with the loud and shrill clash of different

---

[21] See Dmitri Nabokov, 'Nabokov and the Theatre', 19–20. A character called Engel reappears in far more concrete manner in Nabokov's later story 'A Busy Man' ('Zaniatoi chelovek', 1931), where the name clearly indicates the character's role as a guardian angel from the otherworld.

[22] Dmitri Nabokov links Napoleon and the waiter Fedor who has also been an artillery officer, suggesting that Fedor is perhaps 'being groomed to march, like Napoleon […] on Russia' ('Nabokov and the Theatre', 21).

worlds in the self-consciously meta-theatrical *The Event*, written some ten years later. Yet the theatrical reality is as much a concern here as in the later play, as Nabokov inscribes the fleeting existence of the Russian emigration and the exile condition into the precarious theatrical reality which is being created only for the brief duration of the play.

STEPPING THROUGH THE FRAME: *THE EVENT*

As in *The Man from the USSR*, the closed community of Russian émigrés in *The Event* is depicted – contrary to its title – in an eventless, almost static condition behind the façade of erratic bustle and high-strung emotions. The concrete émigré situation rooted in 1920s Berlin which had been portrayed in *The Man from the USSR*, however, has disappeared in *The Event*, which is set in an indeterminate place at an indeterminate point in time. The subtle probing of the theatrical reality in *The Man from the USSR* becomes a thorough examination of the world of the stage in *The Event*.

The meta-theatre of *The Event* provided ample ammunition for that camp of Nabokov's contemporary critics who viewed him as a shallow, cold stylist. Berberova, although coming to Nabokov's defence and presenting him as an innovative, bold playwright, emphasised formal aspects of the play.[23] More recent critics have concentrated on the content side of the play, suggesting an 'ethical' or 'moral' dimension to the play. Karlinsky, for instance, interprets *The Event* as 'a portrait of an artist as a coward'.[24] Boyd also points to Troshcheikin's moral poverty.[25] Dolinin suggests that the real drama takes place in the disintegrating relationship between Troshcheikin and Liubov, who have to deal with the loss of their son.[26] Babikov follows a similar line of argument, defining the death of the son as the actual drama.[27] As in the earlier *The Man from the USSR*, however, a strict separation into content and form would be beyond the point, as the events on stage and the meta-theatrical elements of the performance condition and reflect each other in the play.

In a self-reflexive twist, this play about a painter continuously emulates and merges with the mode of painting, exploiting the affinities in the aesthetic attributes of theatre and painting. Gotthold Lessing in

---

[23] Berberova, *Italics Are Mine*, 350–1.
[24] Karlinsky, 'Illusion, Reality in Nabokov's Plays', 185.
[25] See Boyd, *Russian Years*, 480–5.
[26] See Dolinin, 'Istinnaia zhizn'', 14.
[27] See Babikov, 'The Main Thing', 153–61.

his famous essay on generic boundaries between different arts, *Laokoön* (1766), distinguishes between inherently spatial (e.g. plastic arts) and temporal art forms (e.g. literature). According to the different perception of different art forms, literature develops sequentially (language in time), while plastic and visual art are perceived in an instant (material in space). Joseph Frank, in his seminal work on spatial art forms, has shown how Modernist literature imitates and appropriates the simultaneous, instantaneous perception of plastic art.[28] Nabokov makes a similar observation in his comparison of pictorial art and literary texts, suggesting that the process of re-reading a book overcomes the temporal restrictions of narrative art and replaces them with the spatial mode of pictorial art. In his lectures on literature he states that

[when] we look at a painting we do not have to move our eyes in a special way even if, as in a book, the picture contains elements of depth and development. The element of time does not really enter in a first contact with a painting. In reading a book, we must have time to acquaint ourselves with it … But at a second, or third, or fourth reading we do, in a sense, behave towards a book as we do towards a painting.[29]

Theatre is positioned somewhere between the spatial and the temporal reception process.[30] While the temporal components of a theatre production (the unfolding of the narrative or the action) tie theatre to literature, there is also a strong link between pictorial and theatrical art in the spatiality of their reception processes. Indeed, the link between theatre and painting is neatly reflected in the architecture of the modern proscenium stage, as Murray Krieger points out: 'This critical attitude [which aligns theatre with the pictorial arts] would support the proscenium-arch theatre, in which the action is framed in a way that makes it the moving analogue to the framed painting as a "still life".'[31] The transformation of theatre into a 'living picture', in which figures and things start moving against a static backdrop, finds its reversal in the *tableau vivant*. A device used primarily in nineteenth-century theatre, the *tableau vivant* is 'a form of picture-making' which presents 'a readable, picturesque frozen

---

[28] Joseph Frank, *The Idea of Spatial Form* (New Brunswick, NJ and London: Rutgers University Press, 1991), 3–66.
[29] Vladimir Nabokov, *Lectures on Literature*, ed. Fredson Bowers (San Diego, New York and London: Bruccoli Clark, Harcourt Brace and Company, 1980), 3.
[30] For an excellent discussion of the historical development of changing notions of the semiotic relationship between painting and theatre, see Murray Krieger, *Ekphrasis: The Illusion of the Natural Sign* (Baltimore and London: Johns Hopkins University Press, 1992), 31–64.
[31] Krieger, *Ekphrasis*, 45.

arrangement of living figures', bringing 'stillness to life'.[32] In the *tableau vivant*, theatre becomes painting (frozen in time) while retaining its characteristic three-dimensionality. The *tableau vivant* has a particular significance in the context of Russian theatre, where the 'silent scene' at the end of Gogol's *The Government Inspector*, when the town people freeze in terror, has become a dramatic paradigm – a scene Nabokov refers to by suddenly freezing the action at the end of the second act in *The Event*.

The Event has the texture of one of Troshcheikin's portraits which seems to come alive on stage. The reverse is also true. During the performance of the play, the stage suddenly freezes into a painting of itself. The spectator is cast in a double role as viewer of a theatre performance and viewer of a painting. By literally framing the performance as a painting, Nabokov throws into relief theatre's capacity to present different realities simultaneously and immediately like a painting. At the same time, the pictorial mode arrests the performance intermittently, allowing the audience to observe and recognise the fragile reality on stage.

The stage-as-painting theme is immediately introduced by the initially empty stage in the first act, set in Troshcheikin's studio. The absence of movement invites the audience to contemplate a static, self-referential picture of a painter's studio, framed by the proscenium arch. This painting suddenly comes alive, when a ball rolls across the stage followed by Troshcheikin's entrance. The ball seems to have rolled out of Troshcheikin's unfinished painting (a painting-within-a-painting) of a boy, leaving behind a white, empty outline. Shortly before his work on *The Event*, Nabokov had started revising his *Kamera obskura* for an American publisher as *Laughter in the Dark* (1938).[33] In this new translation he established the cinematic theme of the novel in Albinus's plan of animating old masterpieces: 'How fascinating it would be, he thought, if one could use this method for having some well-known picture, preferably of the Dutch School, perfectly reproduced on the screen in vivid colours and then brought to life – movement and gesture graphically developed in complete harmony with their static state in the picture.'[34] This preoccupation with pictures coming to life continues in *The Event*. While in *Laughter in*

---

[32] Martin Meisel, *Realizations: Narrative, Pictorial and Theatrical Arts in Nineteenth-Century England* (Princeton University Press, 1983), 47.

[33] See Boyd, *Russian Years*, 445; for a detailed discussion of the reworkings and revisions of the Russian original and the earlier English translation by Winifred Roy, see Jane Grayson, *Nabokov Translated: A Comparison of Nabokov's Russian and English Prose* (Oxford University Press, 1977), 23–58.

[34] Vladimir Nabokov, *Laughter in the Dark* (London: Penguin, 1969), 5–6.

the Dark, moving pictures are linked with cinema, in the play, pictures developing their own life become almost naturally theatre.[35]

The pictorial quality of this first scene prepares the subsequent merging of painting and theatre in Troshcheikin's plan to paint a picture of his own studio as part of a stage performance, where his life unfolds before the eyes of an audience:

Here's what I'd like to paint – try to imagine that this wall is missing, and instead there is a black abyss and what looks like an audience in a dim theater, rows and rows of faces, sitting and watching me. And all the faces belong to people whom I know or once knew, and who are now watching my life. Some with curiosity, some with vexation, some with pleasure. This man with envy; that woman with compassion. There they sit before me, so pale and wondrous in the semidarkness. My late parents are there, and my past enemies, and that character of yours with his gun, and my childhood friends, of course, and lots and lots of women – all the ones I told you about: Nina, Ada, Katyusha, the other Nina, Margaret Hoffman, poor Olenka – all of them.[36] (*Plays*, 132)

Написать такую *штуку*, – вот представь себе … Этой стены как бы нет, а темный провал … и как бы, значит, публика в туманном театре, ряды, ряды… сидят и смотрят на меня. Причем все это лица людей, которых я знаю или прежде знал и которые теперь смотрят на мою жизнь. Кто с любопытством, кто с досадой, кто с удовольствием. А тот с завистью, а эта с сожалением. Вот так сидят передо мной – такие бледновато-чудные в полутьме. Тут и мои покойные родители, и старые враги, и твой этот тип с револьвером, и друзья детства, конечно, и женщины, женщины – все те, о которых я рассказывал тебе, – Нина, Ада, Катюша, другая Нина, Маргарита Гофман, бедная Оленька, – все … (*Sobr. soch.*, V, 453–4)

The confusion of different art forms (to paint a play, or to stage a painting) is deepened in the Russian text through the double meaning of the verb *pisat'*, denoting both 'to write' and 'to paint'. In a first probing of the limits of the Fourth Wall convention, Troshcheikin is proposing a picture of the very theatre where his life is being enacted. Although the audience will not consist of Troshcheikin's close relatives and friends, he is closely observed 'with envy and with sympathy' by the guests arriving for the birthday party in the second act, and on another level, by the actual audience present in the auditorium.

---

[35] Dabney Stuart points out that the description of the animation of the pictures foreshadows the development of the novel's subsequent plot, in which Albinus's monotonous life is also set in motion by his affair with Margot (see *Nabokov: The Dimensions of Parody* (Baton Rouge, LA and London: Louisiana State University Press, 1978), 90–2).

[36] Troshcheikin's idea anticipates Pnin's vision of giving a public lecture to relatives and friends some of whom are already dead (see Diment, 'Plays', 593).

The egotistical focus on Troshcheikin himself at the centre of the stage and picture suggests a depiction of events from an equally subjective perspective. In its exclusively inward-looking orientation, Troshcheikin's idea of his intended audience surpasses even Nabokov's frequently declared disdain for his readers: 'I must paint for my monster, my tapeworm, and for it alone' (*Plays*, 228) ['нужно писать для моего чудовища, для моего солитера, только для него' (*Sobr. soch.*, V, 502)]. His method of double-painting is a bizarre compromise to please both his viewers and himself:

I used my double-portrait method again the other day … I painted two versions [of the sitter] simultaneously on the sly: on one canvas as the dignified elder he wanted, and on another, the way *I* wanted him – purple mug, bronze belly, surrounded by thunderclouds. (*Plays*, 134)

на днях применил мой метод двойного портрета … Под шумок написал Баумгартена сразу в двух видах – почтенным старцем, как он того хотел, а на другом холсте, как хотел того я, – с лиловой мордой, с бронзовым брюхом, в грозовых облаках. (*Sobr. soch.*, V, 455)

The double-painting with its muddling of internal and external perspectives becomes a formal model for the play itself. The events on stage are seen through the prism of Troshcheikin's subjective perception, which is set off against an external reality.[37] Babikov sees this staging of Troshcheikin's inner life as a variant of Evreinov's concept of the 'monodrama', a play which depicts events from the singular perspective of one of its protagonists.[38] Although throughout the play Barbashin never appears in person, Troshcheikin's fear of him comes to dominate his mind and the play, as Khodasevich correctly observes: 'according to its content, [the play] could have been called "Fear" … Barbarshin is nothing else but the phantom, the phantasmagoria, the sick product of Troshcheikin's mind … The appearance, development and sudden disappearance of this fear also shapes the basic plot line of the play.'[39] In a variation of Stéphane Mallarmé's famous Symbolist dictum 'to paint not the object, but the effect which it produces',[40] Troshcheikin focuses not on actual objects or sitters, but instead on their effect on him:

[37] The representation of Troshcheikin's subjective perception of reality in the play has been noted by Khodasevich, '"Sobytie" V. Sirina', 425.
[38] See Babikov, 'The Main Thing', 152
[39] Khodasevich, '"Sobytie" V. Sirina', 425.
[40] Quoted in Martin Puchner, *Stage Fright*, 59. In his notes to *The Seagull*, Nabokov paid detailed attention to Treplev's description of Trigorin's strategy of describing not the source of the light but its effect: 'Treplev reads: "[…] Trigorin has created his own tricks; for him it is easy. He will show the neck of a broken bottle glistening on a river-dam and the black shadow under the mill-wheel – that's all the moonlight is ready "[…]" (Here we get, incidentally, a beautifully

the balls have to *glow*, to cast their reflection on [the boy he is painting], but I want the reflection firmly in place before tackling its source. You must remember that art moves against the sun. (*Plays*, 129)

они должны *гореть*, бросать на него отблеск, но сперва я хочу закрепить отблеск, а потом приняться за его источники. Надо помнить, что искусство движется всегда против солнца. (*Sobr. soch.*, V, 452)

In this concentration on the effects of events rather than the events themselves, the play once more resembles one of Troshcheikin's subjective paintings.

The encounter of different realities is played out between the static world of Troshcheikin's life and the dynamic action of his imagined reality, between the pictorial and the theatrical mode. As in a painting, Troshcheikin and Liubov are frozen in the habits and routines of their monotonous life in the provinces. Already in the much earlier short story 'La Veneziana' ('Venetsianka', 1996), Nabokov had juxtaposed monotonous life and motionless painting.[41] Simpson, the protagonist of the story, feels buried alive in the routine of his eventless life, a motionless state which is subsequently realised when he enters and freezes into a painting. Troshcheikin and Liubov's life receives suddenly an impetus and is – together with the drama itself – set in motion by Barbashin's unexpected arrival. This movement is however, illusory, based on Troshcheikin's exaggerated sense of his own importance. His histrionic reaction to Barbashin's release unnecessarily dramatises an actually harmless situation and creates an imaginary event and movement. The supposed threat of Barbashin transforms Troshcheikin from an unremarkable provincial painter into the protagonist of a true drama, occupying centre stage, just as he imagined himself in the projected picture. Yet the play ends in an anticlimax, which presents the real catastrophe, as Boyd argues: '[a] quite unexpected tragedy looms behind the final curtain: that there is no stagy denouement to resolve the Troshcheikins' fortunes; that, as in Chekhov at his best, life's muddle simply continues'.[42] Without the threat of Barbashin's revenge, Troshcheikin and Liubov will never move away from the provincial town and their dreary life. They have missed a

---

defined difference between Chekhov's art and that of his contemporaries)' (*Lectures on Russian Literature*, 293).

[41] 'La Veneziana' was written in 1924 but remained unpublished during Nabokov's lifetime. The story was first published in Dmitri Nabokov's English translation in 1995 (*The Stories of Vladimir Nabokov* (New York: Alfred A. Knopf, 1995)). The Russian original appeared in 1996 (Vladimir Nabokov, 'Venetsianka', *Zvezda*, 11 (1996), 26–41).

[42] Boyd, *Russian Years*, 483.

precious and rare opportunity to escape from the eventless inertia of their 'still lives'.

The opposition of movement and stasis is mirrored in the interaction of two major theatrical subtexts, Gogol's *The Government Inspector* and Chekhov's plays, which emerge, alternate and vanish before coming to the surface once more. The idea of a messenger stirring up the quiet life of a small circle of people with the news of impending doom, is, as nearly all critics of the play have noted, reminiscent of Gogol's *The Government Inspector*.[43] Self-consciously, the characters of the play themselves perceive the obvious parallels between their situation and the play. Antonina Pavlovna suggests that their situation offers plenty of material for a Gogol-inspired play, while Liubov quotes the literary original which is underlying *The Event*: 'In a word: "Gentlemen, Gogol's Inspector General has arrived in our town"' (*Plays*, 176) ['Одним словом: «Господа, к нам в город приехал ревизор»' (*Sobr. soch.*, V, 475)]. The constantly arriving and departing characters who exchange confused pieces of information and rumours is another variation of the Gogol play. Khodasevich remarked that '*The Event* can be seen as a variant of *The Government Inspector*. Troshcheikin waits for Barabashin ... with the same terror with which the Mayor waits for the government inspector.[44] Like the genuine inspector in Gogol's play, Barbashin never appears on stage. Instead in both plays, as Khodasevich points out, an imaginary threat (Khlestakov and Barbashin) is the driving force in the play. Nabokov's reading of Gogol agrees here with Meyerhold's staging of *The Government Inspector* as the Mayor's subjective and insane perception of events.

Underlying the excited Gogolian bustle is another subtext, an amalgamation of several plays by Chekhov, suggesting the static monotonous life which the main characters lead. The setting in an unnamed provincial town is also a recurring motif in *The Seagull*, *The Three Sisters* (*Tri sestry*, 1901) and *The Cherry Orchard*. The name of Liubov's mother, Antonina Pavlovna, is itself the female equivalent of Chekhov's first name and patronymic.[45] Her story about a dead swan at a lake conjures up the motif of the dead seagull in Chekhov's famous play. The characters' boredom,

---

[43] See, for instance, Khodasevich, '"Sobytie" V. Sirina', 425–6; L. Chervinskaia, 'Po povodu "Sobytiia" V. Sirina', *Krug*, 3 (November 1938), 168–70. Reprinted in Mel'nikov and Korosteleva, *Klassik bez retushi*, 173–4 [174]; Karlinsky, 'Illusion, Reality in Nabokov's Plays', 186–7; Boyd, *Russian Years*, 483; Diment, 'Plays', 592; A. Zlochevskaia, 'Teatr N. V. Gogolia i dramaturgiia russkogo zarubezh'ia pervoi volny', *Voprosy literatury*, 2 (March–April 2005), 209–35 [218–26].

[44] Khodasevich, '"Sobytie" V. Sirina', 425.

[45] See Karlinsky, 'Illusion, Reality in Nabokov's Plays', 187.

their inability to communicate and Liubov's nostalgic attachment to the past are further elements which are typical of Chekhov's plays. Again, the characters themselves sense the Chekhovian atmosphere. Liubov is compared to a Chekhovian character, while Troshcheikin thinks of his life as a variant of the monotonous provincial existence of the three sisters: 'we are decaying in this hick-town atmosphere, like Chekhov's three sisters' (*Plays*, 136) ['мы разлагаемся в захолустной обстановке, как три сестры' (*Sobr. soch.*, V, 455–6)]. His gloomy assessment of their situation is accompanied by his fixing of a sketch, evoking once more the parallels between a motionless picture and his own unchanging, frozen life.

The impetus Troshcheikin gives his life generates a drama which during the course of the play, however, turns into ever more absurd farce. The guests arriving at the birthday party have not come to watch his life, as he imagined in his initial picture, but their ghoulish sensationalism and morbid questioning indicate that they are there to witness his murder without much concern for or interest in him.[46] From the second act onwards, grotesque and unreal characters start populating the stage. Vagabundova, who has arrived in a costume for her sitting seems to be the embodiment of her own bizarre portrait, as if she had climbed out of her own picture. Slapstick misunderstandings, absurd arguments and ridiculous competitions for attention mark the beginning of a chaotic vaudeville, to some extent resembling a Russian *balagan*.[47] The three old women in particular appear as a weirdly distorted version of the female trio of Chekhov's *The Three Sisters*. Dressed like the three sisters in blue, white and black, they are anything but the melancholy, delicate sisters of Chekhov's play, resembling, rather, the three ladies who suddenly appear at the end of *The Government Inspector* to enjoy the spectacle of the Mayor's downfall. On yet another level, the three old women in the roles of the young sisters might also be a hidden slight at the Russian émigré actresses who refused to acknowledge their own aging, as Berberova remembered: 'I could never forget the adaptation of *The Brothers Karamazov* where [Mariia Germanova] acted Grushenka and Madame [Ekaterina Roshchina-] Insarova played Katya: on the stage they both looked as if they were grandmothers of Dostoevsky heroines, or as if they were *the very same* Grushenko and Katya who were young in the 1880s and now were still alive.[48] The emerging comedy (also prepared in the description of the play

---

[46] Senderovich and Shvarts see in the scene of the birthday party another instance of what they call 'the balagan of death' (see 'The Juice of Three Oranges', 100).

[47] See Senderovich and Shvarts, 'Balagan smerti', 356.

[48] Berberova, *Italics Are Mine*, 351.

as 'A dramatic comedy in three acts') increasingly resembles the parodies Troshcheikin creates in his double portraits.

The feverish tempo of the second act is suddenly halted in a tribute to Gogol's famous silent scene in *The Government Inspector*. Painting and theatre oscillate in this scene just like the real and the imaginary, recognition and illusion come to the fore only to vanish again in a continuous competition for supremacy. The pictorial and the theatrical merge when the theatrical reality is suspended and the gathering of guests at Troshcheikin's house reverts to a *tableau vivant*, one of Troshcheikin's paintings:

As she [Antonina Pavlovna] reads, her face remains distinct, but she seems to have receded with her armchair into the distance, so that her voice grows inaudible even though her lips continue to move and her hand keeps on turning the pages. The listeners around her, who have also lost all contact with the front of the stage, sit in motionless, drowsy attitudes. (*Plays*, 212)

Она читает с ясным лицом, но как бы удалилась в своем кресле, так что голос ее перестает быть слышен, хотя губы движутся и рука переворачивает страницы. Вокруг нее слушатели, тоже порвавшие всякую связь с авансценой, сидят в застывших полусонных позах. (*Sobr. soch.*, V, 494)

The stage directions stipulate that 'Actually, a scrim ought to descend, or a drop on which the whole group is depicted with all their attitudes exactly reproduced' (*Plays*, 213) ['Собственно, следовало бы, чтобы спустилась прозрачная ткань или средний занавес, на котором вся их группировка была бы нарисована с точным повторением поз' (*Sobr. soch.*, V, 494)]. The use of the curtain recalls once more Meyerhold's production of *The Government Inspector*, where the mute scene was also introduced by a curtain which rose upwards from the orchestra pit.[49] Having stepped out of his own painting into the space beyond the frame of the proscenium arch, Troshcheikin himself dismisses the reality behind him as an illusion: 'It's a kind of mirage. They are extras. They don't exist. Actually, I daubed it all myself. A poor painting, but innocuous' (*Plays*, 216) ['мираж, фигуранты, ничто. Наконец, я сам это намалевал. Скверная картина – но безвредная' (*Sobr. soch.*, V, 496)], while Liubov confirms that her 'husband painted it in very natural colors' (*Plays*, 216) ['муж написал это в очень натуральных красках' (*Sobr. soch.*, V, 496)]. Their return into the picture borders on the magical, Troshcheikin experiences

---

[49] The similarities between *The Event* and Meyerhold's interpretation of *The Government Inspector* was also noted by Nabokov's contemporary critics. See, for instance, Chervinskaia, 'Po povodu "Sobytiia" V. Sirina', 174; Adamovich, '"Russkie zapiski". No. 4', 167.

a sense of sinking when he is close to congealing into the picture again. In the earlier short story 'La Veneziana', a similar sensation accompanies Simpson's entry into the picture: 'He was mired like a fly in honey – he gave a jerk and got stuck, feeling his blood and flesh and clothing turning into paint, growing into the varnish, drying on the canvas' (*Stories*, 111) ['Он увяз, как муха в меду; дернулся и застыл, и чувствовал, как кровь его и плоть и платье превращаются в краску, врастают в лак, сохнут на полотне' (*Sobr. soch.*, I, 105)].

In this 'painted scene', the stage becomes strictly divided into the area 'upstage', into which the guests at the birthday part move, and the area in front of the proscenium arch, occupied by Troshcheikin and Liubov. This division is reinforced by the curtain separating the two spaces. In Nabokov's most radical violation of the Fourth Wall principle, Troshcheikin and Liubov cross from upstage into the transitional space where the auditorium and the stage meet. Separated from the farcical birthday guests, Troshcheikin takes stock of their situation:

Alone on this narrow, lighted stage. Behind us, the old theatrical frippery of our whole life, the frozen masks of a second-rate comedy, and in front a dark chasm full of eyes, eyes, eyes watching us, awaiting our destruction. (*Plays*, 214)

Одни на этой узкой освещенной сцене. Сзади – театральная ветошь всей нашей жизни, замерзшие маски второстепенной комедии, а спереди – темная глубина и глаза, глаза, глаза, глядящие на нас, ждущие нашей гибели. (*Sobr. soch.*, V, 495)

The theatre functions here on different levels simultaneously. The theatre becomes a metaphor for the couple's empty and shallow life built on deception and illusion, the misfortunes of which are observed and enjoyed by their relatives and friends. At the same time, this 'theatrical frippery of our whole life' is mirrored and realised in the concrete theatrical space into which Troshcheikin and Liubov step. Their dialogue therefore simultaneously refers to the shallow, empty life they lead and describes the actual theatrical space they inhabit. They are fictional characters and actors of their roles at the same time. The theatre itself in this scene is both real and illusory, a site of fiction-making and a real space in real time.

This essentially theatrical perception of a twofold reality extends into the auditorium. By crossing onto the forestage which is conventionally designated for asides and audience addresses, Troshcheikin enters a space reserved for encounters between fictional characters and spectators in the same space–time continuum. Stage characters intrude here into the space of the audience, or, rather the audience is drawn into the world of the stage. Stage characters become real, or the audience becomes unreal. Troshcheikin might be referring to the guests who are watching his demise, but at the same time he describes the actual theatre audience in front of him, who are indeed watching him, perhaps expecting that according to Chekhov's maxim of loaded guns on stages, Troshcheikin will be shot at the end. Nabokov's later distinction in his lectures between a fictional, an implied and an actual audience is, although a valid semiotic principle, not thematised in this scene.[50] Instead this scene seeks to create an eerie, unsettling sensation which confuses auditorium and stage, reality and illusion, and raises complex questions about the status of the theatrical reality experienced on stage and in the auditorium.

In the last act, the reality of the stage further disintegrates in parallel with the collapse of Troshcheikin's fantasy and the drama itself. Liubov ceases to be a fictional character and turns into an actress playing the role of Liubov. Marfa's way of acting a servant is criticised: 'That wasn't a very good performance. I'll show you how it ought to be done ... A very common part, actually...' (*Plays*, 219) ['это вы недостаточно сочно сыграли. Я вам покажу, как надо ... это, в общем, очень обыкновенная роль ...' (*Sobr. soch.*, V, 497)]. The detective Barboshin, described as resembling a tragic actor, distributes photographs of himself in the role of King Lear and deals in such absurd props as false cornices. Liubov has played her role so many times, that she experiences a sense of *déjà vu*: 'this has happened before, all of it has happened just like this – you said "shadow", I said "child", and at that point Mother came in' (*Plays*, 230) ['это все было уже раз, все-все так было, ты сказал «тень», я сказала «младенец», и на этом вошла мама' (*Sobr. soch.*, V, 503)]. The late guest Meshaev Two, the twin of the earlier guest Meshaev One, jokes that 'both I and my brother [are] played by one and the same actor, only in the part of my brother he was good, and in mine he was bad' (*Plays*, 249) ['меня и брата играет один и тот же актер, но брата хорошо, а меня худо' (*Sobr. soch.*, V, 513)]. While the stage is becoming increasingly visible, the illusions, lies and deceptions of the characters' lives are openly revealed. Liubov confronts Troshcheikin with his cowardice, their crumbling relationship

---

[50] Confusing actual, implied and fictional audiences, Babikov comes to the contradictory conclusion that the 'silent scene' 'shows Troshcheykin the truth that those "eyes, eyes, eyes" in the audience belong to people whom he does not know, who have been created by some other Author, and thus both he and the public [i.e. audience] are equally characters of some other Drama. Thus in the "tableau vivant scene", the "fourth wall" remains intact, and the stage illusion is intensified because the audience is included in the author's conception' ('The Main Thing', 165).

and his hysterical reaction to an imaginary threat. The play ends with the announcement that Barbashin has left the town forever, which effectively shatters the illusion on which the whole drama was built. Resembling the last acts of *The Man from the USSR*, the stage in *The Event* reveals its underlying mechanisms and operations, while Troshcheikin's dramatic enactment of his own life is exposed as a mere illusion.

The pictorial theme is playfully taken up again by Nabokov before the end of the play. Barboshin's way of walking describes the letter N, suggesting the initials of the real painter Nabokov.[51] Nabokov left his trace also in Meshaev Two's unusually worded suggestion to go to bed: 'Пора, на боковую' (*Sobr. soch.*, V, 517; emphasis added) and in the reference to *Kamera obskura* as the season's best film.[52] This reference to Nabokov's novel would have been even more obvious if plans for a film adaptation of this book had actually reached fruition.[53] Nabokov's signature on the canvas of the play might have been primarily a conspiratorial wink at his friends and informed readers in the audience. On another level, however, his insistence on his rightful ownership of the play – although ultimately futile and merely rhetorical in the context of an actual performance – hints at another world beyond the play and reiterates the twofold reality of the play, of its double portraits and of the stage which brings them to life.

As in *The Man from the USSR*, the stage reveals the pretensions and play-acting of the drama's characters. In *The Event*, however, a further dimension is added, which uses the specific properties of theatre and painting to draw attention to the motionless life depicted. Nabokov's play transforms the stage into a painting, and a painting into a play, criss-crossing between different aesthetic modes. From beneath Troshcheikin's picture of an event in his life, another picture of a static dreary émigré existence, reminiscent of the gloomy world of *The Man from the USSR*, gradually emerges. Behind Troshcheikin's bustling play looms an empty theatre which exposes its own skeleton.

LEAVING THE STAGE: *INVITATION TO A BEHEADING*

Shortly before writing *Invitation to a Beheading*, Nabokov finished the short story 'The Leonardo', where the fictional world itself is undercut by

---

[51] See Andrei Babikov, '"Tol'ko poshliaki khodiat maiatnikom": podpis' Nabokova na kholste *Sobytiia*', *zembla* (www.libraries.psu.edu/nabokov/zembla.htm).

[52] The literal translation of this phrase would be 'Time to get on your side'.

[53] *Kamera obskura* was made into a film only in 1969, directed by Tony Richardson.

an overtly theatrical setting. The story does not try to disguise but openly declares its own artificiality, with the narrator assembling the necessary props to set the scene:

The objects that are being summoned assemble, draw near from different spots … Here comes the ovate little poplar, all punctuated with April greenery, and takes its stand where told, namely by the tall brick wall, imported in one piece from another city. Facing it, there grows up a dreary and dirty tenement house, with mean little balconies pulled out one by one like drawers. Other bits of scenery are distributed about the yard: a barrel, a second barrel, the delicate shade of leaves, an urn of sorts, and a stone cross propped at the foot of the wall.[54] (*Stories*, 358)

Собираются, стягиваются с разных мест вызываемые предметы … Вот овальный тополек в своей апрельской пунктирной зелени уже пришел и стал где ему приказано – у высокой кирпичной стены – целиком выписанной из другого города. Напротив вырастает дом, большой, мрачный и грязный, и один за другим выдвигаются, как ящики, плохонькие балконы. Там и сям распределяются по двору: бочка, еще бочка, легкая тень листвы, какая-то урна и каменный крест, прислоненный к стене. (*Sobr. soch.*, III, 629–30)

The first signs of action are appropriately conveyed in the form of stage directions: 'two live people – Gustav and his brother Anton – already come out on their tiny balcony, while rolling before him a little pushcart with a suitcase and a heap of books, Romantovski, the new lodger, enters the yard' (*Stories*, 358) ['на один из балкончиков уже выходят живые люди – братья Густав и Антон, – а во двор вступает, катя тележку с чемоданом и кипой книг, новый жилец – Романтовский' (*Sobr. soch.*, III, 630)]. Significantly, the props are not especially designed for this story but have been recycled from other productions. A sense of hasty construction is further evoked by the explicit imperative 'Hurry up, please' (*Stories*, 358) ['Поторопитесь, пожалуйста' (*Sobr. soch.*, III, 629)] and the admission that '[all] this is only sketched and much has to be added and finished' (*Stories*, 358) ['все это только намечено и еще многое нужно дополнить и догелать' (*Sobr. soch.*, III, 630)], which draws attention to the function of the objects as props and the implicit sham reality they create.

As soon as the actual story commences, however, the theatrical stage recedes, giving space to the unfolding of the plot without any further intruding reminders of the artificial backdrop against which the events are acted out. On the contrary, the constant persecution of Romantovski and particularly his murder at the end of the story become almost

---

[54] Senderovich and Shvarts point out that 'the story's setting is introduced like a stage set in an avant-garde theater' ('The Juice of Three Oranges', 102).

palpably real, the latter partly through the explicit audibility of the stabbing sounds, as Wyllie points out.[55] The strong effect of these scenes is also achieved by the contrast between the ill-smelling, strong and enormous bodies of the brothers, and Romantovski's weak, soft and almost child-like stature.[56]

The theme of an illusionary world returns with the surprising revelation that Romantovski is not a Romantic artist figure but a counterfeiter, himself a creator of illusions. Simultaneously with the shattering of this illusion, the reality of the story itself collapses, like a theatre set: 'Alas, the objects I had assembled wander away' (*Stories*, 367) ['Собранные предметы разбредаются опять, увы' (*Sobr. soch.*, III, 639)]. The narrator seems to have lost his initial control over the stage settings. His strangely passive stance and his expressed regret ('alas') suggest that his precarious, unstable reality cannot resist the advent of an external reality. This use of theatre recalls the gradual disintegration of stage scenery in *The Man from the USSR* where the disappearing stage coincides with and reflects the gradual shattering of illusions and clichés in the Russian émigré world. A similar use of theatre can be found in *The Defense* (*Zashchita Luzhina*, 1929–30), where the description of the flat of Luzhin's parents-in-law has been modelled on a clichéd view of Russia (just like the tavern in the first act of *The Man from the USSR*):

she made an imaginary Luzhin enter the rooms, talk with her mother, eat home-cooked kulebiaka and be reflected in the sumptuous samovar purchased abroad – and these imaginary calls ended with a monstrous catastrophe, Luzhin with a clumsy motion of his shoulder would knock the house down like a shaky piece of scenery that emitted a sigh of dust.[57]

[она] заставляла воображаемого Лужина входить в комнаты, говорить с ее матерью, есть домашнюю кулебяку, отражаться в роскошном, купленном за границей самоваре, – и эти воображаемые посещения кончались чудовищной катастрофой, Лужин неуклюжим движением плеча сшибал дом, как валкий кусок декорации, испускающий вздох пыли. (*Sobr. soch.*, II, 366)

Ultimately the narrator of 'The Leonardo' has been outwitted by his own preconceptions. Although his Romantic values of individuality and artistic vision are diametrically opposed to the brothers' totalitarian

---

[55] See Wyllie, *Nabokov at the Movies*, 38.

[56] The torturing and killing of children or child-like figures appears frequently in Nabokov's fiction. For instance, Cincinnatus is frequently compared to a small, weak child. This theme is epitomised in one of the cruellest scenes in the whole of Nabokov's fiction, the killing of David in *Bend Sinister*. Another instance is, of course, Humbert's repeated rape of Lolita.

[57] Vladimir Nabokov, *The Luzhin Defense*, trans. Michael Scammell in collaboration with the author (London: Penguin, 2000), 103–4.

ideal of the collective, just like them he imposes his preconceived ideas on Romantovski. The narrator remarks that 'And I who believed *with them* that you were indeed someone exceptional' (*Stories*, 367; emphasis added) ['я-то думал вместе с ними, что ты и вправду особенный' (*Sobr. soch.*, III, 638)]. Both parties share a simplistic worldview which leaves no space for ambiguity and which consequently cannot accommodate a figure from a grey area like Romantovski. In that sense, the narrator's hurriedly assembled world shows a striking resemblance to the brothers' simplistic unperceptive construction of the reality around them: 'Now this is the way we'll arrange the world: every man shall sweat, every man shall eat' (*Stories*, 359) ['Мы устроим мир так: всяк будет потен, и всяк будет сыт' (*Sobr. soch.*, III, 630)]. A further similarity can be discerned in the brothers' and the narrator's tendency to fill space. Not only are the brothers frequently associated with heavy food (filling themselves), but their presence seems to suffocate Romantovski in whose perception 'the brothers began to swell, to grow, they filled up the whole room, the whole house, and then grew out of it' (*Stories*, 361) ['братья стали раздуваться, расти, они заполнили всю комнату, весь дом и затем выросли из него' (*Sobr. soch.*, III, 633)]. The narrator likewise fills the space with theatrical props and is clearly disturbed by the empty space remaining at the end of the story: 'The world irks me again with its variegated void' (*Stories*, 367) ['Мир снова томит меня своей пестрой пустотою' (*Sobr. soch.*, III, 639)]. Equally revealing is the narrator's regret that '[h]armony and meaning vanish (*Stories*, 367) ['[p]аспадается гармония и смысл' (*Sobr. soch.*, III, 639)], implying as it does that a world in which a completely unmotivated brutal murder takes place makes sense.

The theatrical motifs are combined to undermine the reality of the story and to expose the narrator as a hack writer with limited imagination. Theatre comes to denote the illusionary quality of fiction by analogy with the hack construction of a world which is based on a black and white view. The theatrical reality is employed as a metaphor for fictional instability and artistic imperfection. The real and the theatrical coexist here to some extent, with the theatrical reality undercutting the actual story. This clearly defined opposition between reality and theatre is complicated in *Invitation to a Beheading* where theatrical and external realities are locked in an interdependent relationship.

The theatricality of 'The Leonardo' clearly anticipates the theatrical world of *Invitation to a Beheading*. The theme of a beheading derives from one of Nabokov's first short dramas, *The Grandfather*.[58] The verse play is set in France about forty years after the French Revolution. A passer-by seeks shelter from the rain in the house of a farmer's family. While waiting for better weather he relates how he was sentenced to death during the Great Terror but was saved from the guillotine at the last minute by a fire that broke out. At the end of the play, he meets the 'grandfather', an old, confused man the family has taken in, who unexpectedly attacks the passer-by with an axe. Recognising his former executioner, who is still set on fulfilling his duty, the passer-by kills the grandfather in the ensuing struggle. The gruesome beheading, the executioner's perverted sense of professional duty and the last-minute escape of a man sentenced to death would all be reworked in *Invitation to a Beheading*. The public spectacle of an execution on a stage surrounded by an audience provides a continuous link to the theatre in both the short play and the novel.[59]

The world of *Invitation to a Beheading* is marked as an overtly theatrical space as almost all critics have noted.[60] Characters wearing costumes, wigs and masks play their roles among hastily constructed stage sets. The prison director and Cincinnatus's lawyer wear wigs, the prison guards wear dog-like masks. Cincinnatus, thinking that his execution is near, wonders whether he will be dressed up for the event. The costuming never seems to even aspire to verisimilitude and is riddled with mistakes

---

[58] See Andrew Field, *Nabokov: His Life in Art* (London: Hodder and Stoughton, 1967), 78.

[59] A similar connection between the public spectacle of an execution and a theatre production was also made by Nikolai Evreinov in his lecture, 'The Theatre and the Guillotine', which he gave in 1918 in Odessa (see Nikolai Evreinov, 'Teatr i eshafot: K voprosu o proiskhozhdenii teatra kak publichnogo instituta', in Vladislav Ivanov (ed.), *Mnemozina: Dokumenty i fakty iz istorii russkogo teatra xx veka* (Moscow: GITIS, 1996-), vol. I, 14–44).

[60] See, for instance, Stuart, *Dimensions of Parody*, 55–85; Ludmila A. Foster, 'Nabokov's Gnostic Turpitude: The Surrealistic Vision of Reality in *Priglašenie na kazn*", in Joachim T. Baer and Norman W. Ingham (eds.), *Mnemozina: Studia litteraria russica in honorem Vsevolod Setchkarev* (Munich: Fink, 1974), 117–29 [121–2]. The novel's theatricality has also been noted by other critics. Sergei Davydov sees the novel's theatricality as part of its dualistic structure, which according to Davydov, contains a spiritual plot line enacting the Gnostic myth as well as a theological farce. The latter is represented in the Ukrainian religious puppet theatre, the *vertep* (see *'Teksty-Matreški' Vladimira Nabokova* (Munich: Otto Sagner, 1982), 170–3). Vladimir Alexandrov sees the novel's theatricality as a metaphor for the material world, which 'is an imperfect copy, or a lesser image of a spiritual reality' (*Nabokov's Otherworld*, 106). Robert Alter argues that the novel's theatre set denotes the sham reality of the totalitarian society which has imprisoned Cincinnatus, proving the 'inexorable antagonism between totalitarianism and authentic art' ('*Invitation to a Beheading*: Nabokov and the Art of Politics', *TriQuarterly* 17 (1970), 41–59. Reprinted in Connolly (ed.), *Nabokov's* Invitation to a Beheading, 47–65 [60]). D. Babich argues that the theatricality of *Invitation to a Beheading* serves a double purpose. While creating a distance between the reader and the text, the theatrical elements also create an actualisation of the text ('Kazhdyi mozhet vyiti iz zala: Teatralizatsiia zla v proizvedeniiakh Nabokova', *Voprosy literatury*, 5 (September–October 1999), 142–57).

and incongruities, as in the meeting between Cincinnatus and his mother whose shoes have remained dry although she is supposed to have come in from the rain. The jailer forgets his apron and false red beard in Cincinnatus's cell. Costumes are confused and roles become interchangeable. The prison director Rodrig and the lawyer Roman turn seamlessly into the gaoler Rodion, while Rodion frequently merges with Rodrig. Later Rodrig and Roman become the executioner's helpers Rom and Rod. The characters' behaviour is entirely in tune with the performance they take part in. The jailer brings Cincinnatus a letter 'on a salver as they do in plays' (*IB*, 58) ['на подносе, как в театре' (*Sobr. soch.*, IV, 84)]. The same jailer has shortly before suddenly broken into an operatic libretto, 'having assumed the imitation-jaunty pose of operatic rakes in the tavern scene (*IB*, 26) ['приняв фальшиво-развязную позу оперных гуляк в сцене погреба' (*Sobr. soch.*, IV, 59)]. Cincinnatus's torturer and executioner, Monsieur Pierre, performs circus tricks and appears with a Punchinello puppet. The (prison or theatrical) director delivers speeches and reads out a letter for the benefit of an audience, rather than for Cincinnatus. In the meeting with his mother, Cincinnatus ironically refers to her insufficient acting skills: 'Play your role – go heavy on the prattle and the unconcern – and you won't have to worry, it'll get by' (*IB*, 112) ['Играйте свою роль, – побольше лепета, побольше беспечности, – и ничего, – сойдет' (*Sobr. soch.*, IV, 126)]. And Cincinnatus is several times admonished for his refusal to act his part.

The theatre performance takes place against the background of hastily assembled stage sets and props, recalling the unstable reality of 'The Leonardo'. Cincinnatus perceives his surroundings as 'our hastily assembled and painted world' (*IB*, 44) ['наш сегодняшний наскоро сколоченный и покрашенный мир' (*Sobr. soch.*, IV, 73)]. Outside of Cincinnatus's cell, as if off-stage, a 'summer thunderstorm, simply yet tastefully staged, was performed' (*IB*, 109) ['разыгралась – просто, но с вкусом поставленная – летняя гроза' (*Sobr. soch.*, IV, 124)], and time is painted as Cincinnatus notices: 'every hour the watchman washes off the old hand and daubs on a new one' (*IB*, 114) ['каждые полчаса сторож смывает старую стрелку и малюет новую' (*Sobr. soch.*, IV, 128)]. The Tamara Gardens are not even a theatre set or model anymore but have been reduced to the backdrop of a wind orchestra. In this theatre-world, it is only natural that the execution itself is frequently referred to as a 'spectacle' or 'production' (*predstavlenie*).

Cincinnatus perceives the world around him as both reality and theatrical performance. This essentially theatrical double vision is the principal difference between him and the other characters who cannot see beyond themselves. Although in the role of prisoner Cincinnatus is an integral part of the novel's world, he recognises his own execution as part of a theatrical performance when he asks for a short reprieve: 'a three-minute intermission – after that, so be it. I'll act to the end my role in your idiotic production' (*IB*, 179) ['три минуты антракта, – после чего, так и быть, доиграю с вами эту вздорную пьесу' (*Sobr. soch.*, IV, 177)]. While the other figures consist only of their roles – a one-dimensionality which is underlined by their interchangeablity – Cincinnatus experiences the split nature of an actor who embodies simultaneously his private self and his role and who fulfils the requirements of his role irrespective of his own self: 'the double, the gangrel, that accompanies each of us – you, and me, and him over there – doing what we would like to do at that very moment, but cannot ...' (*IB*, 22) ['призрак, сопровождающий каждого из нас – и тебя, и меня, и вот его, – делающий то, что в данное мгновение хотелось бы сделать, а нельзя ...' (*Sobr. soch.*, IV, 56)].[61]

As an actor, Cincinnatus is constrained by what Nabokov defined elsewhere as the principal convention of theatrical performance: 'the man on the stage, however inactive and mute he is, is absolutely bound by the conspiracy of the stage and by its main convention: that is, he may *not* wander back into the wings for a drink or a chat, nor may he indulge in any physical exuberance that would clash with the idea of his part' ('Playwriting', 316). Cincinnatus's imprisonment becomes the natural result of his participation in the performance; as an actor Cincinnatus is a prisoner on and of the stage. The prison and the theatre become analogous concepts. Cincinnatus's claustrophobic cell, where most of the action takes place, is both the concrete place of his imprisonment and the limited space of a stage where practical necessities preclude frequent scene changes and from where the actor cannot escape.

Cincinnatus's dual identity sustains the ambiguity of the ending, which is frequently interpreted as his merciful release into the 'otherworld' after he has died.[62] Yet, Cincinnatus does not die, or rather, by the end of the

---

[61] Stuart notes in regard to the figures surrounding Cincinnatus that 'if one has no identity apart from that [one] role, then it makes little difference how one's role is merged temporarily with the role of another, or how roles in general can be exchanged' (see *Dimensions of Parody*, 62).

[62] See, for instance, Alexandrov, *Nabokov's Otherworld*, 99; Davydov, *'Teksty-Matreški'*, 138–40; Don Barton Johnson, *Worlds in Regression: Some Novels of Vladimir Nabokov* (Ann Arbor, MI: Ardis, 1985), 41.

novel he is, like Schrödinger's cat, both dead and alive. Cincinnatus splits into his role and his real self, into a fictional character and an actor:

one Cincinnatus was counting, but the other Cincinnatus had already stopped heeding the sound of the unnecessary count which was fading away in the distance; and, with a clarity he had never experienced before – at first almost painful, so suddenly did it come, but then suffusing him with joy, he reflected: why am I here? Why am I lying like this? And, having asked himself these simple questions, he answered them by getting up and looking around. (*IB*, 190–1)

один Цинциннат считал, а другой Цинциннат уже перестал слушать удалявшийся звон ненужного счета – и с не испытанной дотоле ясностью, сперва даже болезненной по внезапности своего наплыва, но потом преисполнившей веселием все его естество, – подумал: «Зачем я тут? Отчего так лежу?» – и, задав себе этот простой вопрос, он отвечал тем, что привстал и осмотрелся. (*Sobr. soch.*, IV, 186)

While Cincinnatus in his role as prisoner is being executed, Cincinnatus the actor lives on. The dual vision is cancelled and Cincinnatus perceives his surroundings no longer as reality but only as a theatrical performance. Confronted with an external reality, the theatrical reality collapses recalling the ending of 'The Leonardo':

The fallen trees lay flat and reliefless, while those that were still standing, also two-dimensional, with a lateral shading of the trunk to suggest roundness, barely held on with their branches to the ripping mesh of the sky. Everything was coming apart. Everything was falling. A spinning wind was picking up and whirling: dust, rags, chips of painted wood, bits of gilded plaster, pasteboard bricks, posters. (*IB*, 191)

Свалившиеся деревья лежали плашмя, без всякого рельефа, а еще оставшиеся стоять, тоже плоские, с боковой тенью по стволу для иллюзии круглоты, едва держались ветвями за рвущиеся сетки неба. Все расползлось. Все падало. Винтовой вихрь забирал и крутил пыль, тряпки, крашеные щепки, мелкие обломки позлащенного гипса, картонные кирпичи, афиши. (*Sobr. soch.*, IV, 187)

Detached from his role and the fictional world of the play, Cincinnatus is able to perceive a reality beyond the stage in the auditorium where 'to judge by the voices, stood beings akin to him' (*IB*, 191) ['судя по голосам, стояли существа, подобные ему' (*Sobr. soch.*, IV, 187)]. The reality off-stage is only audible (just like in *The Man from the USSR*) to Cincinnatus who is still on stage and not able to see the audience in the darkened auditorium. By stepping outside the spectacle and crossing over into the auditorium, Cincinnatus resists the theatre and violates the Fourth Wall convention, which for Nabokov would later become an essential and uninfringeable principle of the theatre.[63] The destruction of the novel's world is only the logical consequence of this shattering of the Fourth Wall convention, or to use Nabokov's own words: 'Destroy the spell, and you kill the play' ('Playwriting', 319).

Like Cincinnatus, the novel is probing its own ontological boundaries, trespassing, as it were, into the space beyond the fictional text in ever closer proximity to the reader. The reader is gradually drawn into the fictional world in a process which Patricia Waugh calls 'the dramatization of the reader'.[64] The reader can perceive Cincinnatus only from a point of view which overlaps with the perspective of Cincinnatus's jailers. Cincinnatus is constantly being watched through the peephole in his cell door, for instance at the beginning of the novel: 'Rodion was standing on the other side of the door and peering with a skipper's stern attention through the peephole. Cincinnatus felt a chill on the back of his head' (*IB*, 12) ['Родион, стоя за дверью, с суровым шкиперским вниманием глядел в глазок. Цинциннат ощущал холодок у себя в затылке' (*Sobr. soch.*, IV, 48)]. Elsewhere Cincinnatus notes: 'I am trembling over the paper … hunching over to conceal myself from the door through which a piercing eye stings me in the nape' (*IB*, 77) ['Дрожу над бумагой … горбом стараюсь закрыться от двери, через которую сквозной взгляд колет меня в затылок' (*Sobr. soch.*, IV, 99)]. His role as a prisoner under observation or as an actor being watched on stage is reflected on another level in his existence as a fictional character who is watched by the reader (following him into his dreams and most intimate thoughts). The reader can see Cincinnatus, but Cincinnatus cannot see the reader, an imbalance in perception which Nabokov noted as 'a unique feature of the dramatic art: under no circumstances of human life can the most secret watcher or eavesdropper be absolutely immune to the possibility of being found out' ('Playwriting', 315). This unequal relationship between the reader and Cincinnatus is also implicitly referred to in the description of Cincinnatus's cell with reference to the theatrical Fourth Wall convention: 'the walls, with their arms around each other's shoulders like a foursome discussing a square secret in

---

[63] Cf. Babikov who argues the opposite, i.e. that 'Cincinnatus is the only being who observes the convention of the "fourth wall", while the others try to penetrate his "monodrama" and involve him in the vile performance' (see 'The Main Thing', 167). Babikov takes the notion of the 'fourth wall' surely too literally when he suggests that Cincinnatus, because of his opacity, is the wall, which is shattered when he is executed.

[64] Patricia Waugh, *Metafiction: The Theory and Practice of Self-Conscious Fiction* (London and New York: Methuen, 1984), 21–2.

inaudible whispers' (*IB*, 29) ['стены, друг другу на плечи положившие руки, как четверо неслышным шепотом обсуждаюших квадратную тайну' (*Sobr. soch.*, IV, 61)]. When Cincinnatus makes an inventory of his cell, he notices the seemingly self-evident: 'This is how matters stood with the walls: their number was unalterably four' (*IB*, 101) ['Со стенами дело обстояло так: их было неизменно четыре' (*Sobr. soch.*, IV, 117)]. The setting of the novel in Cincinnatus's cell is here transformed into a theatrical space, the Fourth Wall of which is a one-way glass, real and opaque for the characters on stage but illusory and transparent for the spectators. The reader's eavesdropping on fictional characters is an inevitable effect of the reading process. In *Invitation to a Beheading*, however, the reader's privileged position as an invulnerable spy is brought to the fore and probed as a specifically theatrical convention. At the close of the novel, the reader's last glimpse of Cincinnatus is on stage, moving 'in that direction' (*v tu storonu*) where the auditorium is. The novel breaks off before the reader can follow Cincinnatus's arrival on the other side. Cincinnatus finally escapes the preying gaze of the watching reader that has kept him arrested on the stage of the novel.[65]

With its title directly appealing to and addressing the reader, the novel announces itself as a public spectacle. The reader is explicitly invited to witness and participate in Cincinnatus's execution. Dale Peterson has elegantly argued that the title '[advertises] the complicity of anyone who has accepted [the invitation]'.[66] Already in the second paragraph of the first chapter, the novel announces its own end:

So we are nearing the end. The right-hand, still untasted part of the novel, which, during our delectable reading, we would lightly feel, mechanically testing whether there were still plenty left (and our fingers were always gladdened by the placid, faithful thickness), had suddenly, for no reason at all, become quite meagre: a few minutes of quick reading, already downhill, and – O horrible! (*IB*, 11–12)

Итак – подбираемся к концу. Правая, еще непочатая часть развернутого романа, которую мы, посреди лакомого чтенья, легонько ощупывали, машинально проверяя, много ли еще (и все радовала пальцы спокойная, верная толщина),

---

[65] Nabokov had already examined the relationship between spying and reading in his earlier novella *The Eye*, where Smurov together with the reader clandestinely watches his own performance as the main character of the book. At the end of the book he steps out of his role as silent observer and addresses his readers directly.

[66] See Dale Peterson, 'Nabokov's *Invitation*: Literature as Execution', *PMLA*, 96 (1981), 824–36 [826]. Reprinted in Connolly (ed.), *Nabokov's* Invitation to a Beheading, 66–92.

вдруг, ни с того ни с сего, оказалась совсем тощей: несколько минут скорого, уже под гору чтенья – и… ужасно! (*Sobr. soch.*, IV, 47–8)

In Peterson's reading, the reader becomes an accomplice who takes part in the execution of Cincinnatus by merely reading the novel: 'we assist inevitability by thinning the fat right-hand text, slicing it away one razor-thin page at a time'.[67] The novel draws attention to its own material being as the book which exists in the world of the reader. The square object held by the reader is transformed into an interface between the fictional and the reader's world. The fictional world seems to break through to the external reality. Crossing over the threshold of the book, the novel trespasses into the external reality, becoming present in the reader's world. In a dazzling twist, literature's mediated reality of the past becomes theatre's mode of the present. The book becomes a truly theatrical object which is both fictional and non-fictional at the same time, confronting the reader with the essentially theatrical double perception of objects. Through the theatricalisation of the novel as book, the reader becomes an integral part of the theatrical world of *Invitation to a Beheading*. The novel stretches the limits of its own aesthetic conventions in emulating a performance situation in which the reader becomes a spectator.

The identical space and time continuum of the auditorium and the stage is exploited by Nabokov in his plays and adapted to his novel which also muddles any clear distinctions between reality and fiction. In *Invitation to a Beheading*, Nabokov moves beyond the use of theatrical metaphors and realises (or anticipates) the meta-theatrical performance of his plays. The reader's participation becomes almost palpably real in the turning of the pages towards Cincinnatus's execution. Through the shattering of the illusion, theatre is defined negatively against something which it is not. By drawing attention to the fact that the illusion in the theatre is never perfect, that another reality is always visible through the chinks in the (fourth) wall, Nabokov focuses on one of the essential characteristics of theatre. This twofold vision provides the structural principle for *Invitation to a Beheading* where, transposed into fiction, the theatre becomes almost automatically a self-reflexive, visible medium, since, if the theatrical illusion were all-encompassing, the theatrical mode would be indistinguishable from the literary mode. Here the reader witnesses the creation of a fictional reality, a world under construction which is also evident in 'The

---

[67] Peterson, 'Literature as Execution', 827.

Leonardo' and Nabokov's two plays of disillusionment. Underlying the image of collapsing theatrical structures in all of these works is the idea that theatre produces an inferior reality of readily assembled clichés and artless illusions, which disintegrates as soon as it is confronted with the more stable reality of the auditorium.

4

Theatre dreams: The Tragedy of Mr Morn, The Waltz Invention *and* Invitation to a Beheading

With the dazzling effect of an Escher drawing, *The Man from the USSR* and *The Event* simultaneously create and erase their own reality. In similar fashion, *Invitation to a Beheading* seems to remove the very boards on which it is being staged. In doing this, they throw into relief the theatrical construction of dream worlds in *The Tragedy of Mr Morn* and *The Waltz Invention*, one in the shape of a lyrical fairytale, the other in the guise of a grotesque chaotic reverie. Both are linked – if not by manner and tone – through their fantastic theme. In *The Tragedy of Mr Morn*, the co-existence of different realities in the exile's mind is reflected in the play's dualistic world, where the enchantment of dreams, poetry and nostalgia is set in opposition to a violent historical reality. Although entirely different in tone and mood, *The Waltz Invention*, written fourteen years later, retains this theme of dual worlds and lost kingdoms in the construction and reality of an imaginary dreamland ruled by Waltz, the insane king and dreamer of Nabokov's last play. While in *The Tragedy of Mr Morn* this dream is still shaped by Nabokov's recent experience of flight and exile, in *The Waltz Invention*, theatre, dream and exile are linked at a more abstract level, whether it is in the form of the poet's exile from his imaginary territory, or the madman's exile from reality.

The same association of theatre and dreams which is evident in Nabokov's theoretical thinking on drama also shapes his practice as a dramatist. The dreamer's powerlessness over the course of the dream together with the immediacy of the experience (or what Nabokov calls in his lectures 'the power to move the spectator') align the theatrical performance with a dream. The absence of any clearly recognisable author or organising principle gives the theatre performance a certain autonomy similar to a dream, which develops outside the control of the dreamer. With distant echoes of Calderón's *Life is a Dream* (1635) and Shakespeare's *The Tempest* reverberating in Nabokov's dream plays, *The Tragedy of Mr Morn* and *The Waltz Invention* let the theatrical performance overlap

with the dream of one of the protagonists, constructing a stage reality which seems to exist by itself. In both plays, the imaginary and the
ephemeral become enduring realities, a paradox which is also at the core
of *Invitation to a Beheading* and 'Lik', where the dramatic and the dreamy
become terrifyingly real. Here, life is not so much a dream as a horrifying
world which Prospero might have described as 'such stuff as nightmares
are made on'.

DREAM REALITIES: *THE TRAGEDY OF MR MORN*

Nabokov's first extensive piece of work, *The Tragedy of Mr Morn*, is a colourful fabrication of dream realities and fantastic worlds which penetrate
and envelop each other. Behind the Romantic drama, with its melodramatic dilemma of honour and the love for life, looms the much more real
tragedy of Russian exiles in the 1920s, longing for an irretrievable past. In
his Stanford lecture 'The Tragedy of Tragedy', Nabokov illustrates the audience's perception of a tragic character through the example of an exile:

> you happen to meet … a character to whom you would never dream of applying
> the adjective 'tragic'; then you learn that this person several years ago had been
> placed by force of circumstance at the head of some great revolution in a remote,
> almost legendary country, and that a new force of circumstance had soon ban-
> ished him to your part of the world where he lingers on as the mere ghost of his
> past glory. Immediately, the very things about the man that had just seemed to you
> humdrum … now strike you as the very features of tragedy. ('Tragedy', 324–5)

This 'hypothetical' protagonist had already been realised almost twenty
years earlier in Mr Morn, the tragic hero of *The Tragedy of Mr Morn* who
creates, loses and finally regains a kingdom by giving it up. Still close to
Symbolist ideas and notions, Nabokov links the king and his kingdom
with the poet and his imaginary realm, suggesting the exile of the poet
from his imaginary territory. The coexistence of different realities in the
exile's mind is reflected in the play's dualistic world, where the enchantment of dreams, poetry and nostalgic memory is set in opposition to the
historical reality.

The play's motifs, plot line, characters and metaphors foreshadow
recurring themes in Nabokov's subsequent work, many of which would
undergo repeated reworkings and transformations over the next decades.[1]

---

[1] See Gennady Barabtarlo, 'Nabokov's Trinity (On the Movement of Nabokov's Themes)', in
Julian Connolly (ed.), *Nabokov and His Fiction: New Perspectives* (Cambridge University Press,
1999), 109–38; A. Iu. Meshchanskii, '"Tragediia Gospodina Morna" kak predtecha russkoiazych-
noi prozy V. V. Nabokova', *Voprosy filologii*, 11/2 (2002), 100–8.

The famous 'magic carpet' from Nabokov's autobiography, for instance, is for the first time folded over in this early play, as Gennady Barabtarlo's perceptive reading of the play has demonstrated.[2] The main character Morn, a king incognitus, an impostor and a 'noble coward' as Nabokov describes him in his initial outline, would undergo numerous reincarnations, emerging as the king in the unfinished novel *Solus Rex*, Humbert searching for his lost kingdom by the sea in *Lolita*, and the famous king (or madman) Kinbote in *Pale Fire*.[3]

The Tragedy of Mr Morn was not published during Nabokov's lifetime. In the late 1950s Nabokov gave an incomplete typescript and manuscript and an outline in prose sketching out the initial conception of *The Tragedy of Mr Morn* to the Library of Congress.[4] These materials were published in the Russian original posthumously in an edition of *Zvezda*.[5] The *Zvezda* publication of *The Tragedy of Mr Morn* retains a number of inaccuracies when compared with the manuscripts and typescripts at the Library of Congress. While none of the mistakes which appeared in the *Zvezda* edition changes the fundamental reading of the play, as a scholarly tool the recent Azbuka edition of Nabokov's plays is without doubt superior in that the archival materials are rendered faithfully and accurately and a reliable text has been created.

The plot line of *The Tragedy of Mr Morn*, structured by a feverish succession of violent revolutions, coups d'état and counter-revolutions, depicts the recent political turmoil of the Russian Revolution through the prism of literary tradition, pointing to Shakespeare's history dramas and Pushkin's *Boris Godunov*. The fast pace of these scenes of bustling action is, however, halted in the interspersed dreamy soliloquies and dialogues on exile, poetry, the realm of the imagination and the nature of happiness, betraying Nabokov's youthful engagement with Russian Symbolism. Between these two poles of headlong action and meditation, Nabokov places the essential plot line of jealousy, duels and betrayals, reminiscent once more of Shakespeare and his tragedy of jealousy, *Othello*, as well as its reworking in Lermontov's *Masquerade*. Morn's tragedy, the moral dilemma between honour and life and the choice between country and self, are also modelled on Shakespeare's tragedies rather than man's struggle with predetermination and fate in classical Greek tragedy. Also Shakespearean

---

[2] Barabtarlo, 'Nabokov's Trinity', 126–7.
[3] Barabtarlo points out specific parallels in the plot of *The Tragedy of Mr Morn* and *Pale Fire* (see 'Nabokov's Trinity', 126).
[4] See Boyd, *American Years*, 367.
[5] Vladimir Nabokov, 'Tragediia Gospodina Morna', *Zvezda*, 4 (1997), 9–98.

is the sheer number of characters mingling and rushing through the play. While most of them are intricately connected with each other, two characters stand out in somewhat isolated positions with a chorus function rather than an active part in the plot development. Dandilio, the old wise man interprets the course of events from a particular philosophical and theological perspective, while the Foreigner (*Inostranets*), a poet from the twentieth century, gives the play a metafictional dimension, perceiving the world of the drama and its characters as his own invention.[6]

The play is set in an imaginary kingdom, a prosperous, harmonious and beautiful place, which has been created out of revolutionary anarchy by the present ruler who hides behind a mask. It soon becomes clear that this king incognitus is no other than the protagonist of the drama, Morn. Morn is at the height of achievement, power and enjoyment of life when his impending tragedy is set in motion by the return of Ganus, a former revolutionary who has escaped from imprisonment in a labour camp. Ganus's expectations of a loving reunion with his wife Midiia are, however, disappointed. Far from a life of loneliness and grief, Midiia is happily betraying her husband with no other than Morn. Outraged, Ganus confronts his wife's lover only to be challenged to a duel. They agree on a so-called *duel à la courte paille*, a particularly merciless kind of duel which decides by a draw who of the two opponents has to commit suicide. The lot falls on Morn whose initial manly resolution to fulfil this deed of honour vanishes as soon as he has to face the barrel of his gun in the solitude of his palace. Instead of pulling the trigger, Morn flees the country allegedly for the sake of romantic love and Midiia who cannot live without him, as he explains to his friend and servant Edmin. The flighty and superficial Midiia, however, can live as easily without him as without her husband. Bored by the eventless repetitive life in exile, she leaves Morn for his friend Edmin. Abandoned and betrayed by the two people closest to him, Morn is overcome by melancholy. Meanwhile back in the kingdom, the former revolutionaries have discovered that the king has disappeared and taken over the country in a bloody revolution, the aftermath of which turns into a cruel dictatorship. Ganus, who has half-heartedly joined his former fellow revolutionaries, finds out that Morn has not committed suicide but fled. He abandons the revolution in order to kill Morn. Ganus arrives at Morn's hiding place and secretly takes aim at Morn. Owing to several missing pages in the typescript, it is difficult

---

[6] For a discussion of how Dandilio's theological world-view might reflect Nabokov's own, see Barabtarlo, 'Nabokov's Trinity', 132–4.

to establish a precise course of events in the following scenes. The initial prose outline suggests that Nabokov planned for Morn only to be injured but not killed by the shot, while the now avenged Ganus was to join a remote monastery. From the fragments of the final act that have survived, whatever fate Nabokov might have finally decided to bestow on Ganus, a few crucial developments become clear. Morn does not die at Ganus's hand. The revolution is overthrown by counter-revolutionary royalists, preparing the return of their king. Having received the good news, fellow émigrés arrive at Morn's place to celebrate. The occasion is, however, a rather subdued affair during which Morn disturbs his guests with his enigmatic remarks and erratic behaviour. The play ends with Morn stepping outside and shooting himself, finally fulfilling the conditions of the duel and honouring the agreement.

The world of *The Tragedy of Mr Morn* is an unreal, dreamy and alluring construct. Its setting in an imaginary place, at an undetermined point of time, recalls the timelessness of fairytales. This sense of enchantment is reinforced by the almost unbelievable all-embracing joyfulness in the kingdom, an impression which Nabokov explicitly intended, as the description of the play's initial atmosphere in the outline suggests: 'Romantic ennui has turned into Romantic joy of life' ['Романтическое уныние перешло в романтическую радость жизни' (*P'esy*, 283)].[7] The capital of this fairytale country is marked by an exquisite beauty. Its wide spaces, light architecture and white squares suggest a stylised image of St Petersburg. This atmosphere of an ideal St Petersburg is also noted by the Foreigner, a poet from a country reminiscent of contemporary Soviet Russia, who comments on the striking but illusory resemblance between his own home and the capital of Morn's fairytale country:

I find [in the capital] an eerie similarity with my distant native town, that kind of similarity which exists between truth and the most elevated fantasy...

Я нахожу в ней [столице] призрачное сходство
с моим далеким городом родным, –
то сходство, что бывает между правдой
и вымыслом возвышенным... (*P'esy*, 158)

Both countries have emerged from a period of political unrest, but while the Foreigner later admits that 'It's bad in my country, bad ...' ['У нас в стране нехорошо, нехорошо ...' (*P'esy*, 273)], a transparent allusion to the Bolshevik regime, Morn has transformed the country into an enchanting

---

[7] All translations of passages from *The Tragedy of Mr* Morn are my own. I have rendered the verse form of *The Tragedy of Mr Morn* in literal prose translation.

kingdom. Morn's creation, which is and is not Russia, and belongs, in the Foreigner's words, to both truth and fiction (*pravda* and *vymysel*), appears as the émigrés' idealised old Russia which never existed, shaped by nostalgic memory and fantasy.

The initially artistic illusion of Morn's kingdom, however, turns into ever baser deception. Morn cannot live up to the high moral standards demanded of a king. High social standing becomes here a metaphor for unquestionable moral probity and untarnished honour. The notion of play-acting becomes central in Morn's performance as the heroic and noble ruler of the country. The wide gap between Morn and his role is contrasted, for instance, with Ganus disguising himself as an actor playing Othello. Unlike Morn's mask, the disguise as Othello does not hide Ganus but reveals his real self, the jealous husband. Morn's dilemma, between a moral obligation to commit suicide and his wish to live derives from the opposed roles as king and as Morn. Morn's double role finds an equivalent in the stage settings which frequently place him in front of mirrors and large windows that duplicate his image. The stage itself becomes a metaphor for the proximity of truth and deceit.

Morn's dilemma mirrors the predicament of the White emigration. The relief at having survived was soon overshadowed by a feeling of guilt at having abandoned their native country instead of giving their lives to the 'honourable' cause of saving Russia from the Bolsheviks. That decades later in his autobiography Nabokov was still troubled by the death of his much-loved and admired cousin, Yuri Rausch, in combat for the White side suggests the persistence of precisely this kind of guilt. Nabokov's memory of having exchanged clothes with his cousin shortly before Yuri's death underlines the sense that it could or should have been Nabokov who died. The helpless feeling of moral failure in comparison to the distinction of Yuri's honourable death is movingly expressed in Nabokov's tribute to his cousin: 'Had I been competent to write his epitaph, I might have summed up matters by saying – in richer words than I can muster here – that all emotions, all thoughts, were governed in Yuri by one gift: a sense of honor equivalent, morally, to absolute pitch' (*SM*, 156).

Through his eventual suicide Morn fulfils the king's moral duty, essentially becoming his role. In death, reality and illusion, the different identities of Morn and the king merge, as the metaphor of the torch falling towards its own reflection illustrates:

I am just a torch thrown into a well, burning, spiralling, flying, flying down towards its own reflection, which is growing in the darkness, like dawn …

Я только факел, брошенный в колодец,
пылающий, кружащийся, летящий,
летящий вниз, навстречу отраженью,
растущему во мраке, как заря … (*P'esy*, 277)

While Morn perishes like the torch, the king, like the torch's reflection, is associated with a new beginning, the breaking of a new dawn (*zaria*), which suggests the king's resurrection and continuation in people's memory and imagination. Morn is last glimpsed on the other side of the large window, as if he had stepped through a mirror, uniting with his reflection. By merging with the illusion he himself has created, he ensures his survival in the continuing reality of legends and myths. Morn's death is witnessed by the king who lives on, as Edmin's closing lines suggest:

… Nobody shall see how my king reveals to the Heavens the death of Mr Morn

… Никто не должен видеть,
как мой король являет небесам
смерть Господина Морна. (*P'esy*, 278)

Through his death, Morn sacrifices himself for his own illusion, transcending the inherent deceit of his kingdom in this final enactment of his role. His suicide, which essentially cancels his play-acting and removes the theatricality of his situation, very aptly also ends the play.

This preoccupation with the relationship between illusion, deception, dream and reality points once more to Lermontov's *Masquerade* as a model for Nabokov's first play. Yet while Lermontov writes a satire which exposes the hypocrisy and intrigues of his contemporary society, Nabokov creates a self-referential drama about the instability of reality. It is, therefore, not so much Lermontov's play but rather its famous staging by Meyerhold that presents a clear inspiration for Nabokov's drama. It is very probable that together with his father, V. D. Nabokov, a passionate theatre-goer, Nabokov saw the premiere of Meyerhold's production of *Masquerade* on 25 February 1917 at the Alexandrinsky Theatre. According to Boyd, in spite of the revolution V. D. Nabokov went to work as usual until 27 February, which suggests that a few days earlier he would hardly have missed the most important event of the theatrical season.[8] In his drama, Nabokov combines the original setting of *Masquerade* in 1830s Petersburg with Meyerhold's shift to eighteenth-century Venice when he notes in the outline that 'The capital has something of seventeenth-century Venice in the times of Casanova, and of Petersburg in the Thirties' [Есть

---

[8] Boyd, *Russian years*, 123.

в ней [столице] что-то от венецианского XVII столетия времен Казановы и от тридцатых годов петербургской эпохи' (*P'esy*, 283)].[9] As in Meyerhold's production of *Masquerade*, the settings in *The Tragedy of Mr Morn* are dominated by masks, mirrors and candles – symbols which suggest the elusiveness of identities and the illusion of reflections in an illumination that creates more shadows than light. In both cases, these props create a magical atmosphere where the difference between seeming and being, illusion and reality becomes blurred.

Contrary to his initial plans, Meyerhold moved away from the social satire of *Masquerade* during the six-year period of preparation and rehearsals for this production. Influenced by the art historian Pavel Muratov and his work *Obrazy Italii*,[10] Meyerhold noted in preparation for the production that:

> It seems to me that the Romanticism which colours Lermontov's *Masquerade* should be looked for in the sphere which Lermontov found himself in when he became engrossed in Byron ... And isn't it eighteenth-century Venice, which appears between the lines of Byron's poetry, which suggested to Lermontov this world of imagination and enchanted dreams which envelopes *Masquerade*? 'The mask, the candle, the mirror – that is the image of 18th century Venice', Muratov writes. ... Isn't it this very Venetian life, 'pervaded by magic which is hidden in cards and gold', which shines through in the images of Lermontov's *Masquerade*, 'existing on *the border between delirium and hallucination*'.[11]

This sense of uncertainty was underlined by Meyerhold's interpretation of Lermontov's drama as an 'enchanting dream'. He created the impression that 'everything moves before the spectator as if in a dream', as he stated briefly before the premiere.[12] This impression of a dreamy, and towards the end nightmarish, atmosphere was supported by a reworking of Lermontov's Stranger *(Neizvestnyi)*. Whereas in *Masquerade* the initially mysterious stranger turns out to be a former victim of Arbenin's cruelty who wants to take revenge, in Meyerhold's production the Stranger becomes a mystical and supernatural figure, closely linked to fate itself. This new emphasis on the stranger in particular is echoed in Nabokov's play by the fantastic character of the puzzling Foreigner, who underlines the tension between dream and reality. The significance of Meyerhold's *Masquerade* for *The Tragedy of Mr Morn* is even greater when one considers that Meyerhold's production achieved in retrospect

---

[9] Giacomo Casanova (1725–1798) lived during the eighteenth century. In the outline to the play, Nabokov mixes up the seventeenth and eighteenth centuries.

[10] See Edward Braun, *Meyerhold: A Revolution in Theatre* (London: Methuen, 1998), 144.

[11] Vsevolod Meierkhol'd, *Stat'i, pis'ma, rechi, besedy*, 2 vols. (Moscow: Iskusstvo, 1968), vol. I, 300.

[12] Meierkhol'd, *Stat'i, pis'ma, rechi, besedy*, vol. I, 304.

the status of a prophecy. The historical symbolism of the premiere on the eve of the Russian Revolution, which Konstantin Rudnitsky subsequently commented on, must have been even more apparent to a Russian émigré in the early 1920s: 'Meyerhold's production sounded like a dark requiem to the empire, like a solemn and terrible, a tragic and fatal funeral march for the world which perished in those days.'[13] Just as Meyerhold's production was seen as an allegory on the destruction of the old world, so Nabokov's play thematises the irretrievability of old Russia which had grown into an idealised fairytale world in the émigrés' memory.

In *The Tragedy of Mr Morn*, Nabokov aligns the exile's memory with poetic creation in the figure of the king-poet Morn who has apparently single-handedly fashioned this enchanting version of Russia in his kingdom. Significantly, Morn himself juxtaposes poet and king when he states that 'If I was not a king, I would become a poet' [(Когда б я не был королем, то стал бы / поэтом ' (*P'esy*, 268)]. Yet during most of the play, Morn remains outside the borders of his kingdom. Only his suicide, which transforms him finally into the real king, allows him eventually to return from this exile, to re-cross the border into his kingdom.

Morn's position as an exile outside his own creation is thrown into relief by his mysterious double, the Foreigner, who, at the metafictional level, claims the whole world of the drama as his poetic invention and dream.[14] During the course of the play, the Foreigner emerges with increasing confidence as the drama's creator, declaring to a perplexed Morn that 'I invented you well' ['я хорошо вас выдумал' (*P'esy*, 272)]. Like Morn, he cannot enter the realm of his imagination except in his dreams, which become bridges between reality and fantasy. The Foreigner's sudden acts of appearing and vanishing correspond to the different states of dreaming and awakening, as his explanation for his sudden departure indicates:

I woke up. The wind woke me up. The window frame banged. It was difficult to fall asleep again …

Я просыпался. Ветер разбудил.
Оконницу шарахнуло. С трудом
заснул опять … (*P'esy*, 170)

---

[13] Konstantin Rudnitskii, *Rezhisser Meierkhol'd* (Moscow: Nauka, 1969), 203.

[14] For a discussion of the different levels of dream and reality, see R. V. Novikov, '"Tragediia Gospodina Morna" V. Nabokova: k poetike "p'esy-snovideniia"', in L. F. Alekseeva and V. A. Skripkina (eds.), *Maloizvestnye stranitsy i novye kontseptsii istorii russkoi literatury XX v.: Materialy mezhdunarodnoi konferentsii, Moskva, MGOU, 24–25 iiunia 2003 g.*, vol. I (Moscow: Moskovskii gosudarstvennyi oblastnoi universitet, 2003), 181–7.

In his dreams he enters the world of the play and disappears whenever he wakes up. Barabtarlo concludes that 'the whole thing is but [the Foreigner's] dream, an intricate hallucination of a creative mind'.[15] Yet while the Foreigner perceives everything around him as his own illusory dream, his own reality is dismissed as a fairytale; the Foreigner is told by his dream figures that his reality is just a legend from ancient times, a fairytale for children, as Dandelio reminds Midiia:

In children's fairy tales, don't you remember? Visions … bombs … churches … golden *tsarevichi* … revolutionaries in cloaks … snow storms…

[…] В детских сказках, ты не помнишь?
Виденья … бомбы … церкви … золотые
царевичи … Бунтовщики в плащах …
метели… (*P'esy*, 157)

In this twofold vision in which the borders between reality and dream are blurred, it remains unclear which reality is the original and which is the reflection, which is the lost territory and which is the new territory, who is the native and who is the exile, as the Foreigner recognises:

I have walked into a day dream, but you are convinced that I have walked out of a day dream … Very well, I shall believe in your capital, but tomorrow I will call it a dream …

[…] Я в грезу
вошел, а вы уверены, что я
из грезы вышел … Так и быть, поверю
в столицу вашу. Завтра – сновиденьем
я назову ее … (*P'esy*, 157–8)

The poet creates but can never enter his imaginary worlds except in his dreams, just as the exile's imagination shapes his memory of a home country to which he can never return.

In its rather highly-strung, melodramatic subject of tragedy and heroic sacrifice, the play reveals itself to be still an early attempt at drama, without the distanced irony of Nabokov's later work. Yet already this first extensive piece of work contains a number of his later art's pivotal themes: the coexistence of different realities and worlds and the relationship between the artist and his work, to which Nabokov would return over and over again throughout his career as a writer. It is significant that these fundamental concerns of Nabokov's art are for the first time fully articulated in a dramatic work which develops them in analogy with the twofold realities of exile and the stage.

---

[15] Barabtarlo, 'Nabokov's Trinity', 130–1.

CONTROLLING DREAMS: *THE WALTZ INVENTION*

Nabokov's last drama, *The Waltz Invention*, built on the attention his previous play *The Event* had received. It was written again for the Russian Theatre in Paris, with Annenkov, who had also staged *The Event*, as the prospective director in mind. The effect of the play depends on the physical embodiment of the protagonist's dream on stage, so that the spectator actually sees events, characters and places which turn out not to exist (even within the reality of the play). Through this confusion of visual illusion and reality, the play mirrors the twofold reality of the theatre in which it is taking place, displaying a certain affinity with the previous *The Event*, with which it also shares a farcical and burlesque tone. Yet the play's preoccupation with dreams and lost realms links it back to Nabokov's first drama, *The Tragedy of Mr Morn*.

The Waltz Invention comes closest to Nabokov's later notion of dream plays in which 'dream-logic, or … nightmare-logic, replaces … the elements of dramatic determinism' ('Tragedy', 327). Minor characters come briefly into focus and disappear without leaving any discernible trace in the plot development of the play, objects appear out of nowhere, and events take place unexpectedly and without logical preparation or consequence. These surreal incidences as well as the play's circular structure could suggest that the drama is an early precedent of the theatre of the absurd, yet the play's illogical and at times absurd incidences are placed into the realistic framework of a dream, which explains the unexpected appearance of objects, people and events. One of Nabokov's favourite dream plays, Gogol's *The Government Inspector*, resonates in his own play. His reading of *The Government Inspector* not as a political or social satire, but as an absurd and fantastic dream play is close to Meyerhold's interpretation in his staging of Gogol's drama as the Mayor's dream or delirium, which, in Nabokov's opinion, 'in spite of all his distortions and additions, offered a stage version of *The Government Inspector* which conveyed something of the real Gogol'.[16]

Despite its political overtones, the play does not work as a mere satire on Nazi Germany or Stalinist Russia. The ultimate exposing of the drama's absurd reality as a dream in the last act makes it difficult to read the play as a serious moral condemnation of totalitarian systems. Nabokov emphasised in the foreword to the English translation of his play: 'I wish to point out

---

[16] Nabokov, *Nikolai Gogol*, 38. The premiere of Meyerhold's *The Government Inspector* took place on 9 December 1926 at his own theatre in Moscow. Nabokov must have seen this production during Meyerhold's tour of Berlin in 1930.

most emphatically that not only is there in my play no political "message" ... but that publication of its English version today [1966] has no topical import' (*WI*, foreword). Most critics have taken heed of Nabokov's denial and have suggested a close link between totalitarianism and failed artistic creativity.[17] The link between art and an authoritarian regime is, however, established at a deeper structural level in Waltz's aspiration for control over the play. Waltz's dictatorship is confronted and replaced by a more powerful reality which asserts its enduring existence at the end of the play when Waltz's world is cancelled as a mere dream. Totalitarianism as a political system becomes an analogy for a dramatic strategy which seeks to translate the omnipotence of the novelist into the playwright's all-encompassing control over his drama, even in its most defiant and rebellious form as a theatre production. As in Nabokov's other plays, the relationship between different realities and the tension between different perceptions and depictions of the world, proves to be the principal concern of *The Waltz Invention*.

Although Nabokov, presumably in expectation of his move to the United States, had the play translated for an English-speaking audience, it was staged neither in the United States nor in England, and the translation itself remained unpublished.[18] In 1939 Nabokov made some revisions to the original play which became the basis for a second English translation some thirty years later.[19] During 1964 and 1965, Nabokov returned to his last play and prepared, in collaboration with his son Dmitri, a new English translation. Whilst the word play of the Russian title can only be approximated in English, and Russian puns were replaced by English variants, other alterations, like the new emphasis on Waltz's insanity and the more tragic dimension of his character, clarify and explain Waltz's erratic behaviour.

Nabokov wrote the play in the South of France while staying at the House of the Union of the St George Cross for Disabled Veterans.[20] This setting might have inspired some of the characters, especially the farcical generals, but the institutional atmosphere might have also prompted the idea of a mental asylum and Waltz's psychological instability. The play stages Waltz's hallucinatory inner world, which is in constant competition with an outside reality threatening to subvert Waltz's peculiar view

---

[17] Karlinsky, for instance, calls the play a 'portrait of an artist as a madman-politician' ('Illusion, Reality in Nabokov's Play's', 185). For similar views, see Field, *Life in Art*, 210; Dolinin, 'Istinnaia zhizn'', 16; Boyd, *Russian Years*, 489. Against these readings, Diment argues that due to the dramaturgical shortcomings of the drama, if 'the play did not work well as a denunciation of political evil, it seems to work even less well as a play about "art"' ('Plays', 596).

[18] See Vladimir Nabokov, 'The Waltz Invention'. Typescript of early translation of the play, VN Berg. The date given on the typescript (Paris, 1937) is incorrect, as Nabokov did not finish the play before October 1938 (see Boyd, *Russian Years*, 489).

[19] See Boyd, *Russian Years*, 509.   [20] See *ibid*., 488.

and interpretation of reality. The beginning of the drama, however, is still entirely realistic. The minister's scepticism about Waltz's unbelievable claims about the omnipotent weapon reinforces the realism of the first scene. It is only after the first break in the conversation with the minister that the reality of the play is almost imperceptibly subsumed by Waltz's dream. The realistic world turns seamlessly into the fantastic world of Waltz's imagination, in which he can miraculously ascend to become the omnipotent ruler of the country. The growing despotism of Waltz's regime is accompanied by an increasingly absurd and fantastic quality in the play's world. The very first scene sets up this theme of opposed realities. The colonel's attempt to remove a speck from the minister's eye which disturbs his view is contrasted with Waltz's fond recollection of an optical illusion he experienced as a child.[21] While the minister tries to maintain an undistorted, 'realistic' view of the world, Waltz explicitly regrets the loss of this mirage-like vision – a comment on the ultimately deceptive nature of the visible reality created on stage.

The illusionary nature of Waltz's world is initially underpinned by the fairytale motif which pervades the whole play. It appears for the first time in the minister's conversation with General Berg about the death of the old man Perrault. This reference to Charles Perrault, who is best known for his collection of fairy stories for children, *Contes de ma mère l'oye* (1697), is further developed in the English translation where the minister remembers: 'Old Perrault – yes, yes. Seems only yesterday that he was reciting his wonderful fairy-tales at Christmas parties for disabled soldiers and at that wonderful mental home' (*WI*, 19). Berg's daughter Annabella claims that the mountain which Waltz destroyed was inhabited by fairytale creatures.[22] Waltz's own machine is associated with fairy-tales when the minister dismisses Waltz's claim as the 'old story about a fantastic machine that's supposed to produce explosions at a distance' (*WI*, 17) ['Старая история о фантастической машине, которая будто бы производит взрывы на расстоянии' (*Sobr. soch.*, V, 528)].[23] The further

---

[21] This scene also introduces the motif of sleep and dreaming, recalling the Sandman who brings dreams to children by sprinkling sand into their eyes.

[22] Annabella claims that an old enchanter and a white gazelle used to live on the mountain. In a letter to David Bellos, Véra Nabokov stated that '[t]he source of Annabella's line in Act I is VN's imagination' (Véra Nabokov to David Bellos, 28 January 1968, VN Berg).

[23] This remark also refers to the play's theme of an omnipotent ruler of the world and his fantastic machine, which, as Dolinin has pointed out, was a commonplace topic in 1920s and 1930s Russian science-fiction literature (see 'Istinnaia zhizn'', 15). Babikov identifies Aleksei Tolstoi's *The Hyperboloid of Engineer Garin* (*Giperboloid inzhenera Garina*, 1925–7) as well as Andrei Belyi's *The Moscow Eccentric* (*Moskovskii chudak*, 1926)) and *Moscow Under Siege* (*Moskva pod udarom*, 1927) as predecessors of the theme of a miraculous invention (see 'Primechaniia [*Izobretenie Val'sa*]', in *Sobr. soch.*, V, 771–80 [773]).

Waltz drifts into his self-centred dream world, the more his kingdom is revealed to be pure fantasy. While in the first act there are still references to known places like Corsica and Sardinia, in the third act the geography of Waltz's country has become thoroughly fantastic in the name of the pulverised town, Santa-Morgana (which functions as another hint at the Fata Morgana being staged for the audience), or the island Palmora. The intrusion of ever more fantastic elements into Waltz's world underscores the growing unreality of the play.

The world of Waltz's dream is a fragile construct and under constant threat of being disclosed as a mere illusion. Already at the end of the first act, Waltz's dream is exposed to what Nabokov calls 'a sudden thinning of the texture, a rubbed spot in the bright fabric, allowing the nether life to glimmer through' (*WI*, foreword). The sudden appearance of an old school atlas out of nowhere is the first hint that rational cause-and-effect logic has been suspended in a surreal dream world where things and people appear without any logical connection. This souvenir, presumably from Waltz's own school days, prepares the absurd meeting of the generals at the beginning of the second act. This seamless shift from a professional crisis summit to a chaotic school lesson is another instance of the peculiar dream logic which pervades the play.[24]

The slippery reality of Waltz's dream is also manifest in the changeable identities of the characters surrounding Waltz. Each general functions in more than one role. The interchangeability of the minor characters, which is indicated by the similar sound of their names, reveals their lack of individuality.[25] The generals appear also in other roles as reporters, doctors, architects, cooks, gardeners and servants. Waltz's factotum, Viola Trance, or Son in the Russian original, seems to alternate between female and male attributes. Although, in the Russian version, Son uses the masculine form to refer to himself, the stage directions state that 'He may be played by a woman' (*WI*, 29) ['Его может играть женщина' (*Sobr. soch.*, V, 536)]. The absurd logic of dreams where the same people appear in different guises is given a theatrical dimension in the play, where the same actor plays different roles. The unreality of Waltz's dream world is taken to an extreme when, during a governmental meeting, three of the generals are reduced to almost identical dolls, while the president remains invisible. His entry becomes apparent to the spectator only through the reactions of

---

[24] Krug in *Bend Sinister* is also haunted by recurring dreams of school days and exams.
[25] In the English version, the generals are distinguishable only through the first consonant of their name: Bump, Dump, Gump, Hump, Lump, Mump, Rump, Stump, Tump, Ump, Zump.

the other characters: 'The invisible President is led to an empty armchair, and from the motions of Lump and the Minister it is evident that they are seating him' (*WI*, 67) ['Невидимого Президента подводят к пустому креслу, и по движениям Герба и министра видно, что невидимого усаживают' (*Sobr. soch.*, V, 558)]. Adamovich found that Nabokov's use of puppets was derivative, a borrowing from Blok's *The Fairground Booth*: 'The Generals at the minister's meeting are almost a copy of Blok's mystics.'[26] The Mystics in Blok's play, like the three generals, are dolls which fall apart when Columbine enters the stage. In Meyerhold's staging of *The Fairground Booth*, they were simply replaced with dummies. The use of dummies recurred in his production of *The Government Inspector* where in the silent scene the actors were replicated by dummies.[27] Both Nabokov and Meyerhold use this device to reinforce the cardboard quality of the reality on stage. Just as in Meyerhold's production the dummies designate the complete disintegration of the Mayor's dream after the announcement of the real government inspector's arrival, in Nabokov's play they hint at the precarious reality of Waltz's dream. If up to this point the audience has shared Waltz's perception of reality and seen what he sees, then the dolls and the invisible president mark a caesura in the play, where the spectator's perspective becomes dissociated from Waltz's perception.

Waltz's dream finds its personification in Trance (in his Russian incarnation, the character's name is Son, the Russian word for 'dream'), which is suggested in his telling name and his unexpected appearances and mysterious acts of vanishing. One of the generals comments on Trance's special status as a dream when he remarks that: 'He's merely a figment of the imagination. A trance, a daze, a dream' (*WI*, 41) ['Это так – фикция. Ведь это – Сон' (*Sobr. soch.*, V, 542)]. Waltz's fantastic construction naturally depends entirely on the presence of Trance who becomes the sole manager of Waltz's private and public life. Trance's disappearance at the end of the play marks the shattering of Waltz's delusion. He plays an ambivalent role, simultaneously supporting as well as challenging Waltz's reality. He doubts the existence of Waltz's machine and plays along with Waltz's fantasy at the same time. In a similar fashion, he strengthens the illusion of Waltz's imaginary island by providing further details about its size until he exposes the island as a figment of Waltz's imagination

[26] Adamovich, 'Rets.: *Russkie zapiski*, 1938, no 11', 176.
[27] See Nick Worrall, 'Meyerhold Directs Gogol's "Government Inspector"', *Theatre Quarterly*, 2/7 (July–September 1972), 75–95 [94].

when he cannot remember the name of the place.[28] The sceptical distance Trance has from the events around him suggests a certain autonomous status, detached from Waltz's control. That the dream is given a physical embodiment on stage has the effect of an actual manifestation of this independence. While in the first two acts Trance is Waltz's assistant, in the final act Trance is in total control of the events. Trance manages the meeting with the prostitutes, and it is no longer Waltz but Trance who assigns the roles to the former generals, who now turn into a sports instructor, a doctor or a chef. If in the first two acts Waltz has controlled the dream, then in the third act the dream controls Waltz.

Trance's status as a character located at the intersection of reality and illusion is mirrored in his ambiguous gender identity. In the English version of the play, Trance is explicitly aligned with Shakespeare's famous female cross-dressers. In the list of dramatis personae, Trance is given the first name Viola and described as 'a smart woman of 30 in black masculine dress Shakespearean-masquerade style', pointing to Shakespeare's heroine from *Twelfth Night* as a predecessor. Shakespeare's Viola is the only person who both generates and recognises the simultaneous existence of different realities which sustain the drama of *Twelfth Night*. The juxtaposition of Shakespeare's Viola and Trance suggests the powerful illusion both can create in the transformation of things into their opposite. Viola's double existence as both boy and girl, which is complicated by the confusing effect of a boy playing a girl playing a boy in the Elizabethan theatre, becomes a reflection of the different levels of theatrical and visual illusions which are explored in the play. In a similar fashion, Trance is the only character in the play who is able to balance Waltz's insane perceptions with a more realistic assessment of the situation. If acted out on stage, Trance's confusing gender identity invites the spectator to adopt an essentially theatrical 'double vision' which accommodates different realities at the same time, so that the spectator sees something that is and is not there at the same time.

According to Nabokov, the change from Son to Trance in the English translation had primarily practical reasons: '"Trance" was originally "*Son*," which means "dream" in Russian but would have got messed up with "son" and "sun" in an English transcription' (*WI*, foreword). There is, however, no reason why Nabokov could not have chosen the direct

---

[28] Boyd suggests a psychological reading of Son's ambiguous role as 'the mind's sly skepticism that half-realizes this is all a dream but remains prepared, up to a point, to suppress its awareness for the sake of the fantasy' (Boyd, *Russian Years*, 491).

English translation 'dream' for *son*, or the more subtle version 'Sandman', as suggested in an early translation of the play.[29] By changing Waltz's mental state from dream to trance, Nabokov implies a far stronger mental delusion than just a dream from which one can awake. The colonel's constant suspicions about Waltz's sanity are confirmed when Waltz recruits the servants for his magical island. Waltz's sudden recognition of a doctor, who together with Trance attempts to calm his unexplained nervousness and fear, affords a glimpse of the actual medical staff at the mental institution where Waltz is held. The bandage around Waltz's head, seemingly the result of an assassination attempt, is the first indication in the final act that Waltz is in a medical institution. In his argument with Waltz, Trance takes on the role of a caring nurse when he insists: 'Don't touch the bandage. Remember, I was the one to place it and therefore I am responsible for your health. Here, let me fix it' (*WI*, 87) ['Не трогайте повязки. Помните, что наложил ее я и, таким образом, я отвечаю за ваше здоровье. Дайте поправлю' (*Sobr. soch.*, V, 570)]. The impression of a mental institution is further reinforced by the doctor's soothing and patronising attitude towards Waltz, which marks him as the actual doctor of an external reality.[30] Unmoved by Waltz's hysterical orders, he proceeds with the examination. The English translation underscores the impression of a mental institution, when Grob's authority as a doctor is indicated in his decision that 'If this goes on, we'll have to try another injection' (*WI*, 97). The English version thus makes explicit the more subtle hint in the Russian original that Waltz's dream develops against the backdrop of a more believable reality. Waltz is not only a dreamer but a delirious madman in a trance. This indication of Waltz's insanity is once more reminiscent of Meyerhold's *The Government Inspector*, where in the final act the Mayor was led away in a straitjacket.[31]

These competing realities of delirium and external reality recall the shifting narrative levels of another story about a madman in Russian literature, Gogol's 'Diary of a Madman' ('Zapiski sumasshedshego', 1835). Poprishchin's delusions of being the king of Spain are echoed in Waltz's kingly ambitions and his despotic behaviour. Gogol's strategy of imposing two different realities at the same time on the reader in 'Diary of a Madman' is taken up in *The Waltz Invention*. Poprishchin's attempt to

---

[29] See Nabokov, 'The Waltz Invention'. English. Typescript of early translation of the play, VN Berg.

[30] Karlinsky also notes that 'another character almost turns into a psychiatrist from the mental institution where Waltz is being treated' ('Illusion, Reality in Nabokov's Play's', 192).

[31] Braun, *Meyerhold: A Revolution in Theatre*, 227.

integrate the grim circumstances of his present situation into his delusion of grandeur, by transforming inmates into soldiers, the hospital staff into the great inquisition, and the cruel treatment of the institution into exotic ceremonies, foreshadows Waltz's desperate attempt to keep intact his megalomaniac delusion by transforming a psychiatrist into his personal doctor and the other inmates into dim-witted generals.[32] The coexistence of different realities is also thematised in other works by Nabokov, as Karlinsky has pointed out, '[i]n the short story "Terra Incognita" and in *The Gift* (the hero's imaginary conversations with the poet Koncheev), Nabokov had developed a set of subtle devices for indicating that the action or the dialogue described is taking place within a character's reverie'.[33] The different narrative levels of 'Terra Incognita' (1931) in particular, where the delirious narrator in an African swamp perceives the external reality of a European bedroom shining through his fantastic non-existent delusion of a jungle expedition, anticipate the twofold vision the spectator has to adopt to appreciate the different layers of reality in *The Waltz Invention*.

The scene in the mental hospital marks the beginning of the total disintegration of Waltz's dream. The subsequent meeting with the grotesque prostitutes or female inmates of a lunatic asylum instead of the expected foremost beauties of the country indicates that Waltz's dream is dissolving to give way to a different reality. The destruction of his dream is finally sealed when he encounters Berg's stubborn resistance to giving up his daughter Annabella. Waltz's offer of money for Annabella, which mirrors the generals' bargaining for Waltz's machine, emphasises the total reversal of Waltz's situation. While in the first act, Waltz's refusal to sell his machine has been the base for Waltz's becoming the ruler of the world, Berg's resistance to selling his daughter now marks the downfall of Waltz. Waltz's dream is finally shattered by Trance's departure and his revelation that Waltz does not have a machine, which destroys the very basis on which Waltz's illusory construction rests. The abrupt change in scene back to the minister's office marks the end of Waltz's dream. Nabokov himself explained in the foreword to the English translation that 'while he [Waltz] waits outside, in a viking-style armchair – [he] imagines the interview he has managed to wangle through old Gump and its fabulous consequences; an interview which in reality he is granted only in the last scene of the last act'.

---

[32] Nabokov used a similar strategy, also with reference to Gogol's madman, to expose Hermann Karlovich's madness in the earlier *Despair*, which will be discussed in the next chapter.

[33] Karlinsky, 'Illusion, Reality in Nabokov's Plays', 192.

In the story 'A Letter that Never Reached Russia' ('Pis'mo v Rossiiu', 1925), the narrator refers to Pushkin's description of the waltz in *Eugene Onegin* (*Evgenii Onegin*, 1825–33): 'We all remember what Pushkin wrote about the waltz: "monotonous and mad." … And so I enjoy watching, in the *cafes dansants* here, how "pair after pair flick by" to quote Pushkin again' (*Stories*, 139) ['Помнишь, так Пушкин написал о вальсе: «однообразный и безумный» … И вот, в здешних кабачках я люблю глядеть, как «чета мелькает за четой»' (*Sobr. soch.*, I, 162)].[34] This association of the whirling couples in the rotating dance with monotony and insanity informs also the circular structure of the play.[35] Nabokov had used a similar structural device in his earlier novel *King, Queen, Knave*, as Nora Bukhs has pointed out. She notes that 'ten years later Nabokov would write a play whose title entails once again a playful allusion to the waltz: *Izobretenie [V]al'sa*, but here the principle of literary camouflage will consist of the negation of the evolution: Val's will designate not the name of the dance but quite simply the hero's surname.'[36] Yet the waltz provides a model for the structure of the play, which is initially reflected in the different couples of the play: Waltz-Trance, minister-colonel and the majority of generals who can be ordered into couples according to the key vowel in their name (Gerb-Breg, Grib-Brig, Gorb-Grob, Grub-Brug, while Berg, Burg and Grab are left out).[37] The idea of the circular construction of the play is also alluded to in what is presumably Waltz's genuine name, Tourvalski, which suggests a 'tour de valse'.

Applying the model of a circle to the play, it becomes apparent that the first two acts run along the contour of a semi-circle, which is mirrored by its other half in the third act. While the first and second acts still move along a linear structure, the repetitions in the third act turn the first two acts retrospectively into part of a circle. Corresponding to '[t]he repetitive nature of the figures of the waltz, linked to their limited number and the order of their movement, which is apparently free', the key scenes of the

---

[34] See Timenchik, 'Chitaem Nabokova', 47. The fragmented quotations are taken from Chapter 5, Stanza XLI in *Eugene Onegin*: 'Monotonous and mad / like young life's whirl, / the waltz's noisy whirl revolves, / pair after pair flicks by' (Alexander Pushkin, *Eugene Onegin: A Novel in Verse*, trans. Vladimir Nabokov, vol. I (Princeton University Press, 1990), 222).

[35] The relationship between the play's title and the circular structure has also been noted by Dolinin (see 'Istinnaia zhizn'', 16) and Babikov (see 'Primechaniia [*Izobretenie Val'sa*]', 779, n. 583).

[36] Bukhs, 'Novel Waltz'.

[37] Babikov also points out, that Son, who may be played by a woman, is Waltz's dance partner (see 'Primechaniia [*Izobretenie Val'sa*]', 779, n. 583).

first and second act are repeated in the same sequence in the final act.[38] The meeting between the colonel and the general in the first act is mirrored in the meeting between the colonel and Waltz at the beginning of the third act. In both instances the country is in crisis. Waltz's reception by the minister is repeated in the minister's audience with Waltz. The explosion of the mountain is reflected by the explosion of the town. The confused meeting of the generals in the second act is duplicated by the chaotic recruitment of staff (also played by the generals) who Waltz wants to take with him on his island. The government's bargaining for Waltz's machine is reproduced in Waltz's bargaining for Annabella. That the events of two acts are now replicated in only one act increases the speed of the play, just as in the dance: 'Vertigo, the dominant characteristic, multiplies the circles of the waltz in an acceleration of the tempo, until finally the leap into another dimension is effected – exstasis (which is literally reflected in the effect of unreality that the whirling of the waltz produces).'[39] At this point, however, a second rotation of the circle is interrupted. Waltz's failure to impose his will on the general with the telling name Berg – the German word for 'mountain' – reverses the earlier explosion of the mountain; this time the mountain stands firm in the face of Waltz's threat of annihilation. Waltz's ascent at the end of the second act is reversed by his downfall at the end of the play. Trance's departure signalling the end of the dream corresponds also to the end of the dance; Waltz cannot complete another rotation without his dancing partner. The change of linear into circular structure in the third act coincides with Waltz's loss of control over his dream and its direction, as Trance's increasingly controlling role from the third act onwards suggests.

Although Waltz's dream eventually has to succumb to an external reality, it is important to note that he is able to maintain his illusion for the duration of almost the whole play. Trance is the first one to recognise Waltz's creative power when he considers him to be a colleague.[40] Several hints further allude to Waltz's poetic aptitude. Although Waltz states that he burned his youthful verse, some of his poems must have survived, at least in his mind. General Lump, for instance, recites the poem 'To my Soul' by Tourvalski, i.e. by Waltz.[41] The prison song, too, has been written by Waltz himself. His speech to the generals is composed in blank verse, which is another indication of a poetic tendency in

---

[38] Bukhs, 'Novel Waltz'.   [39] *Ibid.*
[40] Field also points to Waltz's creativity (*Life in Art*, 209).
[41] See Petr Palamarchuk 'Teatr Vladimira Nabokova', *Don*, 7 (1990), 147–53 [151].

Waltz's character. Waltz has chosen a telling pseudonym as in Russian his first name Sal'vator combines an anagram of 'Val's' ('Waltz') and 'avtor' ('author'). This idea is supported by Nabokov who in the English list of Dramatis Personae refers to Waltz as 'a fellow author'.[42]

Waltz's creativity is also alluded to in the title, which implies some possible historical theme about the emergence of the dance. Only at the very end of the play when Waltz's dream has fallen apart is the real meaning of the title disclosed. The audience has witnessed the development of Waltz's invention of a whole world. The manuscript of the play shows that Nabokov had initially thought of calling the play 'Otkrytie Val'sa' (Waltz's discovery) and only later opted for the more ambiguous *izobretenie* (invention) suggesting the notion of both technical innovation and fantastic creation (in the sense of the Russian *vydumka*), rather than a mere discovery.[43] The final title is also misleading in its suggestion that Waltz himself developed the machine, yet Waltz is not the inventor but only the owner of the machine, as he explains: 'It has been built by a cousin of mine, a gray-bearded man, also called Waltz, Walter Waltz, Walt Waltz, a genius, a super-genius!' (*WI*, 13) ['Она – работа моего старичка, моего родственника, изобретателя, никому не известного, но гениального, сверхгениального!' (*Sobr. soch.*, V, 525)].[44] The English version complicates the relationship between inventor and owner further by giving both identical names. The machine itself is therefore assigned the ambiguous status of a dream which originates in the dreamer but is not a deliberate and controlled creation.

Waltz's dream is linked with his creative faculties, so that the dream, and as such the play, is to a certain extent his creation, but he is unable to determine the actual shape of his dream. Trance's increasing control over the course of the action is mirrored in the seeming autonomy of a theatre

---

[42] Nabokov used very similar terms to describe the close link between madness and creativity in *Pale Fire*, when John Shade points out that '[one] should not apply it [presumably the word "loony"] to a person who deliberately peels off a drab and unhappy past and replaces it with a brilliant invention'. In response to this, his interlocutor addresses Kinbote, explaining that 'I maintain that what's his name, old – the old man, you know, at the Exton railway station, who thought he was God, and began redirecting the trains, was technically a loony, but John calls him a *fellow poet*' (emphasis added) (Vladimir Nabokov, *Pale Fire* (London: Penguin, 1991), 188).

[43] Nabokov, 'Izobretenie Val'sa'. Holograph. Draft, corrected, undated. VNLOC, Box 6.

[44] Boyd, for instance, does not make this distinction between owner and inventor of the machine when he states that 'Waltz [...] hopes to save the world by means of a device he has invented' (*Russian Years*, 489). Diment also ignores this distinction when she conceives of Waltz as 'a mad scientist who seeks an audience with the country's Minister of Defense in order to tell him about his new invention' ('Plays', 595).

production. Nabokov literally stages Waltz's theatre of the mind. Waltz's dream becomes the actual performance. The twofold nature of the stage reality is crucial in embodying both the reality of Waltz's dream and its fragile illusory nature. While in *The Tragedy of Mr Morn*, the dream is the only precarious reality of the play, the end of which coincides with the end of Morn's dream and life, Waltz's dream develops against a more stable reality which fully emerges in the final scene when he is carried off. Nabokov exposes the inner world of his protagonist on the open stage, while hinting at a different play which has been going on all along in parallel with Waltz's dream. This last scene, almost unnecessary as a means to expose Waltz's dream, determines that Waltz is not the author but an imprisoned madman in somebody else's play. In *The Event*, which preceded *The Waltz Invention* by a year, Nabokov had self-consciously and overtly inscribed his own presence as the ultimate playwright. In *The Waltz Invention* he seems to take a back seat, gently pushing into action characters who, as if in self-perpetual motion, whirl in ever faster circles around the stage, celebrating their own existence as long as the spectators are willing to believe their eyes.

THEATRE OF THE MIND: *INVITATION TO A BEHEADING* AND 'LIK'

Throughout his fiction, Nabokov juxtaposes dreams and theatre productions, which alerts the reader to both the imperfect illusion of dreams and their power to move the dreamer or spectator. The Russian émigré actor Lik, for example, has dreams of his childhood tormentor which are reminiscent of a theatre production:

Dreams … would still occur even now, for there was not control over them. Sometimes Koldunov would appear in person, in his own image, in the surroundings of boyhood, hastily assembled by the director of dreams out of such accessories as a classroom, desks, a blackboard, and its dry, weightless sponge. (*Stories*, 468)

до сих пор бывали, конечно, сны, на них не было управы. И не только случалось, что Колдунов являлся ему в собственном виде, в обстановке отрочества, наскоро составленной сном из таких аксессуаров, как парта, черная доска, сухая легкая губка. (Sobr. soch., V, 385)

Similarly, the narrator of *The Real Life of Sebastian Knight* draws attention to the overtly theatrical setting of his last dream of Sebastian. The hastily assembled stage set of V's dream recalls the hurried construction of the world of 'The Leonardo': 'I was sitting in a large dim room which my dream had hastily furnished with odds and ends collected in different houses I vaguely knew' (*RLSK*, 157), while the people in the dream 'had been placed there by the dream manager – just because anybody would do to fill the stage' (*RLSK*, 158). In *Bend Sinister*, Krug's recurring dream is set, like Lik's nightmare, in his former school and is described as a theatre production in conjunction with interspersed references to the cinematic mode: '[the dream's] somewhat meagre setting was patched up with odds and ends from other (later) plays; but still the recurrent dream we all know (finding ourselves in the old classroom …) was in Krug's case a fair rendering of the atmosphere of the original version' (*BS*, 60). Accordingly, the dream distortions are explained once more by the hasty and careless construction of the stage set: 'the dream stage management having used the first set available for rendering "tunnel", without bothering to remove either the rails or the ruby lamps that glowed at intervals along the rocky black sweating walls' (*BS*, 62). The same link between dreams and a hastily assembled theatre set is established in Nabokov's lecture on Tolstoy's *Anna Karenina* (1875–7):

A dream is a show – a theatrical piece staged within the brain in a subdued light before a somewhat muddleheaded audience. The show is generally a very mediocre one, carelessly performed, with amateur actors and haphazard props and a wobbly backdrop. But what interests us for the moment about our dreams is that the actors and the props and the various parts of the setting are borrowed by the dream producer from our conscious life. A number of recent impressions and a few older ones are more or less carelessly and hastily mixed on the dim stage of our dreams.[45]

Even much later Nabokov would note in his diary to write something on dreams 'with especial stress on the[ir] sloppy production – any old backdrop will do'.[46]

Although the world of *Invitation to a Beheading* is from the beginning revealed to be a theatrical illusion, it remains real to Cincinnatus and the reader for the duration of almost the whole novel. Against Cincinnatus's better judgement, the fictional reality reasserts its strength in every one of his emotional reactions to the disappointments and tortures which his surrounding, obviously illusionary, world deviously invents for him. This theatre of the mind asserts its power until the very end in Cincinnatus's fear shortly before his execution, at a stage when the world surrounding him has already begun collapsing:

---

[45] Nabokov, *Lectures on Russian Literature*, 176.
[46] Quoted in Boyd, *American Years*, 188.

He realized that this fear was dragging him precisely into that false logic of things, that had gradually developed around him … He fully understood all this, but, like a man unable to resist arguing with his hallucination, even though he knows perfectly well that the entire masquerade is staged in his own brain, Cincinnatus tried in vain to out-wrangle his fear. (*IB*, 182–3)

Он понимал, что этот страх втягивает его как раз в ту ложную логику вещей, которая постепенно выработалась вокруг hего … Он вполне понимал все это, но – как человек, который не может удержаться, чтобы не возразить своей галлюцинации, хотя отлично знает, что весь маскарад происходит у него же в мозгу, – Цинциннат тщетно пытался переспорить свой страх. (*Sobr. soch.*, IV, 180)

Invitation to a Beheading advances as such not only a notion of theatre as a sham illusion but also a diametrically opposed view of theatre as a powerful artistic mode which gives life to a fictional reality. As such, theatre becomes a place of almost magical and frequently dangerous enchantment in Nabokov's work, which envelops and literally arrests the spectator.

Throughout *Invitation to a Beheading*, there is a strong suggestion that the whole theatrical world might be only Cincinnatus's dream construct. When he is led to his prison cell, for instance, Cincinnatus is compared to 'a man who has dreamt that he is walking on water only to have a sudden doubt: but is this possible?' (*IB*, 11) ['человек во сне увидевший, что идет по воде, но вдруг усомнившийся: да можно ли?' (*Sobr. soch.*, IV, 47)]. Later Cincinnatus reflects that 'our vaunted waking life … is semi-sleep, an evil drowsiness into which penetrate in grotesque disguise the sounds and sights of the real world (*IB*, 78) ['наша хваленая явь … есть полусон, дурная дремота, куда извне проникают, странно, дико изменяясь, звуки и образы действительного мира' (*Sobr. soch.*, IV, 100)]. The frequency of implausible actions and events, the unexpected shifts in time and space as well as the constantly changing identities of Cincinnatus's jailers (similar to the interchangeable generals in *The Waltz Invention*) can be read as further instances of dream logic.[47] Another parallel with the absurd dream world of *The Waltz Invention* is the sudden transformation of characters into puppets:

Rodrig Ivanovich seemed even more spruce than usual: the dorsal part of his best frock coat was stuffed with cotton padding like a Russian coachman's, making his back look broad, smooth, and fat; his wig was glossy as new; the rich dough

[47] See Foster, 'Nabokov's Gnostic Turpitude', 123–8. Foster links the dreamy or nightmarish atmosphere of the novel to Nabokov's notion of 'dream-logic' in Gogol's writings without, however, considering the specifically theatrical context in which Nabokov uses this term.

of his chin seemed to be powdered with flour, while in his buttonhole there was a pink waxy flower with a speckled mouth. (*IB*, 48)

Родриг Иванович казался еще наряднее, чем обычно: спина парадного сюртука была, как у кучеров, упитана ватой, широкая, плоско-жирная, парик лоснился, как новый, сдобное тесто подбородка было напудрено, точно калач, а в петлице розовел восковой цветок с крапчатой пастью. (*Sobr. soch.*, IV, 76)

Like in a dream, the theatre performance that is surrounding Cincinnatus appears to have sprung from his own mind. Paradoxically, it is Cincinnatus who sustains the illusion in this eerie description of a shadow theatre:

Involuntarily yielding to the temptation of logical development, involuntarily (be careful, Cincinnatus!) forging into a chain all the things that were quite harmless as long as they remained unlinked, he inspired the meaningless with meaning, and the lifeless with life. With the stone darkness for background he now permitted the spotlighted figures of all his usual visitors to appear – it was the very first time that his imagination was so condescending towards them … and by evoking them – not believing in them, perhaps, but still evoking them – Cincinnatus allowed them the right to exist, supported them, nourished them with himself … emerging from the darkness, the lighted figures joined hands and formed a ring – and, slightly swaying to one side, lurching, lagging, they began a circling movement, which at first was stiff and dragging, but then gradually became more even, free and rapid, and now they were whirling in earnest and the monstrous shadow of their shoulders and heads passed and repassed ever more quickly across the stone vaults. (*IB*, 133–4)

Невольно уступая соблазну логического развития, невольно (осторожно, Цинциннат!) сковывая в цепь то, что было совершенно безопасно в виде отдельных, неизвестно куда относившихся звеньев, он придавал смысл бессмысленному и жизнь неживому. На фоне каменной темноты он сейчас разрешал появляться освещенным фигурам всех своих обычных посетителей… впервые, впервые воображение его так снисходило к ним. … вызывая их, – пускай не веря в них, но все-таки вызывая, – Цинциннат давал им право на жизнь, содержал их, питал их собой … выходя из мрака, подавая друг другу руки, смыкались в круг освещенные фигуры – и, слегка напирая вбок, и кренясь, и тащась, начинали – сперва тугое, влачащееся – круговое движение, которое постепенно выправлялось, легчало, ускорялось, и вот уже пошло, пошло, – и чудовищные тени от плеч и голов пробегали, повторяясь, все шибче по каменным сводам. (*Sobr. soch.*, IV, 142–3)

In parallel with the figures' movement becoming more secure and stable, the figures themselves become more real in Cincinnatus's mind and finally take on an independent reality, which is reflected in their growing shadows. The dance, as in *The Waltz Invention*, points to Cincinnatus's imprisonment inside the circle which the figures' movement describes (note that early on in the novel Cincinnatus dances a waltz with one of his jailers). The three themes of theatre, dream and imprisonment converge in this scene, indicating that Cincinnatus's own dream stages a play which keeps Cincinnatus arrested. Cincinnatus's dream or nightmare has detached itself from its creator, just as a theatre production seems to happen outside the control of an organising principle behind it. The ambiguity of Cincinnatus's role as both creator and participant in the dream is mirrored in his role as both maker and victim of puppets and dolls.

The powerful reality of a theatre performance is also the central theme of the short story 'Lik', written at the end of a phase of intense work on drama in November 1938. Despite the low quality of the melodrama *L'Abîme* in which the story's protagonist Lik plays the role of a Russian émigré, in performance it gains an independent reality:

like any piece acted out by live people, it gained, God knows whence, an individual soul, and attempted for a couple of hours to exist, to evolve its own heat and energy, bearing no relation to its author's pitiful conception or the mediocrity of the players, but awakening, as life awakes in water warmed by sunlight. (*Stories*, 465)

как и всякая живыми людьми разыгрываемая вещь, она добирала, Бог весть из чего, личную душу, часа два-три пыталась как-то жить, развивая свою теплоту и энергию, не состоявшие ни в какой зависимости от жалкого замысла автора, от посредственности актерских сил, а просыпавшиеся так, как просыпается жизнь в нагретой солнцем воде. (Sobr. soch., V, 381)

This theatre production is mysteriously realised by the ending of the story, when Lik does not register that he is already part of a new reality that has emerged after he has died of a heart attack.[48] Lik's brief rest by the seaside corresponds with the caesura in his life, after which almost imperceptibly a new reality commences. Dolinin has pointed to the white shoes as a symbol of death and the suddenly implausible topography of Lik's ride in a taxi as markers that Lik has died by the seaside and has entered a new reality.[49]

That Lik, however, steps not only into a new but into a specifically theatrical reality is signalled by his coinciding thoughts of death and theatre: 'The thought of death coincided precisely with the thought that in half an hour he would walk out onto the bright stage' (*Stories*, 478) ['Мысль

---

[48] See Dolinin, 'Istinnaia zhizn'', 12.
[49] See *ibid*.

о смерти необыкновенно точно совпадала с мыслью о том, что через полчаса он выйдет на освещенную сцену' (*Sobr. soch.*, V, 396)]. This association of death and theatre has been anticipated earlier in a paradoxical notion of theatrical revival after death:

Lik imagined for some reason that when he died of heart failure … the attack would certainly come onstage, as it had been with poor Molière, barking out his dog Latin among the doctors; but that he would not notice his death, crossing over instead into the actual world of a chance play, now blooming anew because of his arrival, while his smiling corpse lay on the boards, the toe of one foot protruding from beneath the folds of the lowered curtain. (*Stories*, 465)

Лик почему-то себе представлял, что когда он умрет от разрыва сердца … то это непременно будет на сцене, как было с бедным, лающим Мольером, но что смерти он не заметит, а перейдет в жизнь случайной пьесы, вдруг по-новому расцветшей от его впадения в нее, а его улыбающийся труп будет лежать на подмостках, высунув конец одной ноги из-под складок опустившегося занавеса. (*Sobr. soch.*, V, 381)

Nabokov explained in his foreword to the story that 'Lik' 'attempts to create the impression of a stage performance engulfing a neurotic performer, though not quite in the way that the trapped actor expected when dreaming of such an experience' (*Stories*, 655–6). Ironically, life after death still seems to conform to dramatic and theatrical convention. Adhering to Chekhov's famous dictum, that a gun which has been introduced at the beginning of a drama must be fired at some point during the course of the play, Lik's dramatic sensibility demands that the gun which Koldunov tried to sell earlier is now used in Koldunov's bloody suicide. That Lik speaks his final sentence in French marks the continuation of his role in *L'Abîme* as a Russian émigré who despite his foreign origin speaks almost exclusively French throughout the play. Nabokov noted a similar effect in Ibsen's *John Gabriel Borkman* which also ends with the heart attack of its protagonist. At the end of Ibsen's play, the scenery of an enclosed courtyard is suddenly replaced by a wide expanse of landscape. The stage no longer represents a realistic setting, but instead becomes an imaginary space which visualises Borkman's consciousness after death. This is another instance of a dream-like drama which seems to have developed an autonomous reality outside the control of the playwright, as Nabokov noted while preparing his lectures: 'the stage transcends stage possibilities, slips away into a life of its own, with no contention with the audience – for the scenic effect is beyond the resource[s] of any theatre not specially built for spectacular drama. The play [*Borkman*] begins leading its own life – and the author goes mad.'[50]

Although Lik has died, his consciousness is still alive, producing images which are combined to create a seeming continuation of his life before his fatal heart attack. This idea of death as a dream-like state produced by the powerful delusion of the dead person's consciousness derives from one of Nabokov's earliest works in drama, the verse play *Death* (*Smert'*).[51] Edmond, who has taken poison, considers himself to be dead and is supported in this belief by Gonville, who claims to be the 'echo of your thoughts before death' ['Эхо / твоих предсмертных мыслей' (*Sobr. soch.*, I, 684)]. It remains unclear whether the spectator has witnessed Gonville's deception in this world or whether Edmond's consciousness stages the play the spectator is watching. In 'Terra Incognita', the dying protagonist, in his feverish, hallucinatory state, comes to understand death as 'at best, fictitious: an imitation of life hastily knocked together, the furnished rooms of nonexistence' (*Stories*, 303) ['в лучшем случае фальсификация, наспех склеенное подобие жизни, меблированные комнаты небытия' (*Sobr. soch.*, III, 570)]. Death, dream and theatre merge in the protagonist's final perception: 'Everything around me was fading, leaving bare the scenery of death – a few pieces of realistic furniture and four walls' (*Stories*, 303) ['Все линяло кругом, обнажая декорации смерти, – правдоподобную мебель и четыре стены' (*Sobr. soch.*, III, 571)]. That this theatre of the mind continues after its creator's death reasserts its ultimate independence and its enduring power.

In his 'dream plays' and in *Invitation to a Beheading*, which after all might only be Cincinnatus's dream, the paradoxical position of a dreamer who creates but cannot control the dream provides a twofold analogy, with the spectator's powerlessness to interfere in the action on the one hand, and with the playwright's loss of control over the play in performance, on the other. While Morn is caught in his own or somebody else's dream, Cincinnatus already has a more ambiguous role as both the spectator and ultimately the creator of his own nightmare. By the time Waltz enters the stage, this ambiguity has become the central focus. Waltz's various attempts to establish himself as the dictator of his dreamland only

50 Nabokov, 'Notebook', VN Berg.
51 Nabokov would return repeatedly to this idea, for instance in his short stories 'Details of a Sunset' ('Katastrofa') (1924) and 'Perfection' ('Sovershenstvo') (1932), both of which end with the death of the protagonist, whose consciousness continues to delude him into the assumption that he is still alive. This theme would be reversed in the novella *The Eye*, where the narrator Smurov perceives himself as dead and the reality around him therefore as the mere chimera of his consciousness after his imagined suicide, although he is still alive.

reiterate the dream's autonomous reality and independence. Waltz is at best a spectator of, at worst a mere participant in but never the master of his dream. In Nabokov's 'dream plays' and in *Invitation to a Beheading*, the theatrical performance becomes a suitable artistic form whose formal properties reflect the nature of dreams. The theatre receives here surprisingly positive connotations as a powerful artistic medium which creates an enduring and almost autonomous illusion – a notion which, in some respects, is diametrically opposed to the sham realities of *The Man from the USSR* and *The Event*.

Yet despite its captivating powers, theatre becomes ultimately a harmful and destructive force, in that both dreams and the theatre exert negative control over their subjects, paralysing them or alienating them from reality. Nabokov's theoretical discussion of drama is throughout informed by the principles of individual freedom and imprisonment. While reading is portrayed as a creative process opening up infinite possibilities to the free imagination of the individual reader, seeing a play is equated with a dream, a nightmarish prison in which the spectator's imagination is arrested for the course of the performance without the possibility of shaping the predetermined reality presented. Theatre, dream and prison merge in curious ways in Cincinnatus's dream-like state in the theatre-prison of *Invitation to a Beheading*, in the hallucinatory death experience of the Russian émigré actor in 'Lik' and the trance-like state of insanity Waltz experiences (who at the end of his play is physically arrested). The real and the imaginary prison of the mind come to be reflected in the predetermined course of a theatre performance and the precarious, elusive yet inescapably alluring dreams it stages.

5

Puppets and masks: King, Queen, Knave *and* Despair

Puppets in Nabokov's work have little to do with the romantic notion of enchanting, magical creatures who transport the viewer into a fairy-tale world of wonder. Instead puppets and the related marionettes and automatons are employed to draw attention to the author's control over them and the drab world they inhabit. They resemble the pieces in Nabokov's favourite game, which are moved by players who are above and beyond the chessboard. This lack of control over their own destiny is put into a theatrical context and explored through the trope of the puppet theatre. In the opening chapter of Nabokov's chess novel *The Defense*, the protagonist is disappointed by an automaton which turns out to be broken, hinting at the futility of Luzhin's subsequent attempts to escape his fate: 'Luzhin walked toward the glass case where five little dolls with pendant bare legs awaited the impact of a coin in order to come to life and revolve; but today their expectation was in vain for the machine turned out to be broken and the coin was wasted'[1] ['Лужин пошёл к стеклянному ящику, где пять куколок с голыми висячими ножками ждали, чтобы ожить и завертеться, толчка монеты; но это ожидание было сегодня напрасно, так как автомат оказался испорченным, и гривенник пропал даром' (*Sobr. soch.*, II, 312)]. The dolls' inability to control their own movements foreshadows, of course, Luzhin's failure to control his own life. While he can move the figures on the chessboard he himself turns out to be just another chess piece whose movements are controlled by someone else. The playing of a game intersects with the playing of a performance throughout the novel (which is accentuated in the Russian version through the identical Russian word for game and performance, *igra*). Luzhin finally exits the novel through a star-shaped hole in the bathroom window, re-enacting Pierrot's departure in Blok's Modernist adaptation of a Russian puppet play, *The Fairground Booth*.

[1] Nabokov, *The Luzhin Defense*, 20.

Examples of other puppets who pop up in Nabokov's worlds include the mannequins in *King, Queen, Knave*, Cincinnatus's torturers in *Invitation to a Beheading* or the puppet-like Pnin. In Nabokov's last two plays, in a Meyerholdian twist, puppets rather than characters appear on the stage, as the generals in *The Waltz Invention*, or Madame Vagabundova in *The Event*, whose name alludes to travelling players and who speaks in the doggerel verse of Russian puppet theatres. The metaphor of the puppet theatre is too tempting not to be frequently evoked in Nabokov criticism, usually to denote the author as an omnipotent force in his fictional world. Alfred Appel, for instance, uses the example of his own puppet theatre performance to illustrate the artifice of a tightly controlled world in Nabokov's novels.[2] Senderovich and Shvartz have also investigated the importance of the Russian puppet theatre, the *balagan*, for Nabokov's fiction as a unifying theme of his wider work.[3]

Nabokov's interest in masks and puppets has to be seen in the context of a revived interest in the puppet theatre and the *commedia dell'arte* in European and Russian culture at the turn of the century. Adopted from Western models and transformed into a distinctly Russian form of puppet theatre, the originally rather coarse *balagan* with its rude and violent hero Petrushka was subsequently appropriated by the elite culture of Russia's Silver Age. The *balagan* became part of the nostalgic project in the art of that era, evoking a dreamy world of fairytales and childhood. The Symbolists and members of the World of Art movement achieved an aesthetic refinement of the *balagan* by conflating it with the more elegant Italian *commedia dell'arte*, a theatre of masks.[4] Based on invented cultural traditions rather than on historical evidence, the *balagan* and the commedia were linked by virtue of the similarity of their protagonists' name (Petrushka and Pierrot) and by the fact that most commedia masks had marionette counterparts.[5] Emblematic of this twinning of the *balagan* and the commedia is Blok's play *The Fairground Booth* which ironically plays out a harlequinade in a traditional *balagan* setting. It inspired Igor Stravinsky's ballet *Petroushka*, which also aligns its protagonist Petroushka with the melancholy artist figure Pierrot.[6]

[2] See Appel, 'Introduction', in Vladimir Nabokov, *The Annotated Lolita*, ed. Alfred Appel, Jr (London: Penguin, 1995), xvii-lxxiii [xxxi-xxxii].
[3] See Senderovich and Shvarts, 'Balagan smerti'.
[4] See Kelly, *Petrushka*, 164.
[5] Pierrot himself was already a further development of an original commedia character, the zanni Pedrolino (see Kelly, *Petrushka*, 164).
[6] Nassim W. Balestrini has shown a number of parallels of thematic motifs and plot structure between Stravinsky's Petroushka and *Invitation to a Beheading* ('Vladimir Nabokov's *Invitation*

The pronouncedly anti-Realist quality of the puppet theatre and the *commedia dell'arte* made them particularly attractive for the self-conscious interrogation of artistic modes in Modernist art. The relationship between the author and his work is accentuated in both theatre forms, so that the puppet theatre and the commedia came to frame Modernist inquiries into processes of textual creation and control and the author's relationship to his characters and their imaginary habitat. The puppet theatre in its most essential form cancels the collaborative element of theatre, allowing an unmediated relationship between the author and his world, where the puppet master is in total control, combining the roles of playwright, director and actor. Scott Cutler Shershow points out the puppet's metaphorical function in the discussion of key Modernist concerns: 'As a literally inanimate object, passive matter available for authorial form, the puppet was … well suited to the intense reaffirmation of a sovereign author.'[7] Frequently depicted as a sinister figure, the puppet master appears, for instance, as Petroushka's nemesis in Stravinsky's ballet and as a marked presence in Blok's *The Fairground Booth* where one of the characters is suddenly pulled back from the stage by a higher force holding the strings. The distinction between puppets, marionettes and automatons is merely technical, since the ontological status of the performing objects remains the same regardless of their respective mechanisms. The tension between the seeming autonomy of the performing object which seems to have a life of its own and the tight control of the puppeteer over the performing object is exploited throughout Nabokov's works.

The *commedia dell'arte* complicates this relationship of the author and his created world by introducing the element of improvisation. While the actor's ability to improvise has been a central feature of the theatre for most of its history (in the comic interludes of the miracle plays as well as in early farces and comedies in the folk tradition), improvisation was developed into an artistic skill by the *commedia dell'arte*, which originated in the sixteenth century in Italy.[8] The term *commedia dell'arte* denotes

to a Beheading and Igor Stravinsky's *Petrushka'*, in Lisa Zunshine (ed.), *Nabokov at the Limits: Redrawing Critical Boundaries* (New York and London: Garland, 1999), 87–110).

[7] Scott Cutler Shershow, *Puppets and 'Popular' Culture* (Ithaca, NY and London: Cornell University Press, 1995), 189.

[8] The account in this paragraph is based on the following studies: Douglas J. Clayton, *Pierrot in Petrograd: The Commedia dell'Arte/Balagan in Twentieth-Century Russian Theatre and Drama* (Montreal: McGill-Queen's University Press, 1993), 16–43; Martin Green and John Swan, *The Triumph of Pierrot: The Commedia dell'Arte and the Modern Imagination* (New York: Macmillan, 1986), 1–13; Robert Henke, *Performance and Literature in the Commedia dell'Arte* (Cambridge University Press, 2002), 12–30; David Mayer III, *Harlequin in His Element: The English Pantomime, 1806–1836* (Cambridge, MA: Harvard University Press, 1969), 1–18; Allardyce Nicoll,

the professional actor's art of improvising his role from a given plot or theme, in contrast to the fixed *commedia erudite* which was performed by amateurs who would learn their lines from a script. A rudimentary plot outline would direct the course of the action, but its realisation would depend entirely on the improvising skills of the actors. The action was frequently interrupted by so-called *lazzi*, more or less spontaneous acrobatic tricks and comic interludes loosely or not at all connected to the main action.

The reception of the commedia by the Modernists remained fragmentary, and they freely selected, adapted and changed characteristic features of the original commedia. The art of improvisation of the original commedia takes on an entirely different meaning in the modern Western theatre with its tension between the property of the playwright's fixed written text and its appropriation by the theatre performance. While the original commedia relied on improvisation as the actualisation of its scenarios, improvisation in modern theatre is perceived as a violation of the fixed play text which is to be performed. The relationship between script and improvisation is the principal theme of Blok's *The Fairground Booth*, the story of which develops against the intentions of its enraged author.[9] Refuting Pierrot's speech, which suggests an Italian setting, the author enters the stage to assure the audience that 'this actor is cruelly mocking my authorial rights. The action [of my play] takes place in Petersburg in winter. Where exactly did he take the window and the guitar from? I did not write my drama for a puppet theatre [*balagan*].'[10] The performance, however, moves ever further away from the author's written drama. Later the author appears again to present his version of the play, appealing to the spectators:

Ladies and gentlemen! I sincerely apologize to you, but I am not responsible for this in any way. They are mocking me. I wrote a most realistic play, the essence of which I feel obliged to set out for you in a few words. The play is about the mutual love of two young souls. A third person bars their way, but in the end

The World of Harlequin: A Critical Study of the Commedia dell'Arte (Cambridge University Press, 1963); Allardyce Nicoll, *Masks, Mimes and Miracles* (London: G. C. Harrap, 1931), 214–98; Giacomo Oreglia, *The Commedia dell'Arte* (London: Methuen, 1968).

9 W. Gareth Jones points out that a 'mark of the *commedia dell'arte* was the autonomy of the professional actors, uncontrolled by the tyranny of the dictatorial author, and this is brought out in *The Puppet Booth* by the failure of the distraught Author to control his copyright' ('Commedia dell'arte: Blok and Meyerhold, 1905–1917', in David J. George and Christopher J. Gossip (eds.), *Studies in the Commedia dell'Arte* (Cardiff: University of Wales Press, 1993), 185–97 [194]).

10 Aleksandr Blok, *Sobranie sochinenii v vos'mi tomakh* (Moscow: Gosudarstvennoe izdatel'stvo khudozhestvennoi literatury, 1960–13), vol. IV, 10.

the obstacles are removed, and the lovers are forever united in lawful wedlock! I never dressed my heroes in fools' clothes. Without my knowledge, they are playing out some old legend.[11]

In this context, improvisation becomes a distorted copy of an original with which it has little in common. While improvisation in the original commedia represented a faithful realisation of a scenario, in the modern theatre which is determined on one side by a fixed play text, improvisation becomes a violation of textual property, an appropriation of the text and an assertion of the performer's independence from the playwright.

Commedia themes pervade the whole of Nabokov's work, in the acrobatic tricks and somersaults of Nabokov's prose, the glimpses of Harlequin's diamond-shaped colourful patterns, reworkings of the eternal love triangle of Pierrot, Harlequin and Columbine and the triple harlequins which the narrator of Nabokov's last published novel tries to create.[12] Martin Green and John Swan have pointed to the debt Nabokov owes to the Modernist reception of the commedia in such works as 'The Leonardo', 'Spring in Fialta' (1936), 'Ultima Thule' and 'Solus Rex' (1940), *Laughter in the Dark*, *Conclusive Evidence* (1951), *Lolita* and *Look at the Harlequins!*[13] Their assertion that 'the rich colors and wild humors of Nabokov's art come from a commedia source … and he is as a whole clearly a commedia artist' is based on their notion of 'the fundamental theatricality of Nabokov's world view, which is his deepest debt to the commedia'.[14] While the commedia certainly shapes the playfulness and irreverence of Nabokov's work in general, it also provides a concrete theatrical model which facilitates Nabokov's increasingly complex inquiry into authorship and narrative control which runs through all of his works.

MIRACLES AND AUTOMATONS – *KING, QUEEN, KNAVE*

In autumn 1927 – only a year after he had finished his second play, *The Man from the USSR*, and less than six months after he had been involved in its production – Nabokov began the novel *King, Queen, Knave*. Despite this proximity in time, the works differ fundamentally both in content

---

[11] *Ibid.*, 14.
[12] Senderovich and Shvarts have traced the theme of the commedia throughout Nabokov's work (see 'The Juice of Three Oranges').
[13] See Green and Swan, *Triumph of Pierrot*. 233–40.
[14] *Ibid.*, 240; 235.

and in tone. The melancholy play about the disintegration of the Russian émigré community in Berlin has little in common with the funny and shrill novel of adultery which Nabokov himself called a 'bright brute' (*KQK*, v). And while the characters of the play inhabit a forlorn world devoid of any stable ordering force behind it, the world of the novel is carefully controlled by the all-pervasive, authorial principle behind it.

Despite these differences between the works, *King, Queen, Knave* appears to have retained a distinct sense of theatricality from Nabokov's work on his play. Only one study concentrates on the use of a specific theatrical form in the English version of the novel, suggesting that the *commedia dell'arte* might have inspired the character constellation (juxtaposing Dreyer, Martha and Franz with Harlequin, Columbine and Pierrot, respectively) and the plot of the novel, and serves as a comment on the novel's artifice.[15] While this observation is applicable not only to *King, Queen, Knave*, and the general theme of the commedia can be found in a number of Nabokov's novels as Green and Swan have demonstrated, *King, Queen, Knave* develops an explicit theatrical motif which has not received any critical attention yet. A distinctive historical type of performance, the European and Russian religious theatre, underlies the novel, various elements of which are merged with the puppet theatre. This peculiar combination vaguely recalling the Ukrainian religious puppet theatre, the *vertep*, becomes the framework in which Nabokov explores the relationship between the author and his fictional world.[16] *King, Queen, Knave* is still an early work, and the ambiguities in the interplay between an author and his text which mark Nabokov's later work are still absent. Instead *King, Queen, Knave* presents an instance of unequivocal authorial domination over the text. Correspondingly, Nabokov assimilates into his novel the puppet theatre and its omnipotent puppet master.

This frivolous novel about adultery and attempted murder develops ironically against the backdrop of a rather more sombre theatrical mode, the religious drama. The medieval European theatre was exclusively religious in subject matter, staging parts of the Gospel or the Old

---

[15] See Stephanie L. Merkel, 'Vladimir Nabokov's *King, Queen, Knave* and the Commedia dell'Arte', *Nabokov Studies*, 1 (1994), 83–102.

[16] The *vertepnyi teatr* consisted of a box which opened to the front and contained a stage divided into a higher and a lower level (see B. N. Aseev, *Russkii dramaticheskii teatr ot ego istokov do kontsa XVIII veka* (Moscow: Iskusstvo, 1977), 141–3; S. S. Danilov, *Ocherki po istorii russkogo dramaticheskogo teatra* (Moscow: Iskusstvo, 1948), 57–8). Davydov has also found the *vertep* a useful model in the context of *Invitation to a Beheading* (see 'Teksty-Matreški', 170–3).

Testament as well as episodes from the lives of the saints.[17] The different
scenes were performed on wooden scaffolds or pageants. From the perspective of the audience, Heaven (where God, played by an actor usually
with a gilded mask, was seated) was represented by a booth or house on
the left (east), while Hell was located on the right (west), usually in the
form of a gaping hell-mouth, through which the devils could exit and
enter.[18] The closeness of Heaven and Hell and the physical presence of
God and the devil reflected a distinctly medieval understanding of life,
as David Wiles points out: 'In the medieval world, true reality was otherworldly. God and the Devil were omnipresent spectators of human lives,
and the actor/audience boundary was fluid because all humans were con-
ceived as ultimately players.'[19] This fundamentally theatrical view of the
world, which was reflected in the medieval theatre, points to the topos
of *Teatrum Mundi*, the notion that man's struggle in the theatre of life is
watched and directed by higher powers.

The subtext of the miracle play is introduced immediately in the first
chapter of the novel.[20] In the third-class carriage of the train which takes
him to Berlin, Franz encounters a disfigured man who at least for him
clearly represents Hell.[21] Franz's flight from third to second class is compared with the transition of an actor from Hell to Heaven in a miracle
play:

The transition from the third-class compartment, where a noseless monster
reigned in silence, into this sunny plush room appeared to him like the passage
from a hideous hell through the purgatory of the corridors and intervestibular

---

[17] The account in this paragraph is based on the following studies: John Addington Symonds,
Shakespeare's Predecessors in the English Drama (London, 1900), 78–91; R. George Thomas, *Ten
Miracle Plays* (London: Arnold, 1966), 6–11; David Wiles, 'Theatre in Roman and Christian
Europe', in John Russell Brown (ed.), *The Oxford Illustrated History of Theatre* (Oxford University
Press, 1995), 49–92 [72–88]; Phyllis Hartnoll, *A Concise History of the Theatre* (London: Thames
and Hudson, 1968), 32–50.

[18] As an alternative to the horizontal structure, the basically three-tiered stage could also be
arranged vertically, where between the upper level (Heaven) and the lower level (Hell), Earth
presented the main acting area.

[19] Wiles, 'Theatre in Roman and Christian Europe', 82.

[20] Nabokov's references to the miracle play in the novel show that he was well acquainted with the
conventions of a medieval theatre production. He might have learned about the miracle plays
and their staging initially during his time at Cambridge, where he studied medieval and modern
French.

[21] The function of the disfigured man as a figure of doom is highlighted in the underlying *Madame
Bovary* subtext. Franz's fellow-traveller on the train alludes to an equally disfigured character
with a similar function in Flaubert's novel. He appears for the first time after one of Emma's
meetings with her lover in Rouen and again outside the window after Emma has taken the
arsenic. In Flaubert's novel, the man anticipates the impending catastrophe of financial debts
and suicide (see Grayson, *Nabokov Translated*, 91).

clatter into a little abode of bliss. The old conductor who had punched his ticket a short while ago and promptly vanished might have been as humble and omnipotent as St. Peter … He transformed the conductor's click into that of a key unlocking the gates of paradise. So a grease-painted gaudy-faced actor in a miracle play passes across a long stage divided into three parts, from the jaws of the devil into the shelter of angels. (*KQK*, 11)

Переход из третьего класса, где тихо торжествовало чудовище, сюда, в солнечное купэ, представился ему как переход из мерзостного ада, через пургаторий площадок и коридоров, в подлинный рай. Старичок кондуктор, давеча пробивший ему билет и срразу исчезнувший, был, казалось ему, убог и полновластен, как апостол Петр … Он обратил кондукторский щелк в звук ключа, отпирающего райский замок. Так, в мистерии, по длинной сцене, разделенной на три части, восковой актер переходит из пасти дьявола в ликующий парадиз.[22] (*Sobr. soch.*, II, 137–8)

In this analogy, Franz's third-class and the Dreyers' second-class compartments represent the scaffolds respectively for Hell and Heaven on a medieval stage.[23] This reference to the medieval play at the very beginning of the novel foreshadows the subsequent development of the plot. In his affair with Martha, Franz moves ever closer to Hell, only to be miraculously saved and liberated at the end of the novel by her death.

The spatial distinction between the Heaven and Hell of the miracle play becomes a stable point of reference throughout the novel. The second-class train compartment is conflated with Heaven and Franz's room during the first sexual encounter between him and Martha. Franz's locking of the door recalls also the conductor, who in the train scene is compared with St Peter unlocking paradise. Martha is compared to the Madonna and describes their sexual encounter as 'paradise' (*KQK*, 98). The implicit link between this scene and the second-class compartment through the 'paradisiacal' quality, is reinforced by comparisons of the room and the train. When Franz places Martha's coat onto the bed, he notices that 'this was like a train passenger marking the seat he is about to occupy' (*KQK*, 95) ['вот так пассажир в поезде отмечает место, которое сейчас

---

[22] Apparently, Nabokov does not distinguish between mystery and miracle play. The Russian 'misteriia' is not translated as 'mystery play' but as 'miracle play' (*KQK*, 11), the Russian equivalent of which would be 'mirakl'. It is tempting to speculate that Nabokov opted for 'miracle play' because of its potential to create an ironic tension between its religious, pious connotation and Martha's use of the word when referring to any incident which furthers her scarcely pious aim to kill her husband as 'a miracle' (for instance, *KQK*, 133; 160).

[23] In this depiction of a medieval stage Nabokov might have relied on an actual drawing which reconstructed the Valenciennes stage of 1547 (reproduced, for example, in John Russell Brown (ed.), *The Oxford Illustrated History of Theatre* (Oxford University Press, 1995), 83). The stage in this picture is unusually long and included the Sea of Galilee, associated with St Peter who in the novel is aligned with the train conductor.

займет' (*Sobr. soch.*, II, 192)]. The parallel between the bed and a train compartment is taken further in the following description: 'Presently, the bed stirred into motion. It glided off in its journey creaking discreetly as does a sleeping car' (*KQK*, 97) ['Постель тронулась, поплыла, чуть поскрипывая, как ночью в вагоне' (*Sobr. soch.*, II, 194)]. Later, 'the bed returned to Berlin from Eden' (*KQK*, 98) ['Постель медленно приехала обратно' (*Sobr. soch.*, II, 194)].[24]

From this seeming paradise, however, the action moves back towards Hell. Correspondingly, the hellish third-class compartment provides a point of reference in the description of Franz's room, once he has tired of his affair with Martha. At the point when Martha's dominance starts to suffocate Franz, a discoloured display dummy reminds him of the encounter with the disfigured man on the train, signalling Franz's movement towards Hell. Correspondingly, Franz's formerly paradisiacal room turns into the hellish third-class train compartment, as a comparison of his moving out with his earlier departure from the compartment suggests:

He donned his raincoat and hat … picked up the suitcases, and, bumping against the doorjamb as if he were a clumsy passenger in a speeding train, went out into the corridor. (*KQK*, 229)

Он надел макинтош, шляпу … подхватил чемоданы и, слегка пошатнувшись, стукнувшись о косяк двери, словно неловкий пассажир в скором поезде, вышел в коридор. (*Sobr. soch.*, II, 278)

This is an exact replica of his earlier hasty flight from the train compartment:

He rose quickly, he lifted like a martyr his pale face, shook loose and pulled down his humble suitcase, collected his raincoat and hat and, banging his suitcase awkwardly against the doorjamb, fled into the corridor. (*KQK*, 4)

Быстро встав, запрокинув побелевшее лицо, он расшатал, стащил сверху свой чемодан, надел пальто и шляпу и, неловко стукнувшись чемоданом о косяк, вышел в коридор.[25] (*Sobr. soch.*, II, 133)

The motif of a miracle play recurs in Franz's sensation before he returns from Berlin to the seaside 'as if two forces were fighting over his soul, tearing him now to one side, then to the other' (my translation) ['как будто спорили за его душу две силы, рвущие то в одну сторону, то в другую' (*Sobr. soch.*, II, 303)], which recalls a famous French miniature of

---

[24] The link between bed and train is stronger in the Russian original where a verb of motion ('priekhala') is used.
[25] Note that in the English version of the novel, the theme of the miracle play is prepared here in the reference to Franz as a martyr.

a theatre performance in which several actors pull a saint in the opposite directions of Heaven and Hell.[26] In the tradition of the medieval theatre, Franz has become an entirely passive character steered by a more powerful but unknown entity which is determining his life.

Throughout the novel, the three main characters, especially Martha and Franz, are given an overtly mechanical quality. They are depicted as empty and shallow people whose daily life is a sequence of automated responses and reactions. Jeff Edmunds counts that 'the adverb "mashinal'no" [automatically] … applied to all three of the central characters, occurs no less than fifteen times in the course of the book, an average of more than once per chapter'.[27] Martha makes up for the lack of any form of authentic emotions by conventional standard responses. In her thinking, the affair with Franz is merely part of a conventional marriage, with the standard adultery being committed. Tellingly, the bizarre role play in which Martha and Franz pretend to be married to each other is depicted as a 'dress rehearsal of future happiness' (*KQK*, 155) ['генеральную репетицию уже недалекого счастья' (*Sobr. soch.*, II, 231)]. Once Martha takes over Franz's life and demands total submission from him, he becomes another automaton:

a curious debility blurred his movements as if he were existing only because existing was the proper thing to do; but one did it unwillingly and would have been glad to return at any moment to a state of animal stupor. His day ran its course automatically … The morning jolt of his alarm clock was like a coin dropped into a vending machine. (*KQK*, 200)

какая-то слабость была во всех его движениях, – как будто он существовал только потому, что существовать принято, но делал это нехотя, был бы рад всякую минуту вернуться в сонное оцепенение. Ход его дня был машинальный. Утренний толчок будильника был как монета, падающая в автомат. (*Sobr. soch.*, II, 260)

Earlier he is explicitly associated with a puppet: 'there still existed the store, where he bowed and turned like a jolly doll, and there still were the nights when like a dead doll he lay supine on his bed' (*KQK*, 152–3) ['был магазин, где он, как веселая кукла, кланялся, вертелся; но были ночи, когда он, как мертвая кукла, лежал навзничь в постели' (*Sobr. soch.*, II, 230)].

[26] This passage exists only in the Russian version of the novel. See Jehan Fouquet, *Le Martyre de S. Appolline* (c. 1460). Reproduced, for example, in Brown (ed.), *The Oxford Illustrated History of Theatre*, 80.

[27] Jeff Edmunds, 'Look at Valdemar! (A Beautified Corpse Revived)', *Nabokov Studies*, 2 (1995), 153–71 [161].

The metaphor of the three protagonists as puppets is realised in the inventor's creation of automated mannequins for Dreyer's department store.[28] Corresponding with Franz and Dreyer, two of the mannequins are initially presented in a theatre performance:

Pulling at a cord, the Inventor drew open a black curtain, also an innovation, and a pale dignified gentleman in a dinner jacket, with a carnation in his buttonhole, walked out of the side door at the left, crossed the room at a life-like though somewhat somnambulic gait, and left by the side door at the right. (*KQK*, 218)

Изобретатель раздвинул за шнур черный занавес, и из боковой двери слева вышел бледный мужчина в смокинге, пошел, с той особенной нежной медлительностью, которой отличается походка лунатиков или движение людей в задержанном кинематографе, – и ушел в боковую дверь направо (*Sobr. soch.*, II, 271)

The final performance of the mannequins (which in the English version includes a mannequin resembling Martha) is less successful. Anticipating the impending end of the novel, the automatons collapse and fall apart, so that Dreyer realises that the 'automannequins had given all they could give … now they had lost all significance, all life and charm' (*KQK*, 263) ['все, что могли дать эти фигуры, они уже дали, – что теперь они уже больше не нужны, лишены души, и прелести, и значения' (*Sobr. soch.*, II, 296)].

These performances of the automatons become an obvious theatrical paradigm for the author's creation and destruction of fictional worlds and his control over the characters within his fiction. In the foreword to *King, Queen, Knave*, Nabokov states that 'the fairytale freedom inherent in an unknown milieu [of Germany] answered my dream of pure invention' (*KQK*, vi), which closely aligns the author and the inventor. The inventor is, however, clearly subjected to the author's will and becomes unwittingly the tool for the author's grander design:

[the] inventor happened to live in the very same room where Franz had spent the night of his arrival … It is significant that Fate should have lodged him there of all places. It was a road that Franz had travelled – and all at once Fate remembered and sent in pursuit this practically nameless man who of course knew nothing of his important assigment, and never found out anything about it, as for that matter no one else ever did. (*KQK*, 107–8)

---

[28] The analogy between the mannequins and the novel's characters becomes neater in the English translation, where the three mannequins (two male and one female) correspond more clearly to each of the protagonists (see Grayson, *Nabokov Translated*, 93).

[изобретатель] жил случайно как раз в том номере, где по приезде переночевал Франц … То, что судьба поселила изобретателя именно там, – знаменательно. Этот путь проделал Франц, – судьба вдруг спохватилась, послала – вдогонку, вдогонку – синещекого человека, – который об этом, конечно, ничего не знал, и никогда не узнал, – как вообще об этом никогда не узнал никто. (*Sobr. soch.*, II, 200)

Through this deliberate exposure of the artificial construction of 'fate', the author reveals his ultimate control over his world. Just like the inventor, the author moves his puppets and determines the course of the plot and the characters' fate.[29]

Both Dreyer and Franz seem briefly to sense the presence of an alien force in their lives. On his own in the dining room and without any apparent reason, Dreyer feels suddenly watched: 'He turned around quickly as though feeling that someone was watching him' (*KQK*, 61) ['Он быстро обернулся, будто почувствовал, что кто-то смотрит на него' (*Sobr. soch.*, II, 170)]. Unlike Dreyer, Franz is worried that his affair with Martha might be discovered, which at first sight explains his anxiety in the following scene:

He did not trust the pictures on the wall – the old baron in the frock coat and his redoubtable double staring down, ready to pounce. The glittering sideboard was all eyes. Cloaked eavesdroppers lurked in the folds of the drapery … He had the awful sensation that at that very instant Dreyer would suddenly step from behind a curtain. (*KQK*, 122–3)

Он не доверял стенам. Пристально уставился на него старик в сюртуке на темном портрете. Буфет, поблескивая, смотрел во все глаза. Что-то было напряженное в складках портьеры … Ему показалось, что вот теперь из-за портьеры вдруг выступит Драйер. (*Sobr. soch.*, II, 211)

Ironically, Franz's seemingly irrational fear that Dreyer might be behind the curtains is justified in Dreyer's subsequent masquerade when he bursts

---

[29] The author's omnipotence is also reflected in the three playing cards of the title. Leona Toker points out that the 'images of playing cards refer […] to Lewis Carroll's *Alice in Wonderland* and the obnoxious Queen of Hearts, who orders heads off until Alice cancels her illusion of grandeur together with the whole Wonderland dream' (*Nabokov: The Mystery of Literary Structures* (Ithaca, NY and London: Cornell University Press, 1989), 57). The notion of the characters being played with alludes also to the religious drama where human beings are played with by God and the Devil. In Georg Büchner's play *Leonce and Lena* (1836), the idea of human beings as playing cards is put into a religious context, when one character states that '[the] sun looks like a sign over an inn and the fiery clouds above it like the inscription: "The Golden Sun." The earth and water down below are like a table on which wine has been spilt, and we're lying on it like playing cards with which God and Satan are having a game out of boredom; you're the king, and I'm the knave, all we need is a queen, a lovely queen, with a big ginger-bread heart on her breast and an enormous tulip in which her long nose is drowning sentimentally' (*Leonce and Lena, Lenz, Woyzeck*, trans. Michael Hamburger (University of Chicago Press, 1972), 20).

through the curtains, just as his fear of being watched is realised in the author's God-like all-seeing eye.

Franz's miraculous rescue coincides with the author's appearance at the end of the novel. This advent of the artist inside his own creation has already been anticipated by the photographer in the ski resort, whose shadow can be seen in the picture he takes of Dreyer. This photographer reappears at the seaside, exclaiming "'The artist is coming! The divinely favoured, *der gottbegnadete* artist is coming!'" (*KQK*, 234) ['«... вот грядет художник Божией милостью»' (*Sobr. soch.*, II, 280)], which places the artist close to God, and sounds like an announcement of the god-like appearance of the author among his own creations:[30]

At that moment the puzzling foreign couple overtook him. They were both in beach robes and walked rapidly, rapidly conversing in their mysterious tongue. He thought that they glanced at him and fell silent for an instant. After passing him, they began talking again; he had the impression they were discussing him, and even pronouncing his name. (*KQK*, 258–9)

[Мимо [Франца] прошла уже знакомая ему чета. Оба были в халатах, шли быстро, громко говорили на неизвестном языке. Он заметил, что они на него взглянули и на мгновение умолкли. Потом, удаляясь, заговорили опять, и ему показалось, что они его обсуждают, – даже произносят его фамилию.[31] (*Sobr. soch.*, II, 294)

The ease with which the author enters the world of his novel here (even dragging his wife with him) is an integral part of the underlying structure of the religious theatre. The idea of God inside the world he has created is one of the essential elements of the religious theatre, where '[mingling] with [the] mortals [of the drama] on the easiest of terms are God, the Virgin Mary, archangels, angels, saints, and devils. Petit de Julleville says cogently: "Rien ne paraît plus naturel dans ces drames que le surnaturel".[32] The English version introduces the author into his own work in an explicitly theatrical context through the playwright Goldemar and his play *King, Queen, Knave*: 'once you imagined that god in the role of a novelist or a playwright, as Goldemar had in his most

---

[30] That this is the same photographer is indicated in a passage where he is mentioned together with swimmers at the seaside who move their legs as if they were on skis, thus recalling his first appearance in the ski resort (see *KQK*, 260). In the English version, the photographer receives the near-anagrammatic name 'Vivian Badlook' which is the author's first attempt to sidle into his own novel (*KQK*, 153).

[31] The English version gives further indications which identify the couple even more clearly with Véra and Vladimir Nabokov (see Grayson, *Nabokov Translated*, 95).

[32] Grace Frank, *The Medieval French Drama* (Oxford: Clarendon Press, 1954), 121.

famous work' (*KQK*, 224). The playwright's name is a combination of 'god' and 'Waldemar', the latter being a descendant of the founder of the Russian state and bringer of Christianity to Russia, the saint Vladimir.[33] The author becomes here the god of the play who determines the lives of his characters.[34]

King, Queen, Knave merges the puppet theatre and the religious drama in its presentation of an omnipotent author in his own fictional world. While the characters are reduced to puppets or automatons whose every movement is controlled by their author, the author aligns himself with the God of medieval drama. By taking on the function of a puppeteer, the author abolishes the tension between the drama text and its realisation, which is inherent in other forms of theatre. Whatever free will the characters believe they have is ultimately subsumed in the omnipotent author's entrance into his own novel, claiming total control over the fate of its world and characters.

HARLEQUIN PERFORMANCES: *DESPAIR*

King, Queen, Knave is still a work which espouses a rather simple relationship between the author and his text, without any interfering entities. The immediacy of the link between the author and his fiction is made possible through a rather unobtrusive third-person narrator who is not involved in the action. Yet this changes into a far more complicated and complex relationship with the entrance of first-person narrators into Nabokov's novels, who stand between the author and the text and compete with the author for control over the text. Nabokov used the device of an unreliable first-person narrator for the first time in the novella *The Eye* (*Sogliadatai*) (1930) and would exploit the dynamic rivalry between

---

[33] See David Hugh Farmer, *The Oxford Dictionary of Saints*, 5th edn (Oxford University Press, 2003).

[34] The notion of the author as God in his own works has become a topos of Nabokov criticism, deriving in part from Nabokov's own statements about his dictatorial, god-like status as author (for instance, *SO*, 69; 95). Alexandrov, for example, states that 'Nabokov's characteristic aesthetic practices resurrect the Romantic idea that the artist is God's rival, and that man's artistic creations are analogues to God's natural world' (*Nabokov's Otherworld*, 18). Davydov combines a metafictional with a metaphysical reading of Nabokov's works, suggesting that 'in Nabokov's teleological poetics [...] the author is the sole God of this cosmos-book, which he himself has created' ('*Teksty-matreški*', 200). In regard to *Bend Sinister*, Richard R. Patterson offers a detailed narratological analysis relating the God-like presence of the narrator and fictional author to different narratological levels in the novel ('Nabokov's *Bend Sinister*: The Narrator as God', *Studies in American Fiction*, 5/2 (autumn 1977), 241–53).

the different narratives of the narrator and the authorial principle behind the text frequently throughout his writing career. In *Despair*, this competition is sharpened by Hermann's role not only as the narrator but also as the writer of the tale. Throughout the novel, Hermann's strategies to control the written text are seen in an overtly performance-oriented context. The constant tension between a written fixed text and its more fluid improvised performance is linked with the *commedia dell'arte*, references to which frequently pop up during the course of the novel just as its irreverent playful characters do during the performance.

Historically, the performances of the *commedia dell'arte* would be given by small itinerant troupes who carried with them the necessary props, costumes and a small platform stage to perform their plays in public areas. The actors wore masks or half-masks designating specific character types. The commedia scenarios were comparatively simple, with the plot usually revolving around cuckolded husbands, mistaken identities, rival suitors, forbidden love and more or less harmless crime. Over the next centuries the commedia spread all over Europe and underwent major developments. Replacing the earlier principal masks of the commedia, the initially minor characters, the servants Harlequin, Pierrot and Columbine, gained prominence and came to present the eternal love triangle. In modern presentations of the commedia, the characters and their features are fluid and sometimes 'you can find ... one figure so played as to have the other's (opposite) personality'.[35] Therefore, the characters of the commedia are defined mainly in relation to each other; both the brutal trickster Harlequin and the more sensitive, artistically minded Pierrot compete for the love of the superficial sex object Columbine.

In *Despair*, Nabokov employs the commedia in typically Modernist fashion, conflating loosely connected fragments lifted from the wide tradition of the commedia, including the original Italian comedy of the sixteenth century and its later adaptations by the English pantomime. Basic elements of the commedia tradition are woven into the plot structure of *Despair*. The love triangle as the central motif of the commedia becomes in *Despair* part of the underlying plot of the love affair between Hermann's wife Lydia and her cousin Ardalion, which remains unnoticed by Hermann. Lydia has certain features of the frivolous Columbine, while Ardalion, although hardly the romantic melancholy, moon-struck Pierrot, is, in comparison to Hermann, the real artist, and his love for Lydia is as

---

[35] Green and Swan, *The Triumph of Pierrot*, 8.

sincere as Pierrot's for Columbine.[36] His poverty, his inclination to get drunk as well as his laziness are traditional characteristics of the Pierrot figure.[37] In this love triangle, Hermann consequently fulfils a Harlequin-like function, as the cruel, cunning and, for his audience, highly entertaining trickster. The most striking commedia feature to be adopted in *Despair* is Harlequin's stick (sometimes the stick has magic transforming powers), which becomes a defining attribute for Hermann.[38] The magic wand with which Harlequin can transform the reality around him represents in itself an important motif in *Despair*, pointing to a whole complex of themes which are linked with Hermann's attempt to transform the world around him and change his identity.

The story of the love triangle in the commedia is usually accompanied by a plot line relating to some crime. While Hermann's attempt to claim life insurance money for his own alleged death places the plot in close proximity to the original commedia tradition of fraud and thievery, the murder of Felix represents a form of serious crime which increasingly enters later forms of the commedia from the nineteenth century onwards.[39] The murder scene itself is clearly signalled to be comedic by Felix miming in jest a fop and subsequently performing an improvised pantomime, pretending to look at himself in the mirror just before he is shot by Hermann. The basic features of this scene are loosely based on the so-called 'dark scene' which is an essential structural element of the nineteenth-century English pantomime.

> This scene, because it invariably occurs in a gloomy or macabre setting, a cave, a ruined tower, a submarine grotto, a desolate heath, is called 'the dark scene'. Here Harlequin completes his quest, and exulting in obtaining his goal … forget[s] his magic bat. Pantaloon manages to recover the forgotten bat … and threatens Harlequin with dire punishment.[40]

Just as in the 'dark scene', Hermann's murder takes places in an oppressive and forbidding locale, in the forest on Ardalion's land on a grey winter's afternoon. The 'dark scene' occupies usually the penultimate scene of a pantomime, just as the murder happens in the ninth chapter, which would have remained the next-to-last scene in Hermann's tale had he not

[36] Senderovich and Shvarts also noticed the 'triangular paradigm' of the commedia in *Despair* ('The Juice of Three Oranges', 99).

[37] See Maurice Sand, *The History of the Harlequinade*, 2 vols. (London, 1915), vol. I, 219.

[38] Senderovich and Shvarts have also pointed to the association of Harlequin and Hermann through the attribute of the stick ('The Juice of Three Oranges', 85).

[39] See Green and Swan, *The Triumph of Pierrot*, 6; Mayer, *Harlequin in His Element*, 262.

[40] Mayer, *Harlequin in His Element*, 31.

been found out.[41] The most important parallel, however, is the adaptation of the stick motif, which in both cases is forgotten and makes the central figure vulnerable in the subsequent pursuit.

In this general comedic context, Hermann introduces himself as a 'stage performer' (*artist*) a notion which merges with 'breaker of the law' and 'poet' (*Despair*, 13). Felix also considers Hermann to be a performer – an assumption which is gladly taken up and developed with an overtly theatrical association by Hermann: 'at our first meeting you thought: "Ah, he is probably one of those theatrical blokes, the dashing kind, with funny fancies and fine clothes; maybe a celebrity"' (*Despair*, 71) ['ты … так примерно подумал: "Э, да он, вероятно, играет в театре, человек с норовом, чудак и франт, может быть, знаменитость"' (*Sobr. soch.*, III, 442)]. His constant play-acting supports this impression of him as an actor. He takes, for instance, the role of a near-sighted man much further than necessary: '[I] crossed the street, slitting my eyes (that ought to be noted) as if I really did not see well: art for art's sake, for there was no one about' (*Despair*, 108) ['пересек улицу, – щурясь (то следует отметить), как будто действительно плохо видел, и это было искусство ради искусства, ибо я уже отошел далеко' (*Sobr. soch.*, III, 473)]. This penchant for spontaneous performance is also reflected in Hermann's boasting of his versatile talent: 'But although I have never been an actor in the strict sense of the word, I have nevertheless, in real life, always carried about with me a small folding theatre and have appeared in more than one part (*Despair*, 82) ['Хотя я актером в узком смысле слова никогда не был, я все же в жизни всегда носил с собой как бы небольшой складной театр, играл не одну роль, и играл отменно' (*Sobr. soch.*, III, 452)]. Apart from the idea of flexibility, the image of a 'folding theatre' implies a clear comedic context of wandering theatres and the itinerant life of the commedia performers. Hermann's improvisation is mirrored in the text itself, which is frequently interrupted by spontaneous *lazzi*, diversions from the actual narrative. The dramatic impact of the discovery of Felix, for instance, is heightened by the reference to an acrobatic trick: 'Trumpets, please! Or still better, that tattoo which goes with a breathless acrobatic stunt' (*Despair*, 16) ['Оркестр, играй туш! Или лучше: дробь барабана, как при задыхающемся акробатическом трюке!' (*Sobr. soch.*, III, 400)]. Hermann's frequent impromptu addressing of the audience is equally

---

[41] Davydov shows that Hermann's attempt to follow a strictly symmetrical, mirror-like structure for his story (Chapters 1–5 being reflected in Chapters 6–10) is undermined by the actual author of the novel, who forces Hermann to add another, eleventh chapter (*Teksty-Matreški*, 57–60).

reminiscent of commedia practice: 'These conversations with readers are quite silly too. Stage asides' (*Despair*, 54) ['Эти разговоры с читателем тоже ни к чему. Апарте в театре' (*Sobr. soch.*, III, 429)].

Hermann's impulse to improvise is set in an explicitly theatrical context when he recalls his participation in an amateur performance:

I had to speak only a few words: 'The prince bade me announce that he would be here presently. Ah! here he comes,' instead of which, full of exquisite delight and all aquiver with glee, I spoke thus: 'The prince cannot come: he has cut his throat with a razor'; and, as I spoke, the gentleman in the part of the prince was already coming, with a beaming smile on his gorgeously painted face. (*Despair*, 82)

я должен был сказать всего несколько слов: «Его сиятельство велели доложить, что сейчас будут-с… Да вот и они сами идут», – вместо чего я с каким-то тончайшим наслаждением, ликуя и дрожа всем телом, сказал так: «Его сиятельство прийти не могут-с, они зарезались бритвой», – а между тем любитель-актер, игравший князя, уже выходил, в белых штанах, с улыбкой на радужном от грима лице. (*Sobr. soch.*, III, 451–2)

In the Russian version, the same complete inversion of an original text takes place in Hermann's school essay on Pushkin's 'The Shot' ('Vystrel', 1831), where he lets Silvio kill his opponent without further ado, thus destroying the actual story line, while in the English version Hermann adapts *Othello*, making 'the Moor sceptical and Desdemona unfaithful' (*Despair*, 47).[42] Through these distortions, Hermann asserts his autonomy as a performer against canonical texts. Hermann's improvisation of original texts finds its logical development in his notoriously unreliable narrative. Hermann's refusal to admit his wife's unfaithfulness, despite obvious evidence, 'borders on the subhuman', as one critic has pointed out.[43] In a similar vein, Hermann's portrayal of himself as a cultured, witty and refined artist is subverted by an alternative image of him as a vain, violent and vulgar cad, which becomes ever more visible during the course of the novel. Although the original text can only be deduced from Hermann's improvisations, its existence is crucial as an implicit touchstone against which Hermann's deviations and manipulations can be measured.

The desire to control his own emerging text shapes Hermann's perception of himself as the director of a theatre performance. In the description of the New Year's dinner in the manner of stage directions, Hermann determines the alternation of movement and freezing: 'Good, now you

[42] This reworking of *Othello* points clearly to the actual infidelity of Hermann's wife.
[43] William C. Carroll, 'The Cartesian Nightmare of *Despair*, in J. E. Rivers and Charles Nicol (eds.), *Nabokov's Fifth Arc: Nabokov and Others on His Life's Work* (Austin: University Of Texas Press, 1982), 82–104 [84].

may move again, be quick with that bottle, the clock is going to strike' (*Despair*, 96) ['Кончено, разрешаю вам двигаться, скорее сюда бутылку, сейчас пробьют часы' (*Sobr. soch.*, III, 463)]. The literal staging of the murder scene is also carefully prepared and controlled by Hermann, who orders Felix to wear a certain costume and make-up. The roles of actor and director merge with that of a spectator in the overtly theatrical description of a bizarre sexual experience, during which Hermann mentally dissociates himself from the sexual act he is performing:[44]

I longed to discover some means to remove myself at least a hundred yards from the lighted stage where I performed; I longed to contemplate that bedroom scene from some remote upper gallery in a blue mist under the swimming allegories of the starry vault; to watch a small but distinct and very active couple through opera glasses … one April night, with the harps of rain aphrodisiacally burbling in the orchestra … I was sitting at my maximum distance of fifteen rows of seats and looking forward to an especially good show – which, indeed, had already started, with my acting self in colossal form and most inventive. (*Despair*, 33)

The distribution of theatrical roles in this scene serves as a precise analogy with the different functions Hermann fulfils simultaneously in the production of the book. The novel becomes a theatrical performance in which Hermann performs the role of the protagonist, directs the narrative and observes his own performance when he later reads his own account. Writing and reading are depicted as distinctly theatrical activities.[45]

This notion of writing as performance has startling implications for the reality of the novel. Boyd sees the novel ultimately as an artistic failure, commenting that

Hermann's unwarranted supposition that another face looks like his remains a brittle and meager basis for a whole novel. It never quite convinces, and page after page that would make one tingle with excitement in another context can here only intermittently overcome one's remoteness from a story whose central premise fails to merit the suspension of disbelief.[46]

Not only is the premise unbelievable, but also the meetings between Felix and the completely hysterical Hermann lack credibility. During the course of the novel, Felix's existence becomes increasingly doubtful, as

---

[44] The quoted passage existed in the original Russian manuscript but was censored in the 1930s and was reinstated only subsequently in the English version (see *Despair*, 10; Grayson, *Nabokov Translated*, 78–9; Boyd, *American Years*, 489).

[45] This blurring of spectator and actor into one role had already been probed in Nabokov's depiction of the self-conscious narrator Smurov in *The Eye* who spies not only on other people but constantly observes himself with the distance of a detached theatre spectator.

[46] Boyd, *Russian Years*, 389.

nobody apart from Hermann ever sees him. It is telling that Hermann describes the night they spend together with the imagery of masturbation, suggesting a rather lone encounter with nobody but himself. In a similar vein, the letter he receives subsequently from Felix has the hyperbolic style of Hermann's own writing. It is the same letter which he shows to Orlovius as evidence that he is being blackmailed. Orlovius's suspicious questions about the sender, and his later statement that Hermann writes letters to himself, indicate that Felix never existed outside of Hermann's imagination. In a variation of these self-addressed letters, towards the end of the novel Hermann receives a letter supposedly from Ardalion. Just like the message from 'Felix', this letter is written in the hysterical tone which is characteristic of Hermann's own writing. That this is another one of those letters Hermann writes to himself is neatly reflected in the absurd situation where Ardalion would address his letter to Hermann's *poste restante* incognito 'Ardalion'.[47] Tellingly, the murder scene itself has the sham reality of a theatre set: 'The yellow post was very yellow indeed. To my right, beyond the field, the wood was painted a flat grey on the backdrop of a pale sky' (*Despair*, 137) ['Желтый столб был очень желт. Справа за полем театральной декорацией плоско серел лес' (*Sobr. soch.*, III, 496)], and in the foreword to the English translation, Nabokov refers to Felix's murder merely as 'great fun' (*Despair*, 11). Hermann's imaginary murder of his double foreshadows Humbert Humbert's ambiguous murder of Quilty at the end of *Lolita*. In both cases the murderer cannot bring himself to check whether the alleged victim is actually dead and both murder scenes are depicted as explicitly theatrical performances.[48] These merely imaginary crimes might be a further reason, apart from their similar names and criminal scheming, why Nabokov links these two protagonists in the foreword to the English translation of *Despair*, stating that 'Hermann and Humbert are alike only in the sense that two dragons painted by the same artist at different periods of his life resemble each other. Both are neurotic scoundrels, yet there is a green lane in

---

[47] In the foreword, Nabokov does not identify the sender of the letter as Ardalion but alludes merely to 'the writer of the rude letter in Chapter Eleven' (*Despair*, 10).

[48] For discussions of the implications of the chronological discrepancy which betrays Humbert's purely imaginary crime, see Christina Tekiner, 'Time in Lolita', *Modern Fiction Studies*, 25 (1979), 463–9; Julian W. Connolly, '"Nature's Reality" or Humbert's "Fancy"? Scenes of Reunion and Murder in Lolita', *Nabokov Studies*, 2 (1995), 41–61; Aleksandr Dolinin, 'Nabokov's Time Doubling From The Gift to Lolita', *Nabokov Studies*, 2 (1995), 3–40. Against these interpretations, Boyd argues that the discrepancies in the chronology can be explained by a mistake on the part of Nabokov ('"Even Homais Nods": Nabokov's Fallibility, or, How to Revise *Lolita*', *Nabokov Studies*, 2 (1995), 62–86).

Paradise where Humbert is permitted to wander at dusk once a year; but Hell shall never parole Hermann' (*Despair*, 11).[49]

Inconsistencies continue to govern the novel after the alleged murder. It remains unclear, for instance, how Hermann was able to cross the border to France with the passport of Felix, who, as it will turn out, has no resemblance to him. The novel suggests that Hermann might have never arrived in Iks, or Aix in the English version of the novel (incidentally a mere reproduction of the last syllabus of Fel*iks* or Fel*ix*); instead, he has crossed mental rather then geographical or national borders. From the moment Hermann leaves the house to kill Felix, the novel takes on an unreal quality. The drive to the forest has a certain dreaminess to it – Hermann calls it 'my sleepy transportation' (*Despair*, 134) ['мое сонное перемещение' (*Sobr. soch.*, III, 494)]. This sense of unreality continues during Hermann's stay in Iks after the murder. Reality is substituted by a stage set in this description of Hermann's hotel room:

I took a room in a second-rate hotel, a huge room, with a stone floor and walls like cardboard, on which there seemed to be painted the sienna-brown door leading into the next room, and a looking glass with only one reflection. It was horribly cold; yet the open hearth of the preposterous fireplace was no more adapted to give heat than a stage contrivance would be. (*Despair*, 150)

Я снял комнату в гостинице второго разряда, – огромную, с каменным полом и картонными на вид стенами, на которых словно было нарисована рыжеватая дверь в соседний номер и гуашевое зеркало. Было ужасно холодно, но открытый очаг бутафорского камина был не приспособлен для топки. (*Sobr. soch.*, III, 507)

Even the gendarme of the next town Hermann moves to appears to be part of an opera performance.

The emerging story of Felix's murder and Hermann's escape is an improvisation on Hermann's actual situation as a patient in a lunatic asylum. Already during his drive to the forest, Hermann has a sensation of bustling people around him: 'the feeling grew upon me that there was a great number of people around, all speaking together, and then falling silent and giving one another dim errands and dispersing without a sound' (*Despair*, 135) ['и потом мне начинало казаться, что кругом много людей, и все говорят сразу и замолкают, и, дав друг другу смутные поручения, беззвучно расходятся' (*Sobr. soch.*, II, 495)]. The long white

---

[49] That Humbert is granted some sort of delivery could be explained by his sense of another entity, another artist beyond himself who has created Humbert's world and Humbert himself, while Hermann frequently denies the existence of any God.

corridors in his lodgings are reminiscent of a mental institution rather than a hotel. The doctor who is supposed to be at the hotel as a guest and the hotel manager clearly resemble a psychiatrist and a warden who try to calm down a hysterical patient.[50] Despite Hermann's statement that he moves three times, from a hotel in Iks to the hotel in the mountains and finally to another village where he takes a room, his actual lodgings never seem to change from his initial freezing room. Much earlier, an acquaintance of Hermann prophesied that Hermann would go mad later in life. References to Russian literature place Hermann in the good company of two of Russia's most famous literary madmen. Hermann shares his first name with the protagonist of Pushkin's 'Queen of Spades' ('Pikovaia dama', 1834), who also loses his sanity.[51] Poprishchin, Gogol's well-known madman, is alluded to indirectly in a description of the picnic on Ardalion's plot in the summer, as Dolinin and Skonechnaia have ingeniously discovered.[52] And once at the hotel, Hermann notices a wind from Spain, the alleged kingdom of Gogol's madman. Just like Poprishchin (and later Waltz), Hermann revises the reality of his own situation as a patient in a mental hospital to fit his fantasy of a perfect crime.

Writing becomes an actually performative act in the context of Hermann's imaginary crime, something of which the reader has been warned in the very opening paragraph of the novel:

> If I were not perfectly sure of my power to write and of my marvellous ability to express ideas with the utmost grace and vividness … had I lacked that power, that ability, et cetera, not only should I have refrained from describing certain recent events, but there would have been nothing to describe, for, gentle reader, *nothing at all would have happened* [emphasis added]. (*Despair*, 13)

> Если бы я не был совершенно уверен в своей писательской силе, в чудной своей способности выражать с предельным изяществом и живостью … не будь во мне этой силы, способности и прочего, я бы не только отказался от описывания недавних событий, но и вообще нечего было бы описывать, ибо, дорогой читатель, не случилось бы ничего (*Sobr. soch.*, III, 397)

Writing and acting overlap in this paradoxical statement, where events are only actualised and performed through language. In the logic of the novel where events only take place as written words, the murder of Felix

---

[50] This episode is reminiscent of the scene in *The Waltz Invention* where the protagonist considers the staff of the mental institution where he is held, to be his servants.

[51] See Carroll, 'The Cartesian Nightmare of *Despair*', 86.

[52] See Aleksandr Dolinin and Olga Skonechnaia, 'Primechaniia [*Otchaianie*]', in *Sobr. soch.*, III, 755–78 [763].

becomes therefore a writer's whim.[53] In the same way as the sexual act never actually takes place outside of Hermann's dissociated imagination, so the murder of Felix is performed only in Hermann's imagination and writing. The act of creating a stable text is crucial in transforming Hermann's tale into reality. Significantly, it is again a printed text which is cited for the corroboration of Hermann's story, a French newspaper which – even to Hermann's surprise – reports a German murder. Yet when put to the test, the text seems to vanish before Hermann's eyes:

> Then, from under the bed, I pulled out the paper; but now I could not find in it what I had just been reading. I examined it from beginning to end: nothing! Could I have *dreamt* reading it? I started looking through the pages afresh; it was like a nightmare when a thing gets lost, and not only can it not be discovered, but there are none of those natural laws which would lend the search a certain logic, instead of which everything is absurdly shapeless and arbitrary. No, there was nothing about me in the paper. Nothing at all. (*Despair*, 155)

> Вытащил из-под кровати газету, – но уже не мог найти в ней то, что читал только что. Я ее просмотрел всю: ничего! Неужели мне приснилось? Я сызнова начал ее просматривать, – это было какъ в кошмаре, – теряется, и нельзя найти, и нет тех природных законов, которые вносят некоторую логику в поиски, – а все безобразно и бессмысленно произвольно. Нет, ничего в газете не было. Ни слова. (*Sobr. soch.*, III, 511)

Another newspaper article appears, hinting at a fatal mistake in the execution of the crime (or Hermann's written story of it), which, on re-reading the tale, Hermann discovers to be the forgotten stick. That the very basis on which Hermann's tale rests, the resemblance between himself and Felix, is not noted in any of the newspaper stories, worries him less than the actually secondary mistake of the forgotten stick. Hermann shares this artistic problem of a forgotten stick with the protagonist of the short story 'Lips to Lips' ('Usta k ustam', 1956), written about six months before *Despair*.[54] Just as for Hermann, for the inexperienced and untalented writer Ilya Borisovich, a cane which he has invented for one of

---

[53] Stephen Suagee also doubts the truth of Hermann's tale: 'we can only guess how much of Hermann's complicated plot is pure fancy' ('An Artist's Memory Beats All Other Kinds: An Essay on *Despair*', in Carl R. Proffer (ed.), *A Book of Things About Vladimir Nabokov* (Ann Arbor: Ardis, 1974), 54–62 [60]).

[54] 'Lips to Lips' was written in 1931, but its planned publication in *Poslednie novosti* in 1932 was cancelled when the editors realised that Nabokov's story was based on a real-life literary scandal involving the émigré journal *Chisla* and the talentless writer Aleksandr Burov. The story appeared only in the 1950s in Nabokov's collection of short stories *Vesna v Fial'te i drugie rasskazy* (New York: Chekhov, 1956).

his fictional characters, presents unforeseen problems in the subsequent development of the plot:

Writing meant to him an unequal contest with indispensable objects … having ponderously finished with the cloakroom fuss and being about to present his hero with an elegant cane, Ilya Borisovich naively delighted in the gleam of its rich knob, and did not foresee, alas, what claims that valuable article would make, how painfully it would demand mention, when Dolinin, his hands feeling the curves of a supple young body, would be carrying Irina across a vernal rill. (*Stories*, 313)

Писание было для Ильи Борисовича неравной борьбой с пердметами первой необходимости … тяжело покончив с возней у гардероба и готовясь героя наделить тростью, Илья Борисович чистосердечно радовался блеску ее массивного набалдашника и, увы, не предчувствовал, какой к нему иск предъявит эта дорогая трость, как мучительно потребует она упоминания, когда Долинин, ощущая в руках гибкое молодое тело, будет переносить Ирину через весенний ручей.[55] (*Sobr. soch.*, V, 340)

While the actual resemblance between Hermann and Felix cannot be verified or disproven by a reader (as the text is despite Hermann's painterly aspirations not a visual picture of his imagination), the stick is a clearly recognisable mistake in the plot construction, which any reader, just like Hermann himself, can discover on re-reading the story.

Hermann's hasty composition of his tale (writing a chapter per day) is a desperate attempt to realise his fantasy in a fixed, written text. The notion of improvisation changes in this context from something free and creative to an elusive, unstable and provisional construct. In terms of writing, this improvisation is much closer to a first draft than to a polished novel despite Hermann's assertion that an 'author does not show people his first draft' (*Despair*, 35) ['писатель не читает во всеуслышание неоконченного черновика' (*Sobr. soch.*, III, 414)]. Yet this unrevised draft, riddled with contradictions, inconsistencies and such crucial oversights as Felix's stick becomes the written record of Hermann's tale, holding him to account. He also has to add another chapter when he realises he will be caught (at least in his own text) which, as Sergei Davydov has shown, destroys the symmetrical structure of the novel he had in mind.[56] The written text resists improvisation, giving Hermann's words a finality which they do not warrant and which ultimately works against Hermann, for by fixing

---

[55] Just as Ilya Borisovich has forgotten his character's cane, he later forgets his own cane in the theatre (see Davydov, '*Teksty-matreški*', 22).
[56] See *ibid.*, 57–60.

his narrative in writing, Hermann also fixes his aesthetic rather than criminal mistake.

In the Russian version, the ending of the novel is suspended while Hermann is contemplating improvising a speech to the gathering crowd.[57] Once more Hermann is in the role of an actor, but this time he is awaiting his performance from behind the curtain: 'I have peeped again. Standing and staring … absolute quiet; only the swish of their breathing. How about opening the window and making a little speech' (*Despair*, 176) ['Я опять отвел занавеску. Стоят и смотрят … полное молчание, только слышно, как дышат. Отворить окно, пожалуй, и произнести небольшую речь' (*Sobr. soch.*, III, 527)]. The novel is broken off before he can leap into another of his improvised performances. Instead this last scene with Hermann at the window stops short of re-enacting Harlequin's frequent leaps out of windows during the pursuit scenes, which was adapted in Blok's *The Fairground Booth*, where Harlequin jumps through a window only to find that the window itself is painted scenery. Hermann, however, does not jump but remains at the close of the book behind the window and arrested in movement within the novel.

One of the central features of the *commedia dell'arte*, the constantly improvised speeches and tricks of the actors, is turned on its head in Nabokov's treatment of the theme. While improvisation marks the artistic skill and creative autonomy of the performers, Hermann's need to improvise underlines only his lack of control and freedom in a preconceived world where his attempts to write and perform his own scenario are frustrated by an underlying text which works ever stronger against his improvised performance. Hermann's improvisation leads only to his imprisonment not as a great artist but as a deluded madman in the best tradition of Russian literature.

In Nabokov's fiction, the theatrical theme evolves from an initially rather clear-cut authoritarian relationship between the writer and his fictional world in the puppet theatre of *King, Queen, Knave* and moves on from there towards ever more complex forms of interplay between the text

---

[57] This speech is given only in the second English translation, prepared by Nabokov himself in 1964 (see Boyd, *American Years*, 489). In this second translation, the reference in this last scene has partly shifted to cinema, when Hermann appeals to the crowd outside the window to protect him against the police, claiming to be a film actor, shooting an escape scene. The delivery of the speech itself, however, would still be a theatrical event in the immediate confrontation of Hermann and his audience. The element of improvisation has disappeared in this scene as Hermann writes the speech out, which repeats his strategy of fixing his improvisations in written text.

and its enactment. Nabokov's next novel, *The Defense*, already presents a hero who gradually develops a certain degree of awareness of his status as a puppet in a *balagan*-like world. Luzhin's jump through the window at the end of the novel is suspended by Hermann in *Despair*, who not only develops a much clearer idea of his fictional status but also challenges the author by improvising on the original text. The puppet theatre and the *commedia dell'arte* recur in later works. The puppet theatre, for instance, provides once more a theatrical context for the creation and manipulation of the fictional world in *Pnin*. The protagonist manages to escape the advent of the cruel fictional author and narrator only at the last moment, climbing out of the proscenium frame of a painted stage. Nabokov's last published novel also announces itself as an overtly comedic text with its title *Look at the Harlequins!* The novel's narrator Vadim, a personage assembled from the different masks of real and fictional authors tries frantically to fix his fluid identity by writing down his tale. Both novels suggest a continuation and firm establishment of the theatrical theme in Nabokov's art in the second half of his writing career. Yet, it is in the earlier novels, the work of a younger and perhaps less subtle novelist, that the mechanics which drive the puppet shows are deliberately laid bare. In this sense, Luzhin's encounter with the broken puppets in the glass case offers a more general commentary on the experience of reading Nabokov: the disappointment that the puppets fail to perform is compensated for by the fact that they can be seen in their limp state in the first place. The fictional worlds of Nabokov's novels become momentarily transparent and allow a tantalising glance at what lies behind the scenes.

6

Shakespeare's ghost: The Real Life of Sebastian
Knight, *"'That in Aleppo Once ...'"*
and Bend Sinister

Nabokov's first works in English present, to some extent, the continuation of his theatrical works and his dramas in the 1930s. *The Real Life of Sebastian Knight* was written only a few months after he had finished his last Russian play *The Waltz Invention*, while "'That in Aleppo Once ...'" and *Bend Sinister* seem to have absorbed a great part of Nabokov's research into drama, in particular his ideas on 'dramatic determinism' and on Shakespeare's plays, which had accumulated during his preparation for his 1941 Stanford lectures on theatre. In these works, Nabokov continues to employ theatre, yet it is adapted to a new cultural context, manifesting itself in the constant presence of Shakespeare. Here, reflecting Nabokov's switch in language, a distinctly English theatre opens its doors for a new readership. Shakespeare's dramas and their performance on the Elizabethan stage become the model for Nabokov's exploration of the most complex and intricate relationships between different authors and the realisation of their texts in his English narrative fiction. While *The Real Life of Sebastian Knight* develops the theme of elusive identities and a shifting authorship against the backdrop of *Twelfth Night*, "'That in Aleppo Once ...'" raises questions of control and authorial property in the context of *Othello*, concerns which are taken up again and reworked in *Bend Sinister*, where *Hamlet* provides the theatrical underpinning to questions of legitimate authorial claims.

Shakespeare is intimately associated with questions of origin and identity in Nabokov's mind. After his switch from Russian to English, Nabokov seeks to position himself in a new literary tradition, in which Shakespeare comes to be perceived as one of the rich sources from which Nabokov's own English grows. Nabokov traces this link between Shakespeare and origin further in the related issues of textual property, literary ownership and authorship. Shakespeare and his plays come to encapsulate these questions in an explicitly theatrical context in Nabokov's work. As a playwright and man of the theatre, Shakespeare combines the two competing entities of the play text and the stage, illustrating questions of origin which are inscribed in the relationship between the text and the stage in the theatre itself: To what extent does a theatre production originate in a written text? Can theatrical performance ever be reliably traced back to an original text? This problem becomes more intricate when the text itself, as in Shakespeare's case, constitutes a borrowing from and reworking of preceding texts and narratives. Further complications arise from the entirely vague status of the texts themselves, which were never authorised by Shakespeare in the form in which we read them today. The playwright's mysterious identity, which has become a source for all sorts of fantastic and wondrous speculations, throws these concerns into relief. In the three works by Nabokov which are the focus of this chapter, Shakespeare provides not a mere literary subtext, but a structural principle which exposes an ultimately theatrical dimension in the production of a text.

From the very beginning of Nabokov's writing career, Shakespeare belongs to the small and exclusively selected group of cherished literary ideals. Nabokov's first play, *The Tragedy of Mr Morn*, is evidently indebted to Shakespeare's tragedies and history plays, if not directly then at least through Pushkin's and Lermontov's readings of Shakespeare. His poem 'Shakespeare', written in February 1924 while Nabokov was completing the drama, apostrophises the 'god of iambic thunder / you hundred-mouthed, unthinkably great bard!' ['бог ямбического грома, / стоустный и немыслимый поэт!'].[1] In the 1930s, Nabokov translated several passages from *Hamlet* into Russian, including Hamlet's famous soliloquy.[2] He would rework parts of these translations in the *Hamlet* chapter in *Bend Sinister*. Although Nabokov repeatedly insisted on the superiority

---

[1] Vladimir Nabokov, 'L'Envoi: Shakespeare', trans. Dmitri Nabokov, in Jane Grayson, Arnold McMillin and Priscilla Meyer (eds.), *Nabokov's World*, vol. I: *The Shape of Nabokov's Word* (Basingstoke: Palgrave, 2002), 216–19. Vladimir Nabokov, *Stikhi* (Ann Arbor, MI: Ardis, 1979), 156–7. (All further quotes from the poem 'Shakespeare' are from these editions.) The original Russian version, undated (published in *Zhar-Ptitsa*, 12 (1924), 32), was later corrected in the posthumous collection *Stikhi* which had been prepared by the author before his death. There is a poem is dated 'December 1924'. M. E. Malikova notes, however, that the poem was enclosed in a letter to Elena Nabokov dated 26 February 1924 (Vladimir Nabokov, *Stikhotvoreniia*, ed. M. E. Malikova (St Petersburg: Akademicheskii proekt, 2002), 587, n. 353). Dmitri Nabokov's translation was republished with minor revisions in the *Nabokov Online Journal*, 3 (2009) (http://etc. dal.ca/noj/volume3/articles/11b_Dmitri%20Nabokov_Transl_SHAKESPEARE.pdf).

[2] See Vladimir Nabokov, 'Dva otryvka iz "Gamleta"', *Rul'*, 19 October 1930 [translations of excerpts from Act IV, Scene 7, where the queen informs Laertes about Ophelia's drowning and parts of Act V, Scene 1, Laertes' and Hamlet's fight at Ophelia's grave]; Vladimir Nabokov, 'Gamlet', *Rul'*, 23 November 1930 [translation of Act III, Scene 1, Hamlet's soliloquy].

of Shakespeare's language over his dramaturgy,[3] he called the canonical dramas *Hamlet, Othello, Macbeth* and *King Lear* 'the great series of
Shakespeare's incomparable tragedies'[4] and referred to Shakespeare frequently as 'a genius'.[5] His admiration for Shakespeare is also evident in
his persistent claim that his birthday on 10 April 1899 in the Julian calendar becomes 23 April in the Gregorian calendar, which is conventionally
accepted as Shakespeare's date of birth (and death). That this is strictly
speaking a miscalculation is less important than Nabokov's clear intention to juxtapose himself with Shakespeare.[6] The same purpose is apparent in his list of favourite writers which was cited by the *Wellesley College
News*: 'Pushkin, Shakespeare and himself constitute his three favorite
writers.'[7]

This continuous fascination with Shakespeare finally seems to have
found an outlet in the novels written after Nabokov's switch to English.
Pushkin, the touchstone of literary greatness in the Russian works,
moves into the background to be replaced by Shakespeare, who occupies centre stage in the English works.[8] Yet this stable point of reference
against which all literary art is measured turns out to be a most elusive
and artificial construct. The fragmentary nature of the documented life of
William Shakespeare of Stratford-upon-Avon leaves many blanks and few
filled pages in his biography. The confusion surrounding the entry relating to his christening in the church register as well as the inconsistencies
between the entry regarding the marriage license and the marriage bond,
or the black hole into which Shakespeare seems to disappear only to suddenly emerge as an established playwright and actor in London, have
given rise to all sorts of speculation about the personality and identity

---

[3] In an interview with Alfred Appel, Nabokov asserted that the 'verbal poetical texture of
Shakespeare is the greatest the world has known, and is immensely superior to the structure
of his plays as plays. With Shakespeare it is the metaphor that is the thing, not the play' (*SO*,
89–90).

[4] Nabokov, *Lectures on Don Quixote*, 6.

[5] In his lecture on tragedy, Nabokov remarked that '[the] charm of tragic genius, the charm of
Shakespeare or Ibsen, lies for me in quite another region' ('Tragedy', 341).

[6] In the nineteenth century the Julian calendar lagged twelve days behind the Gregorian calendar,
while in the twentieth century this gap widened to thirteen days. Nabokov's birthday on 10 April
1899 (old style), therefore, corresponds to 22 April 1899 (new style). Only if Nabokov had been
born a year later, in the twentieth century, would his date of birth in the old style have corresponded to what is conventionally taken as Shakespeare's birthday, 23 April. For a discussion of
Nabokov's calculation of his date of birth and its occurrence in his writings, see Pekka Tammi,
Russian Subtexts in Nabokov's Fiction (Tampere University Press, 1999), 106–8.

[7] Quoted in Boyd, *American Years*, 122.

[8] Johnson also comments on the replacement of Pushkin with Shakespeare in the English novels
(*Worlds in Regression*, 202).

of the poet. The wide-ranging knowledge of literature, culture, science, politics and law which is displayed in his works, without any evidence that he enjoyed an outstanding education or that he ever travelled abroad, has left many biographers and literary critics equally puzzled. Out of these apparent contradictions and uncertainties, a widespread controversy about the authorship behind the plays has sprung up.[9] The Shakespeare plays have been attributed among others to Francis Bacon (due to his thorough and professional knowledge of the law), and to the nobleman Edward de Vere, seventeenth Earl of Oxford (due to his knowledge of the court and acquaintance with aristocratic society). More important for the present discussion than the playwright's true identity are the questions about the status of a literary text and its author that are generated by the Shakespeare controversy. Marjorie Garber points out that the commencement of this argument in the mid-nineteenth century immediately follows on from a distinctive change in the notion of intellectual property and authorial ownership in the late eighteenth and early nineteenth century, when 'strict copyright rules define the relation between text and author in a new way. It is not until there is such a thing as property that violations of property can occur.'[10] Any property relations or claims are, however, complicated when the owner himself remains anonymous or non-existent.

Shakespeare becomes a merely ghostly presence in his plays, a spectre of himself, fulfilling that 'peculiar characteristic of ghostliness – that the ghost is a copy, somehow both nominally identical to and numinously different from a vanished or unavailable original'.[11] Shakespeare as an apparition of himself is encapsulated in the anecdote that one of his best performances was in the part of Old Hamlet's ghost, sidling on to the stage of his own drama – a story too tempting in its metafictional potential not to be noted by Nabokov, who referred to it in his poem 'Shakespeare' ('that Shakespeare – Will – who played the Ghost in *Hamlet*' (217) ['тот Вилль Шекспир, что «Тень» играл в «Гамлете»'

---

[9] F. E. Halliday gives a very useful and concise survey of this debate (*Shakespeare and His Critics* (London: Duckworth, 1949), 211–31). Marjorie Garber provides an excellent analysis of this controversy and its meaning in a wider cultural context (*Shakespeare's Ghost Writers: Literature as Uncanny Causality* (New York: Methuen, 1987), 1–12). Nabokov was well acquainted with at least one side of this debate, which claims that the real author of the Shakespeare plays is Francis Bacon. L. L. Lee has identified Edwin Durning-Lawrence's monograph *Bacon is Shake-speare* (London: Gay and Hancock, 1910) as the study that is parodied at the beginning of the *Hamlet* chapter in *Bend Sinister* ('*Bend Sinister*: Nabokov's Political Dream', in L. S. Dembo (ed.), *Nabokov: The Man and His Work* (Madison: University Of Wisconsin Press, 1967), 95–105).
[10] Garber, *Ghost Writers*, 4.
[11] *Ibid.*, 10.

(156)]) and much later again in an interview: 'Shakespeare in the part of the King's ghost. That is said to have been one of his best roles. Stalking along, stalking along.'[12] Already in his early poem 'Shakespeare', Nabokov touches upon some of the issues that are raised by the complex relationship between Shakespeare and his work. The poem seems to assume an inextricable link between the text and its author, supplying Shakespeare's elusive biography with details derived from his plays, only to sever this link in the last lines. The poem evokes trips to Italy, a mistress in Verona and even conversations with Shakespeare's contemporary Cervantes.[13] Yet this imaginary construct of the author derived from his texts resists all attempts to prove its validity. Shakespeare remains inaccessible to the pleas of the speaker to reveal himself and his 'real life' behind the mask. The different versions of Shakespeare's life and the ultimate impossibility of determining who Shakespeare really was, however, are reconciled in the idea that Shakespeare the historical person pales in comparison with his great art. He lives on in his works and in his characters:

> … your phantasms' echoes
> still vibrate for us: your Venetian Moor,
> his anguish; Falstaff's visage, like an udder
> with pasted-on moustache; the raging Lear…
> You are among us, you're alive … (217)

> … но гул твоих видений
> остался нам: венецианский мавр
> и скорбь его; лицо Фальстафа – вымя
> с наклеенными усиками; Лир
> бушующий … Ты здесь, ты жив … (156)

Eventually, Shakespeare simply dissolves into his art: 'faceless you'd stay, like immortality / itself – then vanished in the distance, smiling' (219) ['пребудешь ты безликим, как само / бессмертие … И вдаль ушел с улыбкой' (157)]. Nabokov would return to this idea almost thirty years later in his lectures on *Don Quixote*, stating that '[the] only matter in which Cervantes and Shakespeare are equals is the matter of influence, of spiritual irrigation – I have in view the long shadow cast upon receptive

---

[12] Quoted in Boyd, *American Years*, 502. To Appel, Nabokov mentioned the same idea in regard to his playing the part of Nabokov, the butterfly hunter, in Kubrick's adaptation of *Lolita*: '"Yes," says Nabokov, "I was going to play the part. There's a precedent, of course." Hitchcock? "No, I had in mind Shakespeare, as the ghost in *Hamlet*. Kubrick loved the idea. I wonder why he changed his mind"' (Appel, *Nabokov's Dark Cinema*, 250–1).

[13] Nabokov highlighted a similar thought in his lectures on *Don Quixote*: 'Indeed, while Cervantes was making his mad knight, Shakespeare might have been making his mad King' (*Lectures on Don Quixote*, 6).

posterity of a created image which may continue to live independently from the book itself. Shakespeare's plays, however, will continue to live, apart from the shadow they project.'[14]

In the poem, the written text provides the stability which the elusive author behind it lacks. Despite the uncertainty about Shakespeare's life, the poem assumes the existence of one individual source from which the plays have sprung, with all the ramifications this has for authority and authorial intention in the texts. Yet Shakespeare's dramas are hardly reliable texts. The more surprising, therefore, is Nabokov's stipulation for a verbatim theatre production of Shakespeare – an absurd demand for a playwright whose dramas in all their different and never authorised versions naturally defy the modern idea of a definitive text. Nabokov was clearly aware of the battles over different versions of Shakespeare's plays, which are being fought in the textual antechambers of editorial forewords, comments and annotations: 'Footnotes in good editions of Shakespeare are quite as exciting as footlights.'[15] Despite this, Nabokov imposes here anachronistically entirely inappropriate notions of textual property and definitive originality onto Shakespeare's plays. What he considers Shakespeare's original version is in itself a 'garbled version' from different 'foul papers', folios and quartos based on scholarly consensus and editorial convenience rather than an actually authorised text. Halliday, for instance, explains that '[it] would be foolish to maintain that every word of the thirty-six plays in the First Folio was written by Shakespeare, or even that every word in any one play is his; that would be to defend the untenable position of the literary reactionary or fundamentalist. In the early plays there are occasional outcrops of his predecessors' work, in some of the later plays there is undoubted collaboration with his contemporaries, and all of them are liable to have gathered accretions in the course of successful productions.'[16] While lacking historical accuracy, Nabokov's view of Shakespeare recalls Barthes' professed desire for the author and is indicative of the critic's or reader's urge to construct one reliable text and one stable authorial source behind it.

Shakespeare epitomises the complex relationship between a playwright and the stage performance of the drama text. In Shakespeare's case, the relationship between the author's written and theatre's performed text is

[14] *Ibid.*, 8.
[15] Vladimir Nabokov, *The tragedy of tragedy.* Typescript draft. With Nabokov's holograph draft (fragment), VN Berg.
[16] Halliday, *Shakespeare and His Critics*, 219. See also Marjorie Garber, 'McGuffin Shakespeare', in her *Quotation Marks* (New York and London: Routledge, 2003), 147–75.

reflected in the precarious relationship between the playwright and his written texts. In Shakespeare's dramas, the playwright is absent not only on stage, but also as a clear original source. If the playwright himself is only a ghostly and unknown entity, frequently doubted in his individuality, he cannot claim or be claimed for authorship of written texts which are neither definitive nor fixed. In this way Shakespeare comes to be closely connected with the loss of biographical and textual origins in Nabokov's work. Nabokov translates the related theme of belonging (in the sense of both a continuous connection and personal property) into a theatrical context by exploring different forms of the playwright's absence which are represented by Shakespeare: as a playwright from the performance of his dramas, as a clearly identifiable author of the drama texts, and as a historical person without a verifiable biographical record. Without a clearly identifiable author, Shakespeare's texts, embedded in Nabokov's novels, become destabilised and fragmented. Shakespeare enters Nabokov's work not as a mere literary giant or as Nabokov's English Pushkin to measure himself against. After his switch to English, it is as if Nabokov had finally found in Shakespeare an appropriate theatrical framework to explore the metafictional pivotal concerns of his art which only now are developed in their entire complexity.

THE REAL LIFE OF SEBASTIAN KNIGHT
OR, TWELFTH (K)NIGHT

Nabokov's transition from Russian to English raises a series of questions concerning the complex relationship between an author and the different language versions of his texts, whether in the original or in translation. The split of the individual author into a Russian and an English version was sharpened in Nabokov's case by his change in name from Sirin to Vladimir Nabokov, underlining the twofold nature of an author who becomes part of different cultures and speaks and writes different languages. Nabokov constructed, as it were, a double or a twin of himself, similar to the way in which a translation is created as a double of a source text. Notions of 'original' and 'double' become, however, problematic the further the original vanishes into the distance: Is Sirin still the original from which the English-speaking Vladimir Nabokov was moulded? Are the Russian texts written by Sirin legitimately inherited by Nabokov? In the later autobiography, the English-speaking Nabokov would construct an identity which is deliberately distinct from and without discernable connection to the Russian Sirin: 'the author that interested me most was naturally Sirin. He belonged to my generation. Among the young writers produced in exile he was the loneliest and most arrogant one. Beginning with the appearance of his first novel in 1925 and throughout the next fifteen years, until he vanished as strangely as he had come, his work kept provoking an acute and rather morbid interest on the part of critics' (*SM*, 220).

The ensuing rivalry of different authors and translators and between different text versions is presented in analogy with the potential competition for control between the playwright and the theatrical performance. In his first English novel, Nabokov explores precisely this tense relationship that develops with an author's transition from one language to another and the ramifications this has for the relationship between the author and the realisation of his text, the instability of authorship and textual property in the overtly theatrical context of Shakespeare's *Twelfth Night*.

The Real Life of Sebastian Knight is a novel of and about uncertainties. The constant reflections and correspondences between the different narrative and fictional levels of the novel mark the tentative status of Sebastian's biography, of the texts embedded within it and of the author and the narrator.[17] The frequent allusions to a hovering presence of Sebastian inside his own biography as well as the narrator's confusing statement at the end of the novel about his supposed merging with Sebastian further support this sense of disturbing ambiguity. This uncertainty has been resolved by critics in three different lines of interpretation. While the majority assume that V. is the legitimate author of the biography,[18] some critics have suggested that the novel is a fictional biography written by Sebastian himself, posing as his half-brother.[19] A third reading of the novel reconciles these different hypotheses and also adds an occult dimension to the discussion, suggesting that V. is directed in his quest and writing by the spectral

---

[17] For an excellent discussion of the interplay between the different diegetic levels of the novels, see Shlomith Rimmon, 'Problems of Voice in Nabokov's *The Real Life of Sebastian Knight*', in Phyllis A. Roth (ed.), *Critical Essays on Vladimir Nabokov* (Boston: G. K. Hall, 1984), 109–29.

[18] See, for instance, Charles Nicol, 'The Mirrors of Sebastian Knight', in Dembo (ed.), *Nabokov: The Man and His Work*, 85–94; Page Stegner, 'The Immortality of Art: Nabokov's *The Real Life of Sebastian Knight*', *The Southern Review*, 2/2 (1966), 286–96; Anthony Olcott, 'The Author's Special Intention: A Study of *The Real Life of Sebastian Knight*', in Carl R. Proffer (ed.), *A Book of Things about Vladimir Nabokov* (Ann Arbor, MI: Ardis 1974), 104–21; Katherine Tiernan O'Connor, 'Nabokov's *The Real Life of Sebastian Knight*: In Pursuit of a Biography', in Joachim T. Baer (ed.), *Mnemozina – Studia litteraria russica in honorem Vsevolod Setchkarev* (Munich: Fink, 1974), 281–93.

[19] For this line of interpretation, see Field, *Life and Art of Nabokov*, 214; Dabney Stuart, '*The Real Life of Sebastian Knight*: Angles of Perception', *Modern Language Quarterly*, 29 (1968), 312–28 [313]; Brenda K. Marshall, 'Sebastian Speaks: Nabokov's Narrative Authority in *The Real Life of Sebastian Knight*', *Style*, 23/2 (1989), 213–23 [214].

influence of his dead half-brother.[20] In the following discussion, I will argue that the author of the biography is simultaneously V. and Sebastian, a reading which is suggested by the theatrical context of the novel.

Initially, Sebastian's novels are accessible to the actual reader only through V.'s selective quotations. In the course of the novel, however, Sebastian's novels seem to come to life. This eerie sense of Sebastian's fiction taking over V.'s quest is evoked by the numerous correspondences between Sebastian's fiction and V.'s narrative.[21] It is significantly in the magical thirteenth chapter that V. meets for the first time a character from Sebastian's fiction. Mr Silbermann is another version of Mr Siller in Sebastian's short story 'The Back of the Moon', a character V. has previously described appropriately as 'perhaps the most alive of Sebastian's creatures' (*RLSK*, 86).[22] Similarly, Pahl Rechnoy's cousin and the old man at Helen Grinstein's house, for instance, are recognisable as the 'gentle old chess player Schwarz, who sits down on a chair in a room in a house, to teach an orphan boy the moves of the knight' and the 'old man [who] sobs and is soothed by a soft-lipped girl in mourning' (*RLSK*, 147) from Sebastian's last novel, *The Doubtful Asphodel*.

From the thirteenth chapter onwards, V.'s quest itself increasingly resembles Sebastian's fiction. The scene of the wrong Roquebrune in *Lost Property* is repeated at the end of *The Real Life of Sebastian Knight* when V. sits at the bedside of the dying Monsieur Kegan and not next to his half-brother. The mixed-up letters of *Lost Property* reappear as Sebastian's final letter to V., which was initially addressed to someone else. As in Sebastian's book, *The Prismatic Bezel*, the action in the second part of *The Real Life of Sebastian Knight* shifts from a resort hotel (in Blauberg) to a secluded house (belonging to Madame Lecerf) in the countryside, where the reader can easily recognise the 'fashionable trick of grouping a medley of people in a limited space' (*RLSK*, 77). V.'s quest itself echoes *The Prismatic Bezel*, a parody of the detective genre. V.'s interpretation that in the middle of *The Prismatic Bezel* '[a] new plot, a new drama utterly

---

[20] For an 'otherworldly' reading of the novel, see Susan Fromberg, 'The Unwritten Chapters in *The Real Life of Sebastian Knight*', *Modern Fiction Studies*, 13/4, (1967–68), 427–42; William Woodin Rowe, *Nabokov's Spectral Dimension* (Ann Arbor, MI: Ardis, 1981), 21–5; Alexandrov, *Nabokov's Otherworld*, 137–59.

[21] For detailed analyses of the correspondences and analogies between Sebastian's fiction and V.'s quest, see Nicol, 'The Mirrors of Sebastian Knight'; Julia Bader, *Crystal Land: Artifice in Nabokov's English Novels* (Berkeley: University of California Press, 1972), 13–30; Rimmon, 'Problems of Voice', 112–15.

[22] The parallels between Mr Siller and Mr Silbermann have been noted by practically all critics of the story. See, for instance Nicol, 'Mirrors of Sebastian Knight', 90; Olcott, 'The Author's Special Intention', 110–11; Rimmon, 'Problems of Voice', 113.

unconnected with the opening of the story ... seems to struggle for existence and break into light' (*RLSK*, 78) could also be a description for the
shift of focus from Sebastian's life to V.'s quest for his brother's life in the
book.

In correlation to this apparent eerie autonomy of Sebastian's fiction,
the sense of a theatrical performance is evoked. The setting and scene of
Sebastian's first novel, *The Prismatic Bezel* appears to be realised in the
final phase of V.'s quest, which has the distinctive features of a theatre
performance from the moment V. meets Madame Lecerf. The apartment
where she receives V. has the 'unlived-in sham domesticity of a stage-
set', as one critic has pointed out.[23] As in a theatre play, V. feels that 'the
place drove me somehow to affected speech and manner' (*RLSK*, 128).
V.'s description of the setting in *The Prismatic Bezel* as 'a primary cross
between stage-properties and a real-estate agent's nightmare' (*RLSK*, 77)
is equally applicable to Madame Lecerf's country house, as the following
description indicates: '[The] house was large and ramshackle. A score of
unhealthy old trees represented the park ... Everything about the place
had a queer look of weariness, and shabbiness, and dustiness' (*RLSK*, 137).
The impression of a tired-looking stage set is further evoked by the 'green
room' in Madame Lecerf's house and the complete silence in the garden: 'It was all very still. The black branches, here and there studded with
green, seemed to be listening to their own inner life. Something dreary
and dull hung over the place' (*RLSK*, 141). Sebastian's novels become real
only through V.'s enactment of them in his own book. V.'s performance
of Sebastian's texts is crucial for Sebastian's art to develop a life or reality
of its own. In this sense, *The Real Life of Sebastian Knight* is a collaborative
work which is created by both Sebastian and V.

The specific theatrical context of this artistic collaboration is established
in the continuous allusions to Shakespeare who is throughout juxtaposed
with Sebastian. V. establishes a link between a passage from Sebastian's
novel *Success* and the author's personal life at the time of writing it.[24] The
quote contains a clear allusion to Shakespeare and his wife Anne. The
passage focuses on the young man, William, who has a humorous and
at the same time melancholy disposition which is reflected in the pairing
of his predilection for puns with his consciousness of man's immortality
and his idea that man constantly approaches his own death with every

---

[23] Paul B. Morgan, 'Nabokov and the Medieval Hunt Allegory', *Revue de Littérature Comparée*,
60/3 (1986), 321–7 [327].
[24] Alfred Appel, Jr also points out that '[part] of Chapter Ten of *The Real Life of Sebastian Knight* ...
[is] devoted to Shakespeare' (Nabokov, *The Annotated Lolita*, 444, n. 284/4).

moment that passes. That he considers his fiancée Anne as only another temporary affair in his love life recalls Shakespeare's abandoning of his wife Anne Hathway, which in turn is juxtaposed with Sebastian and his subsequent leaving of Clare. This parallel can be taken even further. Like Shakespeare, Sebastian leaves a domestic relationship. The mysterious woman whose identity cannot be established beyond doubt evokes the so-called 'dark lady', who betrays the poet in Shakespeare's sonnets. Significantly, Sebastian's last letter switches between addressees, just as Shakespeare's sonnets are supposed to switch between a young man and the 'dark lady'.[25] The uncertainty of Sebastian's whereabouts at the end of his life with a possible sojourn in Italy recalls the many gaps in Shakespeare's life and the repeated claims that Shakespeare might have gone to Italy, where he acquired the knowledge for his plays. Sebastian's life remains ultimately as uncertain and inaccessible as Shakespeare's biography.

The imitation of a sibling as well as the narrator's initial and Sebastian's name imply a specific Shakespearean connection with *Twelfth Night*, as Page Stegner, Shlomith Rimmon and Aleksandr Dolinin have noticed, albeit without examining the subject any further.[26] Some superficial correspondences in the constellation of the characters further suggest Shakespeare's comedy as a sub-text,[27] while the violet motif which pervades the novel hints at the Shakespearean heroine.[28] The theme of uncertain identities and disguises becomes the central concern in both the play and the novel. In both works, a sibling who through a misfortune happens to be in a strange country, is looking for a lost brother who is believed to be dead. The uncertainty of the 'estate' is a major concern for both Viola and V. Viola disguises herself 'Till I had made mine own occasion mellow / What my estate is!', which refers not only to her social standing but

[25] Halliday, *Shakespeare and His Critics*, 5c4–5.
[26] See *The Portable Nabokov*, ed. and intr. Page Stegner (New York: Penguin, 1977), xxv; Rimmon, 'Problems of Voice', 128; Aleksandr Dolinin, 'Kommentarii' [to *The Real Life of Sebastian Knight*], in Vladimir Nabokov, *Romany: Perevod s angliiskogo* (Moscow: Khudozhestvennaia literatura, 1991), 401–410 [401].
[27] See Márta Pellérdi, 'Nabokov's *The Real Life of Sebastian Knight* or, What You Will', *Kodolányi Füzetek* (*Studies on the 20th Century English Novel, Working Papers*), 5 (1999), www.mek.iif.hu/porta/szint/tarsad/irodtud/engnovel/engnovel.htm#2. Pellérdi identifies both V. and Mme Lecerf with Viola and suggests further analogies between Mr Goodman and Malvolio and between Helene von Graun and Olivia. She argues that the references to *Twelfth Night* prove that Sebastian Knight is writing his own fictional biography, while *Twelfth Night* 'with its comedy of mistaken identities serves as a source for illustrating mistaken textual ownership'.
[28] For a discussion of the violet motif, see Stuart, *Dimensions of Parody*, 7–8; Alexandrov, *Nabokov's Otherworld*, 154–5.

also to the inheritance of her father's estate.[29] V. is protective not only of the interpretation of his brother's life, but also of the financial profit to be gained from his brother's literary estate, as his threat of impending legal proceedings against Mr Goodman indicates, which adds a very practical dimension to the issue of authorial property.

The question of imitation is central to both works. As a woman in a strange country without any money, Viola might be in a more secure position as a boy or man. Yet this reason is never explicitly given in the drama, and her male attire brings her into the precarious situation of almost having to fight a duel. There is also a clearly psychological dimension to Viola's act of cross-dressing. Since Viola and Sebastian are twins, her switch of gender transforms her into her male counterpart, her brother Sebastian: 'For him I imitate.'[30] This impersonation cancels his absence, filling the void left by Sebastian, and, as it were, bringing him back to life. In a similar vein, V. enacts Sebastian's life and work. V.'s quest is intended to 'follow [Sebastian's] life stage by stage without overtaking him' (*RLSK*, 45). V. also writes in English like his brother, although he considers his English to be inferior. The alleged 'psychological affinities' (*RLSK*, 30) between Sebastian and V. are frequently emphasised by V. This emulation of Sebastian reaches its climax in the end of the novel when V. claims to have become Sebastian, essentially bringing him back to life.

Viola's disguise as a boy is the more perfect on the stage which can sustain a deliberate lack of information and hence the ambiguous identity of Cesario/Viola until the final scene. Her androgynous status is maintained even when her name is finally pronounced in the 'mirror' scene with Sebastian. Just as the audience hears Viola's name only at the very end of the drama, so the readers are left in the dark as to which Christian name the narrator's initial stands for throughout the novel. V. is at great pains to disguise himself and his name from his readers, for the sake of secrecy constructing such awkward phrases as 'My name is [I mentioned my name]' (*RLSK*, 172). Viola's identity is deliberately complicated through her switch in gender. As a man, Viola becomes unrecognisable even to her own brother when he sees her: 'Do I stand there? I never had a brother; / Nor can there be that deity in my nature / Of here and everywhere. I had a sister.'[31] V. appears to be equally disguised not only from the reader but also from other characters, who are unable to recognise him. The

---

[29] William Shakespeare, *Twelfth Night Or What You Will* (Cambridge University Press, 1985), Act I, Scene ii, lines 43–4.
[30] *Ibid.*, Act III, Scene iv, line 334.
[31] *Ibid.*, Act V, Scene i, lines 226–8.

confusion surrounding questions of gender in *Twelfth Night* is imitated in
The Real Life of Sebastian Knight in subtle and curious ways. Although V.
clearly identifies himself as Sebastian's brother, the close parallels between
Viola and V. implicitly also obfuscate V.'s gender. The novel plays with the
possibility that, like Shakespeare's heroine, V.'s male gender might actually
be a disguise. This, at least, would explain why in Mr Goodman's biography of Sebastian Knight, V. is 'bound to appear non-existent – a bogus
relative, a garrulous impostor' (*RLSK*, 6), or why even at close distance
in their chance encounter Clare does not identify V., although they met
some years before in person. It is significant in this respect that the book
opens with a reference to a woman (Olga Olegovna Orlova) incognita.
Female disguise is a theme which recurs in Sebastian's last letter when he
refers to Domrémy, where Joan of Arc first heard voices. A reference to
Joan of Arc – a woman disguised in the armour of a *knight* – is also made
in a similar context in *Lolita*, where Humbert remembers seeing Quilty's
assistant Vivian Darkbloom as 'Joan of Arc (in a performance we saw at
the local theatre)'.[32] The play with different genders in Joan of Arc's disguise and in the theatre anticipates the subsequent confusion between
the playwright and his assistant, which Lolita deliberately creates. Later,
Humbert is allowed a glimpse of 'something of the joint authors – a man's
tuxedo and the bare shoulders of a hawk-like, black-haired, strikingly tall
woman'.[33]

Grammatically V.'s gender cannot be unequivocally determined.
Despite what V. calls 'my miserable English' (*RLSK*, 29), the biography
is written not in Russian but in English. Apart from V.'s constant desire
to imitate Sebastian (who also wrote in English), this decision receives
a further meaning when one considers that Russian grammar requires
speakers (or first-person narrators) to determine their gender in the use of
adjectives or verbs in the past tense, a need for precision which is absent
in English. V.'s English translation of a key passage in Sebastian's last
letter, written in Russian, therefore disguises what a retranslation into
Russian would reveal. In the letter which Sebastian addresses initially to
his Russian lover he asks her to come and see him: 'If you can come,
come; if you can't, I shall not be offended; but it might be perhaps better if you came' (*RLSK*, 156). In Russian (as in English) the conditional
form here would be identical with the past tense form and thus require
the speaker to specify the (in this case female) gender of the addressee. In

---

[32] Nabokov, *Annotated Lolita*, 209.   [33] *Ibid.*, 221.

a retranslation into Russian, the sentence would therefore require the use of the female form of the past tense: 'Если можешь приехать, приезжай; если не можешь – я не обижусь, но все-таки лучше бы ты **приехала**'.[34] The switch from a female to a male addressee, which is unproblematic in English, would not be possible in Russian unless both addressees are of the same gender. It is only in V's English translation that this switch can happen smoothly with the different (grammatical) genders securely disguised. Outside the novel, this is mirrored in Nabokov's switch to English, fully utilising the possibilities of his new language. It is only in English that the effect of Viola's disguise on stage can be emulated in V.'s concealment behind the genderless English past tense. V.'s disguise is not only described as part of the narrative but is enacted in a performance which maintains the ambiguity in V.'s gender and identity until the end.

Nabokov plays with different gender identities from the very beginning of his writing career. The mysterious female siren-bird from Russian mythology becomes Nabokov's initial pseudonym and trade mark, creating a fresh identity distinct from his prominent father. In his first literary hoax, Nabokov donned the mask of Vivian Calmbrood, who had allegedly written the English original of the play *The Wanderers*. This female dramatist would later be transformed into Vivian Darkbloom (Vivian Damor-Blok in the Russian translation of *Lolita*), Clare Quilty's personal assistant. The ambiguous gender of Quilty's first name is incidentally exploited by Lolita to shield her lover-playwright from Humbert's suspicious eyes. The play with gender is also evident in *The Waltz Invention*, completed shortly before the work on *The Real Life of Sebastian Knight*, where Nabokov bestowed a fluid gender identity on to Waltz's assistant, Son. The specific reference to *Twelfth Night* would be highlighted in the later English translation where Son becomes a distinctly Shakespearean figure, Viola Trance.

In the more immediate context of writing *The Real Life of Sebastian Knight* and *The Waltz Invention*, Nabokov might have adapted the idea for a character with an ambiguous gender identity from Virginia Woolf's *Orlando: A Biography* (1928), which he read in 1933 in preparation for his

---

[34] In I. Gorianin's and M. Meilakh's translation of *The Real Life of Sebastian Knight* the switch in gender is avoided by opting for an impersonal construction: 'Если можешь приехать, приезжай; если нет – не обожусь; похоже, однако, что лучше приехать' (Vladimir Nabokov, *Romany: Perevod s angliiskogo* (Moscow: Khudozhestvennaia literatura, 1991), 151). In a later translation, Sergei Il'in uses a similar strategy: 'Если можешь прийти, приходи; если не сможешь, я не обижусь; но может быть, лучше будет тебе прийти' (Vladimir Nabokov, *Sobranie sochinenii amerikanskogo perioda v piati tomakh*, vol. I (St Petersburg: Simpozium, 1997), 175).

short story 'The Admiralty Spire' ('Admiralteiskaya Igla') (1933), another story in which a woman writer plays a major role. Predictably, Nabokov thought Woolf's novel to be a 'first-class example of *poshlost*'.[35] The novel purports to be a biography, which follows the life of a poet from the Elizabethan age, travelling through time and finding himself changing into a woman. Apart from *As You Like It*, another of Shakespeare's comedies which plays with shifting gender identities, *Twelfth Night* is a constant subtext in the novel, which comes to the surface, for instance, in Orlando's violet eyes, or when the book ends on the '*twelfth* stroke of mid*night*' (emphasis added).[36] Perhaps Nabokov ironically acknowledges his female colleague in the character of Sebastian's English high-strung, neurotic mother Virginia. There is only one obvious instance where Nabokov slipped into a female role in his writing as the tormented female first person narrator of 'A Slice of Life' ('Sluchai iz zhizni') (1935), who relates the gruesome events of one day in her life. Written 'for myself, my wife, and half a dozen dear dead chuckling friends' (*Stories*, 655), this parody of female confessional writings is in keeping with his general prejudice against women writers.[37] As he confessed to Edmund Wilson: 'I dislike Jane [Austen], and am prejudiced, in fact, against all women writers. They are in another class' (*NWL*, 268).[38]

Much of the effect of the gender switch in Shakespeare's play relied originally upon the complete absence of women on stage, so that a boy actor would imitate a woman imitating a boy. In *Twelfth Night*, this convoluted relationship between the boy actor and his role reflects the underlying transformation of Viola into the role she is acting, as she is strangely reluctant to give up her role even when her conversation with Antonio has given her the almost certain knowledge that her brother is alive in Illyria. Up to the end of the play, she remains a boy in her appearance, embodying her brother. Her retransformation into a woman, is, as Stephen Greenblatt points out, 'not enacted … and the only authentic transformation that the Elizabethan audiences could anticipate when the play was done was the metamorphosis of Viola back into a boy'.[39] What is only hinted at in *Twelfth Night*, is realised in *The Real Life of Sebastian Knight*. V.'s

[35] Boyd, *Russian Years*, 402.

[36] Virginia Woolf, *Orlando: A Biography* (London: Penguin, 1993), 228.

[37] See Maxim D. Shrayer, 'Vladimir Nabokov and Women Authors', *The Nabokovian*, 44 (Spring 2000), 52–63 [62].

[38] He would later revise this judgement, at least in regard to Jane Austen, and include *Mansfield Park* in his lectures on masterpieces of European literature.

[39] Stephen Greenblatt, *Shakespearean Negotiations: The Circulation of Social Energy in Renaissance England* (Berkeley: University of California Press, 1988), 92.

ambiguous (gender) identity is finally fixed when V. and Sebastian merge into one person at the end of the book. V. recognises that 'the soul is but a manner of being – not a constant state – that any soul may be yours, if you follow its undulations ... Thus – I am Sebastian Knight' (*RLSK*, 172). What previously has been a role which was taken on to get closer to Sebastian, to prolong his life, has now become an identity in its own right. It is significant that V. describes this process in explicitly theatrical terms:

I feel as if I were impersonating him on a lighted stage, with the people he knew coming and going – the dim figures of the few friends he had ... They moved round Sebastian – round me who am acting Sebastian – and the old conjuror waits in the wings with his hidden rabbit ... And then the masquerade draws to a close. The bald little prompter shuts his book, as the light fades gently. The end, the end. They all go back to their everyday life ... – but the hero remains, for, try as I may, I cannot get out of my part: Sebastian's mask clings to my face, the likeness will not be washed off. I am Sebastian, or Sebastian is I, or perhaps we both are someone whom neither of us knows. [40] (*RLSK*, 172–3)

The distance between actor and role has diminished until V. has actually become that role, claiming Sebastian's identity and reality. V. has even fulfilled Sebastian's last creative project to write a biography of Mr H., or – if one considers the identical appearance of the Cyrillic letter H which signifies the sound N – the biography of Mr N. which is the first letter of 'Nait', the Russian transliteration of 'Knight'. V.'s imitation has thus turned into metamorphosis, enacting and bringing Sebastian back to life, so that the book has ultimately been written by both V. and Sebastian, turning it into a truly collaborative work. In the very last undulation of the novel, the reader can glimpse Nabokov's own transformation. *The Real Life of Sebastian Knight* is Nabokov's rite (or right) of passage from a Russian to an English-speaking writer, and literally from Europe to the United States, leaving the bird with the face of the woman behind and taking on the identity of a writer with the unpronounceable but clearly male name Vladimir Nabokov.

"'THAT IN ALEPPO ONCE ...'", OR, KILLING A DOG

The problem of authorship recurs in another Shakespearean variation in the short story "'That in Aleppo Once...'". In 1941, while preparing his

---

[40] It is interesting to note that the slight imperfections of the mirror structure of the last sentence in the novel would be removed in Russian translation because of the absence of different forms of the verb *to be*, and the replacement of the English *or* by the Russian palindrome *ili*: Я – Себастьян или Себастьян – я.

lectures on drama, Nabokov appears to have considered writing a book
on the art of drama with the provisional title 'In Aleppo Once', a quote
from Othello's final speech before he kills himself.[41] This idea was possibly inspired by a *nota bene* in the notebook for his lectures on drama:
'The perfect end in Othello's last speech instead of "messenger-speech".[42]
One of the complaints about drama to which Nabokov returns with
unfaltering irritation in his notebooks and subsequent lectures is what
he calls 'dramatic determinism', the predictable development of a dramatic plot which unfolds according to convention and tradition. Such a
play concludes in an ending which does not 'contain any new cause that
would explode [the final scene] somewhere beyond the play' ('Tragedy',
330). With this in mind, it is easily conceivable that Nabokov applauded
Othello's admission of having killed a Turk in Aleppo at the end of the
play as an unexpected but believable confession, yet one without any
discernible consequences for the plot, an instance of 'the irrational and
illogical, … that spirit of free will that snaps its rainbow fingers in the
face of smug causality' ('Tragedy', 326). That Shakespeare avoided the use
of a reliable messenger who confirms for the audience the hero's successful suicide must have met with equal approval by Nabokov.

Nabokov's projected study of drama never reached fruition, but he used
the quote from *Othello* as the title for a short story which he wrote three
years later, '"That in Aleppo Once …"'. The theme of determining the
unfolding plot through literary convention and tradition becomes closely
interlinked with the need to determine the author behind the story.
Already in his first drama *The Tragedy of Mr Morn*, Nabokov had developed the subplot of an exile returning home and discovering his wife's
unfaithfulness against the backdrop of Shakespeare's tragedy. In '"That
in Aleppo Once …"', however, the *Othello* motif is integrated into the
story as a device that goes far beyond a general subtext for the narrator's
jealousy on account of his wife's alleged unfaithfulness. Shakespeare's tragedy becomes an integrated structural device of the story and the decisive
factor in determining who controls the story's narrative.

The story is written in the form of a letter from a Russian émigré poet
to his compatriot V., a writer in America, in which he gives an account
of his brief marriage to a woman who apparently betrayed him. As a poet
himself, the narrator is conscious of the literary tradition within which
he is constructing his narrative. Already at the beginning of the letter,
he aligns himself with Othello indirectly through the comparison with

[41] Boyd, *American Years*, 23.   [42] Nabokov, 'Notebook', VN Berg.

the 'Russian Moor' Pushkin, observing that 'retrospective romanticism ... finds pleasure in imitating the destiny of a unique genius (down to the jealousy, down to the filth, down to the stab of seeing her almond-shaped eyes turn to her blond Cassio behind her peacock-feathered fan)' (*Stories*, 561). A further parallel is suggested in the narrator's speculation that his wife might have been 'solely attracted by the obscurity of my poetry' (*Stories*, 561), which recalls Desdemona's initial attraction to Othello's stories before falling in love with the man. The interrogation of his wife is described by amalgamating excerpts from two different speeches from *Othello* into a single quote: '*The time, the place, the torture. Her fan, her gloves, her mask*' (*Stories*, 564). The first phrase, an excerpt from Lodovico's order to enforce Iago's punishment, suggests that he physically hurts his wife when she reappears, which the narrator later remembers clearly: 'she shook and rattled and dissolved in my violent grasp' (*Stories*, 565).[43] The second part alludes to Othello's suggestive questioning of Desdemona's servant Emilia.[44]

The depiction of his search for his wife also suggests a close link with the dramatic world of *Othello*. From the beginning, his narrative is pervaded by a constant sense of confusion and incoherence. The story of the abandoned dog, for instance, is undermined by the immediate assertion that the poet and the wife never had a dog, and even her imagining that they actually bought a dog is contradicted by the narrator's claim that they never had any intention of buying a dog. In a final twist, this nonexistent dog leaps into existence again when in a later conversation the narrator is accused of having killed the dog. In a similar vein, the narrator insists that despite 'documentary proofs of matrimony, I am positive now that my wife never existed' (*Stories*, 560). Like the dog, the wife's status constantly alternates between appearance and disappearance. She is reduced to a merely 'nebulous' figure in the narrator's memory: 'She would glimmer and fade, and reappear with some trifle' (*Stories*, 565). Like the dog, she reappears in the last scene, with a new husband, and is resurrected once more, waiting for the narrator at the port. These inconsistencies are the product of the narrator's almost pathological jealousy which locks him, just like Othello, inside an irrational, nightmarish inner world. A similar device is also used by Shakespeare. As early as 1850, John Wilson identified temporal inconsistencies in the play's structure as a 'double time' scheme which reflects the discrepancy between historical

---

[43] See William Shakespeare, *Othello* (Cambridge University Press, 1984), Act V, Scene ii, line 365.
[44] *Ibid.*, Act IV, Scene ii, line 8.

or external time ('long time') and Othello's confused inner state of passionate jealousy ('short time') – a manifestation of a mind that is rapidly
retreating into an inner world defined by obsessive jealousy.[45] In the story,
this sense of nightmarish unreality is strengthened in the narrator's perception of his surroundings in terms of a theatre set. He describes the
flight from Paris as 'walking through the stale stage setting of abstract
towns' (*Stories*, 562), and his visa hunting drives him to despair in 'a mock
world where millions of lives were being juggled by the clammy hands of
consuls and *commissaires*' (*Stories*, 565). While his mind unravels, reality
becomes an indefinable, shifting entity in direct correspondence with an
ever-changing dog and an equally elusive wife.

The narrator is acutely aware of the incoherencies in his narrative and
offers his material in exchange for a story, hoping that V. might 'clarify things for me through the prism of your art' (*Stories*, 568). V., however, does not transform the letter into a story but publishes it, apparently
without any textual changes. The only clear interference is V.'s choice of
a quote from *Othello* as the title against the expressed wish of the narrator, who warns V. at the end of the letter not to develop the *Othello* motif
to its logical conclusion: 'It may all end in *Aleppo* if I am not careful.
Spare me, V.: you would load your dice with an unbearable implication
if you took that for a title' (*Stories*, 568). That this reference to Othello's
final speech implies the narrator's suicide after having finished his letters
has been pointed out by most critics of the story.[46] But this allusion to
Othello's speech can be taken further in its additional implication that
the narrator might also have killed his wife, just as Othello has killed

---

[45] See John Wilson, 'Dies Borealis: Christopher Under Canvass, No. VI', *Blackwood's Edinburgh
Magazine*, 67 (April 1850), 481–512; 'Dies Borealis: Christopher Under Canvass, No. VII',
Blackwood's Edinburgh Magazine, 67 (May 1850), 622–39. Nabokov might have been acquainted
with this article, as he noticed a similar dual temporal structure in Tolstoy's *Anna Karenina*
(*Lectures on Russian Literature*, 194–7). Gennady Barabtarlo identifies the merging of different
time structures (following the Georgian and the Julian calendar) in *Pnin* (*Phantom of Fact: A
Guide to Nabokov's* Pnin (Ann Arbor, MI: Ardis, 1989), 121–3, n. 67.3).

[46] Lucy Maddox, for instance, argues that the reference to Aleppo in the title not only implies a
Shakespearean suicide, but also transforms the letter writer into a tragic character (*Nabokov's
Novels in English* (London: Croom Helm, 1983), 8). Gennady Barabtarlo remarks that 'he begs
his friend to spare him by not taking this line for a title, which would then imply that the baffled
and unhappy poet had died a Shakespearean death – or has never existed' ('Nabokov's Little
Tragedies (English Short Stories)', in his *Aerial View: Essays on Nabokov's Art and Metaphysics*
(New York: Peter Lang, 1993), 77–105 [87]). Against this, Victor Strandberg argues that it 'is
unlikely that Nabokov's narrator [...] measures up to the self-punishing grandeur of Othello's
last gesture' ('Nabokov and the "Prism of Art"', in Steven G. Kellman and Irving Malin (eds.),
Torpid Smoke: The Stories of Vladimir Nabokov (Amsterdam and Atlanta, GA: Rodopi, 2000),
189–202 [196]).

Desdemona in a jealous rage, which is further suggested by the narrator quoting Othello's expression of regret at having to kill Desdemona: '*Yet the pity of it*' (*Stories*, 568).

By mentioning specifically Aleppo, the narrator refers not only to Othello's speech but to a particular event which Othello proudly remembers:

> ... that in Aleppo once,
> Where a malignant and a turbaned Turk
> Beat a Venetian and traduced the state,
> I took by th'throat the circumcised dog
> And smote him – thus.[47]

Othello remembers killing a Turk, whom he calls 'the circumcised dog', an image which provides a link back to the notorious dog in Nabokov's story and the narrator's possible killing of it. This version of events has already been hinted at by an acquaintance who, after his wife's disappearance, accused the narrator of having hanged 'that poor beast ... with your own hands before leaving Paris' (*Stories*, 567). The dog and the wife oscillate simultaneously between existence and non-existence in the story. Both come to the fore only to vanish before reappearing again. Their similar status suggests that if the narrator, like Othello, killed the dog, he has also killed his wife.[48] The narrator's implied murder of his wife and subsequent suicide lead to another parallel with Othello. Both men attempt to control the narrative of their lives before they die, explaining and interpreting what has happened. Both rely on someone else to realise their story. Othello implores Lodovico:

> I pray you, in your letters,
> When you shall these unlucky deeds relate,
> Speak of them as they are, nothing extenuate.[49]

In a similar vein, the narrator expects V. to act as a messenger of the events he has related in his story. Like the play, the story contains its own origin in the protagonist's plea to be remembered. The narrator's description of a brief glimpse of a man who cannot be buried in the dry ground and will remain without a grave to remember him by is telling in this context.

---

[47] Shakespeare, *Othello*, Act V, Scene ii, lines 348–52.
[48] Alexander N. Drescher also argues that the narrator has killed his wife ('A Reading of Nabokov's "That in Aleppo Once ...", *zembla* (www.libraries.psu.edu/nabokov/zembla.htm)).
[49] Shakespeare, *Othello*, Act V, Scene ii, lines 341–3.

V. appears to retain the narrator's own voice by publishing the letter supposedly verbatim. This impression of honesty is supported by the quotation marks of the title, signalling the faithful retention of another voice and anticipating that the story itself consists ultimately of one long quotation, the narrator's letter.[50] That V. chooses the title of the story ensures the letter's transformation beyond its original form into a fictional short story. Yet although V. seems to act as a mere publisher, seemingly leaving the narrator's material untouched, he asserts total control over the story by choosing as a title the quote from *Othello*. It is only through V.'s deliberate refusal of the narrator's plea not to use an allusion to Aleppo in his title that the title takes on the 'unbearable implication' the narrator is so anxious to avoid. Ironically V., through the allusion to *Othello*, grants his friend's request for clarification of the unreliable narrative by determining the fate of his friend, the friend's wife and even the dog in the story. The title controls the meaning of the otherwise indeterminate and elusive narrative, killing both the narrator and his wife. It is by handing over control to his friend that the narrator commits the 'fatal mistake' he senses at the end of his letter.

In this story of cultural transition and transfer, Nabokov extends the literary field to include two classic texts of jealousy and murder from the Russian literary tradition, Tolstoy's *Kreutzer Sonata* and Chekhov's *The Shooting Party* (*Drama na okhote*, 1884–5). Nabokov had played the murderous husband of Tolstoy's tale, Pozdnyshev, in the 1920s at one of the literary trials which were staged in the Russian emigration. He prepared in detail his defence taking the audience again through the major events which led to the killing of the wife.[51] Both Tolstoy's and Chekhov's stories are told by hardly reliable first-person narrators, Pozdnyshev conveys his story to a fellow traveller during a train journey, while the narrator of *The Shooting Party* delivers the manuscript of his story to a journal editor. Pozdnyshev's obsessive jealousy leads him to murder his wife – an act which he contemplates for the first time after a disagreement about their dog, the predecessor of the unfortunate animal in Nabokov's story: 'One day as we were talking, the subject of the dog came up. I said it had

---

[50] Drescher argues that V. and Nabokov intersperse the letter with their own writings: 'The letter is a screen. Onto its surface the poet projects his confusing images; from behind V. and his creator provide glimpses, lights and shadow, data and doubts, suggesting a different tale' ('A Reading of "That in Aleppo Once …"'). Drescher's approach is problematic, as it hinges on his subjective evaluation of descriptive passages in the story which are ascribed to either Nabokov or the letter writer according to whether they are 'true poetry' or not.

[51] See Vladimir Nabokov, 'Rech' Pozdnysheva. Holograph draft of mock trial, unsigned and dated July 1927', VN Berg.

won a medal at a dog show. She said it hadn't been a medal, just a special mention. An argument began.'[52] Chekhov's tale is more complex and presents an early experiment with narrative perspective and form, which is reworked in Nabokov's story. Chekhov himself poses as the journal editor who publishes the story of a seemingly unsolved murder of a young, promiscuous girl. The narrator's mental state, bordering frequently on the delirious, shapes the increasingly confused narrative marked by gaps and inconsistencies. Just as in "'That in Aleppo Once …'", it is the editor who ultimately governs and explains the story line, leaving unmistakable clues in a few well-placed footnotes, which reveal the narrator to be also the murderer. The need to live on in art is also reflected in another ambiguous reference to Chekhov's *The Shooting Party*: 'I come to you like that gushing lady in Chekhov who was *dying to be described*' (emphasis added).[53] The wish of the young girl to die a spectacular death (like her mother who was struck by lightning) in order to become famous and be remembered comes true when she is both murdered and immortalised in fiction by the narrator.

In a typically Nabokovian self-reflexive twist, V. not only uses *Othello* but also emulates Shakespeare's method of appropriating already existing narratives for the stage. What emerges is a mysterious palimpsest of Russian and English story lines woven together to reveal the narrator's jealous guarding of his cultural and literary belonging and origin(ality). That the story appears under V.'s name further obscures the textual ownership of the story. The narrator's loss of language and identity is mirrored in the loss of an original primary narrative, which here is replaced with an extended quotation. Faithfulness and infidelity come to function here thematically on several levels. Loss of authorial control and the actual loss of a narrative are equated with the loss of love. Claims to textual property are linked with claims to one's spouse and, finally, unfaithful editing becomes here associated with marital infidelity. It is through V.'s unfaithful editing that the authorship of the story becomes unstable. This is another instance where cultural transition is linked with loss of authorial control and loss of identity – questions which are once more exposed in the theatrical context of Shakespeare's work.

---

[52] Leo Tolstoy, *The Kreutzer Sonata and Other Stories*, trans. David McDuff (London: Penguin, 2004), 81.

[53] Dmitrii Chekalov's Russian translation of the story establishes the same intertextual link in this passage: 'как та чеховская девушка в красном, мечтавшая, чтобы в нее ударила молния, лишь бы умереть на людях' (like Chekhov's girl in red, who dreamt of being struck by lightning to die before the eyes of the world) (Vladimir Nabokov, *So dna korobki: rasskazy*, trans. Dmitrii Chekalov (Moscow: Nezavisimaia gazeta, 2001), 46).

BEND SINISTER, OR, THE MOUSE-TRAP

In *Bend Sinister*, Nabokov continues to explore the self-reflexive theme of textual and authorial property in the context of Shakespeare's *Hamlet*. Just as in *The Real Life of Sebastian Knight* and "'That in Aleppo Once ...'", the very status of the author is at stake in this novel. Yet in *Bend Sinister*, the relationship between the author and the text is complicated by Nabokov's enactment of himself in the role of the fictional author-creator inside the novel, who – as part of the fictional universe –, is controlled by the external author Nabokov.[54] As in *King, Queen, Knave*, the fictional author is assigned a god-like status in the novel, which collapses as soon as he enters its fictional world. Yet the relationship between the text and its creator is far more complex than that between the puppets and their god-like puppet master. Nabokov constructs a theatrical framework in which he develops the relationship between Krug and his author(s), in analogy with the bonds between Hamlet and his ghostly father. What has only been hinted at in the preceding works becomes the central concern in *Bend Sinister*. Questions of textual legitimacy are developed further to include problems of textual and hereditary origin and originality.

Significantly, Nabokov approved of one editor's blurb which explicitly aligns *Bend Sinister* with theatre:

Bend Sinister is a dramatic fantasy of modern man menaced by the rising tyrant State ... From the opening scene in a hospital, where the hero Adam Krug's wife is dying, to the last scene where the author, like Prospero at the end of *The Tempest*, takes command of the creatures of his imagination, there is a drama of mounting, of almost intolerable intensity. The 'color' of this novel has the weird brilliance of a dream seen under Klieg lights.[55]

The conflation of Shakespeare's drama with the notion of 'a dream seen under Klieg lights' fuses the somewhat overlapping imagery of cinema and theatre in the novel. The theatrical and cinematic elements complement each other to produce what Wyllie calls 'denial through art', the

---

[54] Patterson also argues that 'the narrator who appears as a character in *Bend Sinister* is not the "real" Vladimir Nabokov ... a narrator whose existence is limited by the boundaries of the fiction he himself relates can be neither omnipotent nor omniscient' ('The Narrator as God', 248). Johnson defines this concept of 'receding worlds' as a principal element of Nabokov's fiction. In regard to *Bend Sinister*, he points out that '[while the narrator-author] is omniscient with respect to his created world, he is, in his own universe, possessed only of limited consciousness and, like his characters, strives toward the Absolute: infinite consciousness ... Each world is a level of consciousness subsumed within a larger one that creates and contains the smaller one' (*Worlds in Regression*, 203).

[55] The editor was Allen Tate, quoted in Boyd, *American Years*, 108.

exposure of the fictionality of the novel's world, which ultimately liber-
ates Krug from his torturous existence.⁵⁶ In this sense, *Bend Sinister* is
another example of Nabokov's employment of theatre and film to expose
a sham reality, just as he does at the end of *Invitation to a Beheading*,
which is in many respects similar to the collapse of the fictional world in
Bend Sinister. In regard to the question of textual status and legitimacy,
however, both film and theatre become a translating medium, appropriating and adapting an original text for a new context.

Much attention has been paid to the Shakespearean subtext in the
novel. Some obvious parallels between *Hamlet* and *Bend Sinister* have
been noted in a number of critical studies. Krug's inertia and subsequent
madness have been compared to Hamlet's indecisiveness and insanity,
while the usurper Paduk, nicknamed the Toad, seems to derive from
Claudius, whom Hamlet at one point calls 'paddock'⁵⁷ – another word
for 'toad'.⁵⁸ *Hamlet*, however, does not present a clean allegory for *Bend
Sinister*, rather it functions as a rich source from which Nabokov has
taken fragmented pieces which are re-combined in new constellations in
his novel. Don Barton Johnson interprets the Shakespeare allusions as
'part of a larger theatrical motif that pervades the novel in many ways …
the anagrammatic Shakespeare–Bacon allusions evoke the "Who wrote
Shakespeare?" motif that parallels Krug's search for his real author'.⁵⁹

The subtext of *Hamlet* comes most clearly to the fore not in the plot
itself but in the so-called *Hamlet* chapter which contains a sophisti-
cated parody of Shakespeare scholarship and interpretation. Most studies of *Bend Sinister* have paid attention to this chapter without, however,
explaining satisfactorily its relation to and relevance for the novel as a
whole. It is read as an attempt to provide 'psychological relief' for the
characters and 'comic relief' for the readers in a novel growing ever

---

⁵⁶ Wyllie, *Nabokov at the Movies*, 181.
⁵⁷ William Shakespeare, *Hamlet, Prince of Denmark* (Cambridge University Press, 1985), Act III,
Scene iv, line 191.
⁵⁸ See Lee, 'Nabokov's Political Dream'; Samuel Schuman, 'Something Rotten in the State: *Hamlet*
and *Bend Sinister*', *Russian Literature Triquarterly*, 24 (1991), 197–212. Both Lee and Schuman
establish a parallel between Hamlet's inactivity and Krug's lack of decisiveness. Both see the
opposition of the artist and a totalitarian state as a central topic of the novel and the play. Lee
sees the Hamlet motif as 'an element in the satire on the political dream' (102), while Schuman
concludes that '[both] works proclaim that art, including the art which they themselves manifest, stand in opposition to subhuman despots and rotten states' (211).
⁵⁹ Johnson, *Worlds in Regression*, 202–3. Herbert Grabes advances a similar reading, suggesting
that the question of the authorship of Shakespeare's plays 'mirrors a pervasive theme in *Bend
Sinister*, the search for the creator' ('Nabokov and Shakespeare: The English Works', in Vladimir
Alexandrov (ed.), *The Garland Companion to Vladimir Nabokov* (New York: Garland, 1995),
496–512 [501]).

darker,[60] or, in a biographical reading of the novel, it is seen as 'a private joke for Wilson, in which Nabokov parodied and perpetuated their own literary gamesmanship'.[61] Louis Feuer suggests a thematic link in that *Hamlet* provides an 'artistic mirror' for *Bend Sinister*, emphasising the parallel in the relationship between the protagonist and Providence in both the play and the novel.[62]

The central concerns of the *Hamlet* chapter are clearly marked in the dramatic form the chapter takes. The room where the conversation between Krug and Ember takes place is described, emulating stage directions: 'A fluted glass with a blue-veined violet and a jug of hot punch stand on Ember's bedtable. The buff wall directly above his bed (he has a bad cold) bears a sequence of three engravings' (*BS*, 94). Subsequently the stage directions degenerate into a hasty *nota bene* of the narrator: 'Describe the bedroom. Allude to Ember's bright brown eyes. Hot punch and a touch of fever' (*BS*, 95), and finally dissolve: 'Last chance of describing the bedroom. Too late' (*BS*, 95–6). The written stage directions give way to the performance by Ember and Krug, enacting translations, rehearsals and film adaptations of *Hamlet*. The performance character of this scene highlights Ember's and Krug's play-acting in their desperate attempt to avoid any mentioning of Olga's death. This initially artificial conversation, however, takes on an authentic character as the friends enter into 'the spirit of the game' (*BS*, 102).

The theatrical form of this chapter mirrors Krug's and Ember's topic of conversation, *Hamlet* and its possible performances. The tension between the written text and the performance is here taken to its extreme. Neither the theatre production Ember is involved in, with its nationalist-fascist agenda, nor Krug's description of a projected film adaptation, which would give a literal interpretation of the play,[63] bears any resemblance to the Shakespeare play any more.[64] Inspired by the liberty their predecessors

---

[60] Lee, 'Nabokov's Political Dream', 101.

[61] Elizabeth Susan Sweeney, 'Sinistral Details: Nabokov, Wilson, and *Hamlet* in *Bend Sinister*', *Nabokov Studies*, 1 (1994), 179–94 [181].

[62] Louis Feuer, 'The Unnatural Mirror: *Bend Sinister* and *Hamlet*', *Critique*, 30/1 (1988), 3–12 [10].

[63] Schuman has shown that the film director's idea to set Hamlet's first soliloquy in 'an unweeded garden that has gone to seed' (100) derives from a literal reading of the soliloquy itself, where Hamlet compares life to an 'unweeded garden, / That grows to seed' (Shakespeare, *Hamlet*, Act I, Scene ii, lines 135–6) ('Hamlet and *Bend Sinister*', 202).

[64] Beverly Gray Bienstock points out that in this passage, film adaptations are juxtaposed with translations between different languages, concluding that 'verbal language cannot be transformed into cinematic visuals without the loss of its own artistic reality. [...] Translation inevitably means debasement' ('Film Imagery in *Bend Sinister*', in J. E. Rivers and Charles Nicol (eds.), *Nabokov's Fifth Arc: Nabokov and Others on His Life's Work* (Austin: University of Texas Press, 1982), 125–38 [135]).

have taken, Ember and Krug amuse themselves by developing increasingly absurd ideas for performance and lines of interpretation which lead ever further away from any discernible link with the written play *Hamlet*. Ember's mock translation of Hamlet's famous soliloquy is another distortion of the original text, interpreting the first lines not as a contemplation of suicide but of murder ('*Ubit' il' ne ubit'?*' (*BS*, 106)), an interpretation which is enhanced in the French rendering '*L'égorgerai-je ou non?*' (*BS*, 106).[65] Krug's and Ember's mocking of *Hamlet* and their discussion about absurd yet theoretically possible realisations of the play raise the question of how far the text can be removed from the control of its author and maintain a legitimate claim to be still related to the original.[66] The tension between the written text and its performance on stage or screen or in translation thus crystallises questions of authorial property, control and belonging.

These issues have already been hinted at in the three engravings over Ember's bed, described at the beginning of the chapter, which raise the question of Shakespeare's identity:

Number one represents a sixteenth-century gentleman in the act of handing a book to a humble fellow who holds a spear and a bay-crowned hat in his left hand …

Number two shows the rustic (now clad in the clothes of the gentleman) removing from the head of the gentleman (now writing at the desk) a kind of shapska …

Finally, number three has a road, a traveller on foot (wearing the stolen shapska) and a road sign 'To High Wycombe'. (*BS*, 94–5)

Lee has identified the first two engravings as parts of the title page of *Cryptomenytices et cryptographiæ* (1624) by Gustavus Selenus.[67] They were reproduced, as Lee has also shown, in *Bacon is Shake-speare* (1910) by Edwin Durning-Lawrence who argues that Selenus's book was at least partly co-produced by Bacon as a sort of hiding place which would reveal to later generations that Bacon wrote the plays attributed to Shakespeare.

---

[65] In a letter to Wilson, Nabokov explained that '[the] point of *L'égorgerai-je ou non* (To be or not to be) is, of course, the well-known hypothesis that what Hamlet meant by the first words of his soliloquy was: "Is my killing of the king to be or not to be?"'(*NWL*, 212). At the same time the Russian 'Ubit' ili ne ubit'' (To kill or not to kill) is a pun on the Russian translation 'Byt' ili ne byt'' (To be or not to be) of the first line of Hamlet's famous soliloquy.

[66] Grabes points out that 'the cruel distortion [in the various politicised interpretations] of *Hamlet* proves that an author has no control over his own creation. Whatever he intends and writes, some later author, under the guise of interpretation, can re-write his story any way he pleases' ('Nabokov and Shakespeare: English Works', 502).

[67] See Lee, 'Nabokov's Political Dream', 100.

Durning-Lawrence interprets the two figures in these engravings as Shakespeare and Bacon at different stages of a transaction in which Shakespeare pretended to have written the plays which were given to him by Bacon. According to Durning-Lawrence, the first shows Bacon handing over the plays to Shakespeare, while the second picture shows Shakespeare 'lifting from the real writer's head a cap known in Heraldry as the "Cap of Maintenance"', suggesting that Bacon had to pay Shakespeare for lending his name to the plays.[68] The third engraving described in the novel does not have a direct counterpart in Durning-Lawrence's book. It might have been conflated from different elements of the first engraving which in the background shows a man with a spear (presumably the same one who is given the documents in the foreground) walking along a road. The 'road sign to High Wycombe' which is mentioned in the novel might have been inspired also by the first engraving in which an arrow is pointing at a bird in the sky carrying a written document. Durning-Lawrence is quoted verbatim in the *Hamlet* chapter with his claim that Shakespeare's famous portrait on the title page of the 1623 Folio 'is cunningly composed of two left arms and a mask' (*BS*, 95).[69] The two left arms suggest to Durning-Lawrence a clear signal by the engraver that Shakespeare did not write the plays himself.[70] The paraphrased Bacon quotation that 'the glory of God is to hide a thing, and the glory of man is to find it' (*BS*, 95) functions as an ironic comment on the limits of this quest for definite traces of Bacon's authorship in Shakespeare's plays. Much later, Nabokov would compare the 'fundamentally medieval world of Freud, with its crankish quest for sexual symbols' with 'something like searching for Baconian acrostics in Shakespeare's works' (*SM*, 18).

In the foreword which was added later, Nabokov explains that the title was 'an attempt to suggest an outline broken by refraction, a distortion in the mirror of being, a wrong turn taken by life, a sinistral and sinister world' (*BS*, 5). The novel is pervaded by the presence of another entity which creates and controls Krug's world.[71] This force or, in Nabokov's

---

[68] Durning-Lawrence, *Bacon is Shake-speare*, 129.

[69] See *ibid.*, 23.

[70] Lee also links the title with Durning-Lawrence's book but comes to a different conclusion: 'not that Bacon fathered Shakespeare's plays, but rather that the true work of art contains the world, the left as well as the right; it contains contraries that are dialectically related. And, too, like questions of parentage, the world of literature contains mysteries'. Lee goes on to argue that Durning-Lawrence '[denies] Shakespeare in the name of political and economic classes' and concludes that '[both] Paduk and Durning-Lawrence are sinister' (Lee, 'Nabokov's Political Dream', 101 and 102).

[71] For a discussion which traces the different motifs and patterns through which the fictional author reveals his presence, see Johnson, *Worlds in Regression*, 191–7.

words, this 'anthropomorphic deity' (*BS*, 11) sidles into Krug's dream as 'a nameless, mysterious genius who took advantage of the dream to convey his own peculiar code message' (*BS*, 61) and appears clearly as the fictional author of the book in the last scene, when he 'got up from among the chaos of written and rewritten pages' (*BS*, 200), and the world of *Bend Sinister* crumbles like an old theatre set. The disappearence of any link between the happy and sane world of Krug's past and the unrecognisable bizarre hell into which this author has transformed it provides an analogy with the relationship between the original text and its possibly distorted realisation in the theatre. It is not only the Toad who has usurped the state, but the text of Krug's life seems to have been claimed and illegitimately seized by an indifferent author. *Hamlet* itself provides a further analogy for this concern with textual property in its plot of an usurped kingdom, the legitimate owner of which has been murdered.

It is precisely this appropriation which is probed in the *Hamlet* chapter. Just as Hamlet's mouse-trap is designed for Claudius to expose himself, so the *Hamlet* chapter challenges the author to reveal himself. Krug's and Ember's detailed discussion of all the various methods of how to distort a text until it becomes unrecognisable simultaneously mirrors the author's distortion of Krug's life and challenges his authority as the discernible originator of the text. This twofold strategy is reminiscent of Hamlet's method in his mouse-trap, holding up the mirror to Claudius's crime and at the same time threatening him with murder through the character of Lucianus, the nephew to the king, who will murder the king in the play-within-the-play. In a letter to Nabokov, after having read *Bend Sinister*, Edmund Wilson, although entirely missing the point, indirectly confirms this reading: 'I'm sorry that you gave up the idea of having your hero confront his maker' (*NWL*, 210).

Just like Claudius, the author reveals himself by interrupting this play-within-the-play through the arrest of Ember. Significantly, the last excerpt from Ember's translation, which is quoted in full, is from Hamlet's speech after Claudius has left the theatre. The emphasis on the 'curiously bright' light at the beginning of the next chapter recalls Claudius's desperate cry for light before he leaves. The two silent organ-grinders, 'an absurd duality' (*BS*, 108) as Krug recognises, replicate the entrance of Hamlet's treacherous friends Rosencrantz and Guildenstern, 'those gentle interchangeable twins' (*BS*, 101), as Krug ironically calls them. Guildenstern is unable to fulfil Hamlet's request to play on a recorder, which Hamlet uses as a wider analogy of Guildenstern's musical incompetence and his inability to retrieve any relevant information from Hamlet: 'there is much music, excellent voice, in this little organ, yet cannot you make it speak. 'Sblood, do you think I am easier to be played on than a pipe?'[72] Hamlet's mouse-trap is also an attempt to establish the doubtful identity of the apparition. Claudius's reaction confirms to Hamlet that the ghost's claims are correct and thus that the apparition is really the ghost of his father. In a similar vein, Krug's challenge to the author in Chapter 7 is also the attempt to verify the ghostly presence of the 'anthropomorphic deity' in his life and thus his origin.

In the foreword, Nabokov informs the reader that the 'term "bend sinister" means a heraldic bar or band drawn from the left side (and popularly, but incorrectly, supposed to denote bastardy)' (*BS*, 5). This idea of heraldry conveyed in the title hints thus at the idea of a clear genealogical line which can be followed back to its beginning. Krug's attempts, however, are ultimately frustrated. Even at the end when the fictional author releases his character into madness, allowing him to recognise his own fictional nature by proving to him 'that death was but a question of style' (*BS*, 200), Krug has not glimpsed his real creator. He has seen only 'an anthropomorphic deity impersonated by [Nabokov]', as the foreword explains. The idea that Nabokov impersonates a fictional author is once more reminiscent of the Bacon–Shakespeare controversy. This specific coupling of authors is, incidentally, also manifest in the first letters of the title, B. and S. And just like Shakespeare, the ultimate author of *Bend Sinister* remains unknown to Krug whose life becomes thus a text without a clear origin, and after his son's murder, without a continuation. The clear line of ascendancy and descendancy is bent into a circle (hinted at in the Russian meaning of 'krug') without beginning or end in the appropriation of someone else's text, which becomes so distorted that it loses all connection with its past and future. It is in this sense that *Bend Sinister* is a 'bastard text', the original of which has been irrecoverably lost to Krug. Krug has literally lost the plot.

The relationship between the author and his world retains distinctly theatrical features in Nabokov's fiction also beyond his first English works. Shakespeare enters Nabokov's fiction again in *Pale Fire* (1962), a novel populated by actresses, actors and impersonators. The Shakespearean theme is here taken to its extreme in the textual thievery around which the novel revolves. Kinbote's concrete theft of Shade's manuscript literalises his appropriation of the poem in his rather imaginative commentary. The distance between the poem and Kinbote's commentary is so

---

[72] Shakespeare, *Hamlet*, Act III, Scene ii, lines 332–4.

great that Kinbote's actually corollary text becomes an entirely new entity without any connection to Shade's poem. This textual rivalry in turn is crystallised in the pale fire (stolen by the moon from the sun) in the title of the poem and the novel, stolen from *Timon of Athens* by Shakespeare, the king of literary thieves.

Shakespeare's ghost pervades all of Nabokov's English works. The period of Nabokov's linguistic transition coincides with a growing awareness of the limits of authorial control once literary works enter into and are appropriated by the public sphere. That the author's text simultaneously relies on and defies its realisation and appropriation by translations into other languages and other artistic media remains unresolved in Nabokov's fiction. Neither V. nor Sebastian gain ultimate control over their biography, while the publisher V. cannot disguise the tension between his friend's original and his appropriation of it. The gap between the original and its realisation in the world of *Bend Sinister* drives Krug ultimately insane, a situation which is thrown into relief by the fictional author's claim to the novel's world, controlled by someone beyond his awareness.

In Nabokov's own appropriation of Shakespeare, he meets his literary idol on the safe ground of his novels where he is so much more comfortably in control than on the shaky boards of theatre. He pays tribute to Shakespeare by staging his dramas in his own interpretation in his novels, renewing their importance and meaning by relating them to concerns with textual property, authorship and competing authors. Paradoxically though, these clearly Modernist concerns would have hardly been on the mind of an Elizabethan playwright before even the invention of copyright.

The notion of an original text, against which the faithfulness of its performance is measured, vanishes in Nabokov's first English works, since the origin of the text itself comes under scrutiny. The formerly rather conservative notion of one original source dissolves in the indeterminacy of collaborative work where questions of authorship and textual property become impossible to decide. *The Real Life of Sebastian Knight* is written and performed by both V. and Sebastian, the publisher of "'That in Aleppo Once …'" simultaneously reiterates and undermines the writer's narrative, realising Desdemona's alleged unfaithfulness, while in *Bend Sinister* texts and characters are left without clear origin or belonging. Throughout these works, not only Shakespeare's plays but also the vague identity of the playwright himself bring these concerns to the fore.

There is the implicit assertion that in contrast to a theatre production, behind all these convoluted and vague authorships stands the one controlling force of the real author outside his novels. Yet even this affirmation of one reliable source is ultimately undermined by the real author's enigmatic identity and his constant play-acting, constructing his own artificial persona VN. Nabokov cultivates a persona unlocated in time or place, rather like the one Shakespeare has acquired with the patina of centuries. Perhaps it was the prospect of a Shakespearean treatment by later critics and interpreters that led to Nabokov's almost excessive attempts to stay in control of his creations in his numerous forewords and interviews, railing against social, political and psychoanalytical readings of his texts. At the same time these fierce outbursts are part of his carefully created persona, which is enacted by the historical figure Vladimir Nabokov. In a sense, VN is Nabokov's playful monument to himself, a bizarre enactment of 'a cunningly composed [portrait] of two left arms and a mask'.

Conclusion: performing identities

> The I of the book cannot die in the book.
> (*Look at the Harlequins!*)

The theatricality of Nabokov's fiction is not confined to his European period. Theatricality remains a central feature of Nabokov's work after *Bend Sinister*: in the school productions Lolita longs to take part in to escape the shadow theatre of Humbert's sinister fantasies; in the tragicomic character of Pnin, whose tongue and limbs are moved by someone beyond the painted stage; in the Shakespearean drama of textual thievery and mistaken identity in *Pale Fire* and finally, in the shifting harlequin masks Vadim Vadymich tries on in *Look at the Harlequins!* The theatre also shapes Nabokov's exploration of the limits of fiction beyond his texts, in the borderlands between illusion and reality where Nabokov dons and sheds a series of masks, personae and public faces.

What is initially a fictional space clearly delineated within Nabokov's novels gradually pushes its boundaries further and further into the reality outside the book. The fictional text, as it were, creeps into the buffer zone of Genette's paratexts, the title pages, indexes and forewords which together create the transitional space of the book where the real and the imaginary meet. The paratext itself has in some ways distinctly theatrical qualities in that it locates the book as a concrete object in the immediate present tense:

And although we do not always know whether these productions [i.e. the paratext] are to be regarded as belonging to the text, in any case they surround it and extend it, precisely in order to *present* it, in the usual sense of this verb but also in the strongest sense: to *make present*, to ensure the text's presence in the world, its 'reception' and consumption in the form (nowadays, at least) of a book.[1]

---

[1] Gérard Genette, *Paratexts: Thresholds of Interpretation*, trans. Jane E. Lewin (Cambridge University Press, 1997), 1.

Akin to a ghost-like chill drifting into a room, Nabokov's books cautiously make their presence felt in the reader's world. Transgressing the border between the fictional and the real, Nabokov's books betray the reader by becoming fictional objects, written and talked about by fictional characters. Hermann intends to send his manuscript to a Russian émigré writer whose name appears indeed as the author of *Despair* on the title page. V. contemplates sending his biography of Sebastian to his brother's unfaithful lover, referring to the same book the reader is holding in his hands. And in *Invitation to a Beheading*, the very process of reading implicates the reader in Cincinnatus's death. Nabokov's texts test the permeability of the Fourth Wall barrier between their fictional reality and their material existence as books in the reader's world. Just like his plays, his novels probe the medium which conditions their existence.

This vertigo-inducing perception of a fictional world in its immediacy is a theatrical characteristic which Nabokov exploits in ever more playful permutations during the course of his career. Fictional titles overlap with the titles of Nabokov's actual books. *Despair* acts as a double title for a work which is claimed by both Hermann and Nabokov as their own authorial property. A similar confusion of fictional levels and titles also marks *Lolita* which poses simultaneously as a confession by Humbert Humbert (who suggests the alternative title 'Confessions of a White Widowed Male'), an edifying case study edited by John Ray, Jr, or a novel by Nabokov, while *Pale Fire* is at the same time a poem by John Shade, a volume of verse edited and with comments by Charles Kinbote and a piece of dazzling art by Nabokov. The two later novels in particular probe the border between fiction and reality by extending the realm of the fictional which comes to encompass the 'threshold' of fiction, title pages, forewords, commentaries and indexes.[2] Akin to actors addressing the audience from the forestage, Nabokov's books occupy a zone between fictional realities and the space–time continuum of the reader.

Nabokov himself also enters a space somewhere between reality and fiction where identity is both empirical and enacted. From the very beginning of his career, Nabokov would hide behind various masks and disguises, including his convincing performances as the playwright Vivian Calmbrood, the alleged author of *The Wanderers*, or as Vasiliy Shishkov, the melancholy émigré poet who stages and witnesses his own eclipse. These hoaxes might have been just literary games or attempts to get even with his literary rivals, but they also reveal Nabokov's preoccupation

---

[2] *Ibid.*, 2.

with the instability of biographical and textual identities. Playing a part became a necessity for an author who continuously defined and subverted the confines of the worlds he created, as Nabokov acknowledged when he donned yet another surprising mask, that of the fictional reviewer of *Speak, Memory*:

It is true that having practically stopped being a Russian writer, he is free to discuss Sirin's work as separate from his own. But one is inclined to think that his true purpose here is to project himself, or at least his most treasured self, into the picture he paints. One is reminded of those problems of 'objectivity' that the philosophy of science brings up. An observer makes a detailed picture of the whole universe but when he has finished he realizes that it still lacks something: his own self. So he puts himself in it too. But again a 'self' remains outside and so forth, in an endless sequence of projections, like those advertisements which depict a girl holding a picture of herself holding a picture of herself holding a picture that only coarse printing prevents one's eye from making out.[3]

Nabokov perpetually obscured and complicated his authorial self, creating one of his most famous roles in his pseudonym Sirin, the magical bird from Russian folklore. During a life span of twenty-odd years, the Sirin bird rose like a 'phoenix ... from the fire and ashes of revolution and exile', and single-handedly, according to Berberova, saved Russian émigré literature and its old and new writers from oblivion.[4] What was a feat in one language turned out to be an obstacle or perhaps just immaterial in another. Sirin's inextricable link to Russian literature and language made him vulnerable when Nabokov moved on to new shores and a new language, leaving Sirin, together with 'the softest of tongues', behind. In his autobiography, Nabokov himself extinguishes the bright glow of the Sirin (or phoenix) bird: 'Across the dark sky of exile, Sirin passed, to use a simile of a more conservative nature, like a meteor, and disappeared, leaving nothing much else behind him than a vague sense of uneasiness' (*SM*, 221). This astonishing vanishing act coincided with the birth of a new English-speaking writer, Vladimir Nabokov, who became ever more inventive in creating and performing new (frequently anagrammatic) identities.

This essentially theatrical convergence of real and unreal is reflected in the complex relationship of the historical writer Nabokov, his fictional representatives and his public persona VN. In the second half of his career, after his arrival in the United States, Nabokov became increasingly

[3] Vladimir Nabokov, '"Chapter sixteen" or "On *Conclusive Evidence*"', in *Speak, Memory: An Autobiography Revisited* (New York: Alfred A. Knopf, 1999), 247–61 [254].
[4] Berberova, *Italics Are Mine*, 315.

intangible, disappearing behind veils of fiction and myth. The different masks and enactments of different personae were part of a grand project of self-mystification which Nabokov staged in his later years. Autobiographical texts and forewords gradually shaped the contours of an authorial figure behind the text, standing in for its vanished younger forerunner, the unruly Sirin of Russian émigré literature. If Nabokov excelled at one particular role, it was surely in the part of Nabokov playing himself. The fame and publicity which *Lolita* brought allowed Nabokov to cultivate the role of the haughty writer in the public persona VN, his most ambiguous and complex part in which he stepped on and off the stage. From the late 1950s onwards, VN would be continuously promoted in a series of carefully controlled interviews which formed the basis for the later *Strong Opinions*. In this collection of staged conversations, Nabokov systematically collated and enacted the different aspects and traits of VN: the arrogant, pompous and self-important writer in the ivory tower, who lavished praise on some and ridiculed and condemned others. Contrary to its title, *Strong Opinions* is therefore less about Nabokov's opinions than about the creation of a persona or a mask which came to replace Nabokov in public while gaining a life of its own. In this display of what Irina Paperno calls 'deliberate aesthetic organization of behaviour', the writer Nabokov himself becomes a paratextual construct, a guard on the threshold between fiction and non-fiction who deters and entices readers at the same time.[5]

Nabokov's work is pervaded by the awareness that identity is always enacted. This is true not only of Nabokov's characters and narrators, so many of whom try to be someone else, but also of Nabokov himself. His texts incessantly realise Barthes' crucial distinction between different textual voices: '*who speaks* (in the narrative) is not *who writes* (in real life) and *who writes* is not *who is*' (emphasis in original).[6] Even in those instances when he appears as himself, Nabokov as the one *who is* does not coincide with the one *who writes*. The very act of saying 'I' is, like a theatrical performance, inextricably linked to a unique moment in the present tense. The fleeting existence of the 'I' belongs to the utterance of the 'here and now', rather than to the 'then and there' of the written text.[7]

---

[5] Irina Paperno and Joan Delaney Grossman (eds.), *Creating Life: The Aesthetic Utopia of Russian Modernism* (Stanford University Press, 1994), p. 2.

[6] Roland Barthes, 'Introduction to the Structural Analysis of Narratives', in *A Barthes Reader* (London: Vintage, 1993), 251–95 [283].

[7] See Paul Ricoeur, *Oneself as Author*, trans. Kathleen Blamey (University of Chicago Press, 1992), 40–55.

The representational gap between the man and the pronoun, or between the one *who speaks* and the one *who writes*, or between the immediate present and the already encroaching past, transforms the writing of 'I' into a performance, in which Nabokov is and is not himself. The paradox of writing 'I' remains unresolved in his fiction and is playfully explored in Nabokov's first-person narrators such as Hermann or V. who try to write themselves into existence. In *Speak, Memory*, which might be Nabokov's most complex exploration of narrative voice and self, Nabokov both subverts and asserts the stability of his older self who delights in his many younger selves: 'In looking at it from my present tower I see myself as a hundred different young men at once, all pursuing one changeful girl in a series of simultaneous or overlapping love affairs' (*SM*, 185). In some ways a bizarre sequel to his autobiography, *Strong Opinions* provides a site where the man and the writer, or the private Nabokov and the public writer, the one *who is* and the one *who writes*, approach each other but never quite meet.

There are few texts in which the pronoun 'I' seems to designate Nabokov as the one *who is*, and in these cases the 'I' rarely appears without a companion, a 'you' – the Véra Nabokov of *Speak, Memory* and the various (absent) interviewers of *Strong Opinions*. The otherness of the listener and audience is central to the formation and creation of identity, as Paul Ricoeur has argued: 'every advance made in the direction of the selfhood of the speaker or the agent has as its counterpart a comparable advance in the otherness of the partner.'[8] While in *Strong Opinions*, the you of the interviewer creates the (false) impression of a spontaneous conversation in the present tense, in *Speak, Memory*, the 'you' emerges as an interlocutor who anchors the narrative self in the present tense in more than just a grammatical sense. Nabokov's elusive selves appear to create a closed, self-indulgent hall of mirrors which reflects the author's constantly multiplying likenesses, capturing him on a stage where he performs as both player and spectator. Yet, in a typically paradoxical statement, Nabokov finds an escape route by simultaneously dismissing and validating his readers as an integral 'other' or a 'you' of the creative process: 'I don't think that an artist should bother about his audience. His best audience is the person he sees in his shaving mirror every morning. I think that the audience an artist imagines, when he imagines that kind of thing, is a room filled with people wearing his own mask' (*SO*, 18). In Nabokov's fiction, the reader is always implicitly present, an audience that will act as the necessary other in the performance of identity. In public, Nabokov's readers are frequently dismissed, patronised or reprimanded, although – or perhaps because – they play a crucial role in reflecting and sustaining the enduring existence of Nabokov's selves.

Unsteady, flighty and ephemeral, butterflies in Nabokov's work encapsulate the inherent instability of the self in fiction and life. They come into existence through a remarkable transformation from wingless caterpillar into soaring butterfly, and they survive by mimicking something or someone else. With their capacity for enchanting metamorphoses and deceptive imitation, butterflies are suggestive of the essentially theatrical nature of identity. In the famous passage on nature and artifice in his autobiography, Nabokov marvels at the miraculous spectacle of a caterpillar's mimicry in explicitly theatrical terms:

> Consider the tricks of an acrobatic caterpillar (of the Lobster Moth) which in infancy looks like bird's dung, but after molting develops scrabbly hymenopteroid appendages and baroque characteristics, allowing the extraordinary fellow to play two parts at once (like the actor in Oriental shows who *becomes* a pair of intertwisted wrestlers): that of a writhing larva and that of a big ant seemingly harrowing it. … When a butterfly has to look like a leaf, not only are all the details of a leaf beautifully rendered but marking mimicking grub-bored holes are generously thrown in. 'Natural selection,' in the Darwinian sense, could not explain the miraculous coincidence of imitative aspect and imitative behavior. (*SM*, 98)

The changeable identity of butterflies is matched by their constant movement. In the butterfly chapter of his autobiography, Nabokov constructs an extended sentence which mimics the breathless itinerary of a butterfly journey eastwards all the way from Vyra to Boulder in Colorado. Metamorphosis and transition merge in the butterfly – an implicit (and somewhat Romantic) metaphor for Nabokov, the exile, fluttering and flitting between different countries and continents, transforming himself from a Russian into an American writer.

The butterfly's restless, transitory movement is both alluring and vexing for the butterfly hunter. Nabokov's passion for butterflies finds its fulfilment in the singularly pleasurable and satisfying – almost erotic – act of arresting their movement. The detailed description of the professional killing of a butterfly merges with Nabokov's experience of something approaching death. In this scene, Nabokov is both hunter and hunted, killer and killed, collector and butterfly:

> Once, as a grown man, I was under ether during appendectomy, and with the vividness of a decalcomania picture I saw my own self in a sailor suit mounting

a freshly emerged Emperor moth … It was all there, brilliantly reproduced in my dream, while my own vitals were being exposed: the soaking, ice-cold absorbent cotton pressed to the insect's lemurian head; the subsiding spasms of its body; the satisfying crackle produced by the pin penetrating the hard crust of its thorax; the careful insertion of the point of the pin in the cork-bottomed groove of the spreading board; the symmetrical adjustment of the thick, strong-veined wings under neatly affixed strips of semitransparent paper. (*SM*, 95)

The movement of the butterfly which had still *dipped, dodged* and *soared* across the previous paragraph is now halted by distinctly static notions (*ice-cold, subsiding spasms, hard crust, affixed*). The killing of the butterfly, climactic and ecstatic in Nabokov's description, appears to satisfy a deeply felt desire to freeze its movement. Yet the butterfly's death guarantees its ultimate survival. The fleeting beauty of the butterfly is fixed permanently by two different kinds of paper, the semitransparent paper strips fastening its wings and the paper of Nabokov's autobiography. Here they can be observed and preserved for future viewers and readers. Another life continues under the cover of glass cases or books.

Feeling his own death approach, Sebastian Knight disguises the painful destruction of some treasured love letters behind a lyrically wistful contemplation on the life and death of texts:

Some day you may come upon certain papers; you will burn them at once; true, they have heard voices … but now they must suffer the stake. I kept them, and gave them night-lodgings … because it is safer to let such things sleep, lest, when killed, they haunt us as ghosts. One night, when I felt particularly mortal, I signed their death warrant, and by it you will know them. (*RLSK*, 156)

Thanks to Sebastian's conscientious brother and incompetent biographer V., the letters burn eventually at the stake, retaining their mystery. Yet, as if to confirm another Russian writer's famous dictum that 'manuscripts don't burn', Sebastian's mistress, his fiction and ultimately Sebastian himself remain 'laughingly alive' (*RLSK*, 44) throughout V.'s biography. In an aesthetically pleasing twist, *The Real Life of Sebastian Knight* foreshadows the final chapter in Nabokov's life story. His last novel, *The Original of Laura*, has recently come 'laughingly alive' in the author's absence. The book itself, an elaborate affair of removable index cards, allows both a glimpse of an intriguing illusion of originals and reflections and an intimate insight into the workshop of fragmented notes and notions behind it. This twofold view on his art provides a singularly suitable conclusion to the creative work and created life of Vladimir Nabokov – his last work staged in his absence as befits the evasive exiled author and playwright.

Nabokov remains one of the most intangible writers, having successfully dodged several attempts to pin him down biographically on the spreading board of canonised writers. Nabokov, whoever he might be, recedes into the background and dissolves into his art in an ultimately theatrical gesture which asserts the autonomous reality and identity of his art.

Bibliography

WORKS BY VLADIMIR NABOKOV

The Annotated Lolita, ed. Alfred Appel, Jr (London: Penguin, 1995).

Bend Sinister (London: Penguin, 1974).

'"Chapter Sixteen" or "On *Conclusive Evidence*"', in *Speak, Memory: An Autobiography Revisited* (New York: Alfred A. Knopf, 1999), 247–61.

'Chelovek iz SSSR' [Act One], *Rul'*, 1 January 1927, 2–3.

The Collected Stories (London: Penguin, 1997).

'Dedushka', *Rul'*, 14 October 1923, 5–6.

Despair (London: Peng uin, 1981).

Drugie berega (Ann Arbor, MI: Ardis, 1978).

'Dva otryvka iz "Gamleta"', *Rul'*, 19 October 1930, 2.

The Eye (London: Penguin, 2010).

'Gamlet', *Rul'*, 23 November 1930, 2.

Gesammelte Werke, ed. Dieter E. Zimmer (Reinbeck: Rowohlt, 1991–).

The Gift (London: Penguin, 1981).

Invitation to a Beheading (London: Penguin, 1963).

'Iubilei', *Rul'*, 18 November 1927, 2.

'Izobretenie Val'sa', *Russkie zapiski*, 11 (November 1938), 3–62.

King, Queen, Knave (London: Penguin, 1993).

Laughter in the Dark (London: Penguin, 1969).

Lectures on Don Quixote, ed. Fredson Bowers (San Diego, New York and London: Bruccoli Clark, Harcourt Brace Jovanovich Publishers, 1981).

Lectures on Literature, ed. Fredson Bowers (San Diego, New York and London: Bruccoli Clark, Harcourt Brace and Company, 1980).

Lectures on Russian Literature, ed. Fredson Bowers (San Diego, New York and London: Bruccoli Clark Layman, Harcourt Brace and Company, 1981).

'L'Envoi: Shakespeare', trans. Dmitri Nabokov, in Jane Grayson, Arnold McMillin and Priscilla Meyer (eds.), *Nabokov's World*, vol. II: *The Shape of Nabokov's World* (Basingstoke: Palgrave, 2002), 216–19.

Look at the Harlequins! (London: Penguin, 1980).

The Luzhin Defense, trans. Michael Scammell in collaboration with the author (London: Penguin, 2000).

The Man from the USSR and Other Plays, trans. Dmitri Nabokov (San Diego, New York and London: Bruccoli Clark, Harcourt Brace Jovanovich Publishers, 1984).

Nikolai Gogol, corrected edn (New York: New Directions, 1961).

Novels 1955–1962 (New York: The Library of America, 1996).

The Original of Laura (Dying is Fun): A Novel in Fragments (London: Penguin, 2009).

Pale Fire (London: Penguin, 1991).

'Pamiati I. V. Gessena', *Novoe russkoe slovo*, 31 March 1943, 2. Reprinted in Vladimir Nabokov, *Sobranie sochinenii russkogo perioda v piati tomakh* (St Petersburg: Simpozium, 1999–2000), vol. v, 594–6.

'Pamiati Iu. I. Aikhenval'da', *Rul'*, 23 December 1928, 5. Reprinted in Vladimir Nabokov, *Sobranie sochinenii russkogo perioda v piati tomakh* (St Petersburg: Simpozium, 1999–2000), vol. ii, 667–8.

P'esy, ed. Ivan Tolstoi (Moscow: Iskusstvo, 1990).

Pnin (London: Penguin, 1997).

Poems and Problems (New York and Toronto: McGraw-Hill Company, 1970).

'Polius', *Rul'*, 14 August 1924, 2–3; 16 August 1924, 2–3.

The Portable Nabokov, ed. and intr. Page Stegner (New York: Penguin, 1977).

'Pushkin, or the Real and the Plausible', trans. Dmitri Nabokov, *New York Review of Books*, 35/5 (1988), 38–42. Originally published in French as 'Pouchkine ou le vrai et le vraisemblable', *La Nouvelle Revue française*, 25/282 (1 March 1937), 362–78.

The Real Life of Sebastian Knight (London: Penguin, 1995).

Romany: Perevod s angliiskogo (Moscow: Khudozhestvennaia literatura, 1991).

'Rupert Bruk', *Grani*, 1 (1922), 212–3:. Reprinted in *Sobranie sochinenii russkogo perioda v piati tomakh* (St Petersburg: Simpozium, 1999–2000), vol. i, 728–44.

'Shakespeare', trans. Dmitri Nabokov, *Nabokov Online Journal*, 3 (2009) (http://etc.dal.ca/noj/volume3/articles/11b_Dmitri%20Nabokov_Transl_SHAKESPEARE.pdf).

'Shekspir', in Vladimir Nabokov, *Stikhi* (Ann Arbor, MI: Ardis, 1979), 156–7.

Sirin, V. 'Pis'mo v redaktsiiu: Po povodu retsenzii M. Zheleznova', *Novoe russkoe slovo*, 11 April 1941).

'Skital'tsy', *Grani*, 2 (1923), 69–99.

'Smert'', *Rul'*, 20 May 1923, 13; 24 May 1923, 5–6.

Sobranie sochinenii russkogo perioda v piati tomakh (St Petersburg: Simpozium, 1999–2000).

Sobranie sochinenii amerikanskogo perioda v piati tomakh (St Petersburg: Simpozium, 1999–2000).

'Sobytie', *Russkie zapiski*, 4 (April 1938), 43–104.

So dna korobki: rasskazy, trans. Dmitrii Chekalov (Moscow: Nezavisimaia gazeta, 2001).

Speak, Memory: An Autobiography Revisited (London: Penguin, 1969).

Stikhotvoreniia, ed. M. E. Malikova (St Petersburg: Akademicheskii proekt, 2002).

The Stories of Vladimir Nabokov (New York: Alfred A. Knopf, 1995).

Strong Opinions (New York: Vintage, 1990).
'Tragediia Gospodina Morna', *Zvezda*, 4 (1997), 9–98.
Tragediia Gospodina Morna: P'esy, lektsii o drame, ed. Andrei Babikov (St Petersburg: Azbuka, 2008).
Transparent Things (New York: Vintage, 1989).
Vesna v Fial'te i drugie rasskazy (New York: Chekhov, 1956).
The Waltz Invention, trans. Dmitri Nabokov (New York: Phaedra, 1966).

ARCHIVAL SOURCES

BAKHMETEFF ARCHIVE OF RUSSIAN AND EAST EUROPEAN CULTURE, RARE BOOK AND MANUSCRIPT LIBRARY, BUTLER LIBRARY, COLOMBIA UNIVERSITY

Nikolai Nikolaevich Evreinov Papers
Il'ia Dmitrievich Surguchev Papers

BEINECKE RARE BOOK AND MANUSCRIPT LIBRARY, YALE UNIVERSITY LIBRARY

Nina Berberova Papers

DÉPARTEMENT DES ARTS DU SPECTACLE, BIBLIOTHÈQUE NATIONALE DE FRANCE

Fond Nicolas Evreinoff

HENRY W. AND ALBERT A. BERG COLLECTION OF ENGLISH AND AMERICAN LITERATURE, NEW YORK PUBLIC LIBRARY

Vladimir Nabokov Papers

MANUSCRIPT DIVISION, LIBRARY OF CONGRESS, WASHINGTON DC

Vladimir Nabokov Papers

STANFORD UNIVERSITY ARCHIVES

Annual Report of the President of Stanford University

PUBLISHED SOURCES

Adamovich, Georgii, 'Rets.: *Russkie zapiski*, 1938, No. 11', *Poslednie novosti*, 24 November 1938, 3. Reprinted in N. G. Mel'nikov and O. A. Korosteleva (eds.), *Klassik bez retushi: Literaturnyi mir o tvorchestve Vladimira Nabokova* (Moscow: Novoe literaturnoe obozrenie, 2000), 175–6.

'"Russkie zapiski". No. 4', *Poslednie novosti*, 21 April 1938, 3. Reprinted in N. G. Mel'nikov and O. A. Korosteleva, *Klassik bez retushi: Literaturnyi mir o tvorchestve Vladimira Nabokova* (Moscow: Novoe literaturnoe obozrenie, 2000), 166–9.

Alexandrov, Vladimir, *Nabokov's Otherworld* (Princeton University Press, 1991).

Alter, Robert, '*Invitation to a Beheading*: Nabokov and the Art of Politics', *TriQuarterly* **17** (1970), 41–59. Reprinted in Julian W. Connolly (ed.), *Nabokov's* Invitation to a Beheading: *A Critical Companion* (Evanston, IL: Northwestern University Press, 1997), 47–65.

Appel, Alfred, Jr, 'Introduction', in Vladimir Nabokov, *The Annotated Lolita*, ed. Alfred Appel, Jr (London: Penguin, 1995), xvii-lxxiii.

Nabokov's Dark Cinema (New York: Oxford University Press, 1974).

Archer, William, *Play-Making: A Manual of Craftsmanship* (London, 1913).

Aseev, B. N., *Russkii dramaticheskii teatr ot ego istokov do kontsa XVIII veka* (Moscow: Iskusstvo, 1977).

Aston, Elaine and George Savona, *Theatre as Sign-System: A Semiotics of Text and Performance* (London: Routledge, 1991).

Babich, D., 'Kazhdyi mozhet vyiti iz zala: Teatralizatsiia zla v proizvedeniiakh Nabokova', *Voprosy literatury*, **5** (September–October 1999), 142–57.

Babikov, Andrei, '*The Event* and the Main Thing in Nabokov's Theory of Drama', *Nabokov Studies*, **7** (2002/03), 151–76 [trans. from the Russian: '"Sobytie" i samoe glavnoe v dramaticheskoi kontseptsii V. V. Nabokova', in B. V. Averin *et al.* (eds.), *V. V. Nabokov: Pro et contra*, 2 vols. (St Petersburg: Izdatel'stvo russkogo khristianskogo gumanitarnogo instituta, 1997–2001), vol. II, 558–86.]

'Izobretenie teatra', in Vladimir Nabokov, *Tragediia Gospodina Morna: P'esy, lektsii o drame*, ed. Andrei Babikov (St Petersburg: Azbuka-klassika, 2008), 5–42.

'Primechaniia [*Izobretenie Val'sa*]', in Vladimir Nabokov, *Sobranie sochinenii russkogo perioda v piati tomakh* (St Petersburg: Simpozium, 1999–2000), vol. V, 771–80.

'Primechaniia [*Sobytie*]', in Vladimir Nabokov, *Sobranie sochinenii russkogo perioda v piati tomakh* (St Petersburg: Simpozium, 1999–2000), vol. V, 755–71.

'"Tol'ko poshliaki khodiat maiatnikom": Podpis' Nabokova na kholste *Sobytiia*', zembla (www.libraries.psu.edu/nabokov/zembla.htm)

Bader Julia, *Crystal Land: Artifice in Nabokov's English Novels* (Berkeley: University of California Press, 1972).

Balestrini, Nassim W., 'Art and Marriage in Vladimir Nabokov's "Music" and Lev Tolstoy's "The Kreutzer Sonata"', in Steven G. Kellman and Irving Malin (eds.), *Torpid Smoke: The Stories of Vladimir Nabokov* (Amsterdam and Atlanta, GA: Rodopi, 2000), 53–73.

'Vladimir Nabokov's *Invitation to a Beheading* and Igor Stravinsky's *Petrushka*', in Lisa Zunshine (ed.), *Nabokov at the Limits: Redrawing Critical Boundaries* (New York and London: Garland,1999), 87–109.

Barabtarlo, Gennady, 'Nabokov's Little Tragedies (English Short Stories)', in his *Aerial View: Essays on Nabokov's Art and Metaphysics* (New York: Peter Lang, 1993), 77–105.

'Nabokov's Trinity (On the Movement of Nabokov's Themes)', in Julian Connolly (ed.), *Nabokov and His Fiction: New Perspectives* (Cambridge University Press, 1999), 109–38.

Phantom of Fact: A Guide to Nabokov's Pnin (Ann Arbor, MI: Ardis, 1989)

'See under Sebastian', *The Nabokovian*, **24** (Spring 1990), 24–9.

Barish, Jonas, *The Antitheatrical Prejudice* (Berkeley: University of California Press, 1981).

Barthes, Roland, 'The Death of the Author', in Vincent B. Leitch (ed.), *The Norton Anthology of Theory and Criticism* (New York and London: W. W. Norton and Company, 2001), 1466–70.

'From Work to Text', in Vincent B. Leitch (ed.), *The Norton Anthology of Theory and Criticism* (New York and London: W. W. Norton and Company, 2001), 1470–75.

'Introduction to the Structural Analysis of Narratives', in *A Barthes Reader* (London: Vintage, 1993), 251–95.

Baumann, Richard, 'Performance', in Erik Barnow (ed.), *The International Encyclopedia of Communications* (New York and Oxford: Oxford University Press, 1989), 262–66.

Bell, John (ed.), *Puppets, Masks and Performing Objects* (Cambridge, MA and London: MIT Press, 2001).

Bennet, Andrew, *The Author* (London and New York: Routledge, 2005).

Berberova, Nina, *The Italics Are Mine*, trans. Phillipe Radley (New York: Alfred A. Knopf, 1992).

Kursiv moi: Avtobiografiia (Moscow: Soglasie, 1996).

Bethea, David M., *Khodasevich: His Life and Art* (Princeton University Press, 1983).

'Style', in Vladimir Alexandrov (ed.), *The Garland Companion to Vladimir Nabokov* (New York: Garland, 1995), 696–703.

Bienstock, Beverly Gray, 'Film Imagery in *Bend Sinister*', in J. E. Rivers and Charles Nicol (eds.), *Nabokov's Fifth Arc: Nabokov and Others on His Life's Work* (Austin: University of Texas Press, 1982), 125–38.

Biukling, Liisa, *Mikhail Chekhov v zapadnom teatre i kino* (St Petersburg: Akademicheskii proekt, 2000).

Blackwell, Stephen H., *Zina's Paradox: The Figured Reader in Nabokov's* Gift (New York: Peter Lang, 2000).

Blok, Aleksandr, *Sobranie sochinenii v vos'mi tomakh* (Moscow: Gosudarstvennoe izdatel'stvo khudozhestvennoi literatury, 1960–3).

Böhmig, Michaela, *Das russische Theater in Berlin 1919–1931* (Munich: Otto Sagner, 1990).

Borovsky, Victor, *A Triptych from the Russian Theatre: The Komissarzhevskys* (London: Hurst and Company, 2001).

Boyd, Brian, '"Even Homais Nods": Nabokov's Fallibility, or, How to Revise *Lolita*', *Nabokov Studies*, **2** (1995), 62–86.

Vladimir Nabokov: The American Years (London: Vintage, 1991).

Vladimir Nabokov: The Russian Years (Princeton University Press, 1990).

'"Welcome to the Block": *Priglashenie na kazn' / Invitation to a Beheading*, a Documentary Record', in Julian W. Connolly (ed.), *Nabokov's* Invitation to a Beheading: *A Critical Companion* (Evanston, IL: Northwestern University Press, 1997), 141–79.

Braun, Edward, *Meyerhold: A Revolution in Theatre* (London: Methuen, 1998).

Brodskii, Boris 'Chelovek iz SSSR (Na postanovke p'esy V Sirina)', *Rul'*, 5 April 1927, 5.

Brook, Peter, *The Empty Space* (London: McGibbon and Kee, 1968).

Brown, Clarence, 'Krazy, Ignatz, and Vladimir: Nabokov and the Comic Strip', in Gavriel Shapiro (ed.), *Nabokov at Cornell* (Ithaca, NY and London: Cornell University Press, 2003), 251–63.

Brown, John Russell (ed.), *The Oxford Illustrated History of Theatre* (Oxford University Press, 1995).

Büchner, Georg, *Leonce and Lena, Lenz, Woyzeck*, trans. Michael Hamburger (University of Chicago Press, 1972).

Bukhs, Nora, 'The Novel Waltz (On the Structure of *King, Queen, Knave*)', *zembla* (www.libraries.psu.edu/nabokov/zembla.htm) [translated from the French: 'Sur la structure du roman de Vl. Nabokov *Roi, Dame, Valet*', *Revue des études slaves*, **59**/4 (1987), 799–810].

Bunnell, Charlene E., *"All the World's a Stage": Dramatic Sensibility in Mary Shelley's Novels* (New York and London: Routledge, 2002).

Bulgakov, Mikhail, *Dni Turbinykh. Poslednie dni (A. S. Pushkin)* (Moscow: Iskusstvo, 1955).

Byrne, Paula, *Jane Austen and the Theatre* (London: Hambledon and London, 2002).

Carlson, Marvin, 'Theatrical Performance: Illustration, Translation, Fulfillment, or Supplement?', *Theatre Journal*, **37**/1 (1985), 5–12.

Performance: A Critical Introduction (London and New York: Routledge, 1996).

Carnicke, Sharon Marie, *The Theatrical Instinct: Nikolai Evreinov and the Russian Theatre of the Early Twentieth Century* (New York: Peter Lang, 1989).

Carroll, William C., 'The Cartesian Nightmare of *Despair*', in J. E. Rivers and Charles Nicol (eds.), *Nabokov's Fifth Arc: Nabokov and Others on His Life's Work* (Austin: University of Texas Press, 1982), 82–104.

Chekhov, Anton, *Sobranie sochinenii v dvenadtsati tomakh* (Moscow: Gosudarstvennoe izdatel'stvo khudozhestvennoi literatury, 1960–1964).

Chervinskaia, L., 'Po povodu "Sobytiia" V. Sirina', *Krug*, **3** (November 1938), 168–70. Reprinted in N. G. Mel'nikov and O. A. Korosteleva (eds.), *Klassik* *bez retushi: Literaturnyi mir o tvorchestve Vladimira Nabokova* (Moscow: Novoe literaturnoe obozrenie, 2000), 173–4.

Christiansen, Richard, 'A Bizarre but Problematic Tragifarce', *Chicago Tribune*, 7 May 1998, 2.

Clayton, Douglas J., *Pierrot in Petrograd: The Commedia dell'Arte/Balagan in Twentieth-Century Russian Theatre and Drama* (Montreal: McGill-Queen's University Press, 1993).

Connolly, Julian W., 'The Function of Literary Allusion in Nabokov's *Despair*', *Slavic and East European Journal*, **26**/3 (1982), 302–13.

Connolly, Julian W. (ed.), *Nabokov's* Invitation to a Beheading: *A Critical Companion* (Evanston, IL: Northwestern University Press, 1997).

'"Nature's Reality" or Humbert's "Fancy"? Scenes of Reunion and Murder in *Lolita*', *Nabokov Studies*, **2** (1995), 41–61.

Cornwell, Neil, 'Paintings, Governesses and "Publishing Scoundrels": Nabokov and Henry James', in Jane Grayson, Arnold McMillin and Priscilla Meyer (eds.), *Nabokov's* World, vol. II: *Reading Nabokov* (Basingstoke: Palgrave, 2002), 96–116.

Danilov, S. S., *Ocherki po istorii russkogo dramaticheskogo teatra* (Moscow: Iskusstvo, 1948).

Davis, Tracy C. and Thomas Postlewait (eds.), *Theatricality* (Cambridge University Press, 2003).

Davydov, Sergej, '*Despair*', in Alexandrov (ed.), *The Garland Companion to Vladimir Nabokov* (New York: Garland, 1995), 88–101.

"*Teksty-Matreški*" *Vladimira Nabokova* (Munich: Otto Sagner, 1982).

Dear Bunny, Dear Volodya: The Nabokov-Wilson Letters, 1940–1971, ed. Karlinsky Simon, revised and expanded edn (Berkeley: University of California Press, 2001).

Derrida, Jacques, *De la grammatologie* (Paris: Éditions de Minuit, 1967).

de Vries, Gerard and Donald Barton Johnson, *Nabokov and the Art of Painting* (Amsterdam University Press, 2006).

Dickinson, Linzy Erika, *Theatre in Balzac's* La Comédie humaine (Amsterdam and Atlanta, GA: Rodopi, 2000).

Diment, Galya, 'Plays', in Vladimir Alexandrov, (ed.), *The Garland Companion to Vladimir Nabokov* (New York: Garland, 1995), 586–99.

Dolinin, Aleksandr., 'Istinnaia zhizn' pisatelia Sirina: Posle "Dara"', in Vladimir Nabokov, *Sobranie sochinenii russkogo perioda v piati tomakh* (St Petersburg: Simpozium, 2000), vol. v, 9–39.

'Kommentarii' [to *The Real Life of Sebastian Knight*], in Vladimir Nabokov, *Romany: Perevod s angliiskogo* (Moscow: Khudozhestvennaia literatura, 1991), 401–10.

'Nabokov's Time Doubling from *The Gift* to *Lolita*', *Nabokov Studies*, **2** (1995), 3–40.

Dolinin, Aleksandr and Olga Skonechnaia, 'Primechaniia [*Otchaianie*]', in Vladimir Nabokov, *Sobranie sochinenii russkogo perioda v piati tomakh* (St Petersburg: Simpozium, 2000), vol. III, 755–78.

Drescher, Alexander N., 'A Reading of Nabokov's "That in Aleppo Once…"', *zembla* (www.libraries.psu.edu/nabokov/zembla.htm).

Durning-Lawrence, Edwin, *Bacon is Shake-speare* (London: Gay and Hancock, 1910).

Edmunds, Jeff, 'Look at Valdemar! (A Beautified Corpse Revisited)', *Nabokov Studies*, **2** (1995), 153–71.

Elam, Keir, *The Semiotics of Theatre and Drama* (London: Methuen, 1980).

Engel, Christine, 'Andrei Eshpai: *The Event* (*Sobytie*, 2007)', *KinoKultura: New Russian Cinema*, **26** (2009) (www.kinokultura.com/2009/23r-sobytie.shtml).

Esslin, Martin, *The Theatre of the Absurd* (London: Methuen, 2001).

Ettinger, Albert, *Der Epiker als Theatraliker: Thomas Manns Beziehung zum Theater in seinem Leben und Werk* (Frankfurt am Main: Peter Lang, 1988).

Evreinov, Nikolai, *Pamiatnik mimoletnomu (iz istorii emigrantskogo teatra)* (Paris, 1953).

'Teatr i eshafot: K voprosu o proiskhozhdenii teatra kak publichnogo insti-tuta', in Vladislav Ivanov (ed.), *Mnemozina: Dokumenty i fakty iz istorii russkogo teatra xx veka*, (Moscow: GITIS, 1996–), vol. I, 14–44.

Farmer, David Hugh, *The Oxford Dictionary of Saints*, 5th edn (Oxford University Press, 2003).

Feuer, Louis, 'The Unnatural Mirror: *Bend Sinister* and *Hamlet*', *Critique*, **30**/1 (1988), 3–12.

Field, Andrew, *Nabokov: His Life in Art* (London: Hodder and Stoughton, 1967).

Nabokov: His Life in Part (London: Hamish Hamilton, 1977).

VN: The Life and Art of Vladimir Nabokov (London: Futura, 1988).

Foster, Ludmilla A., 'Nabokov's Gnostic Turpitude: The Surrealistic Vision of Reality in *Priglašenie na kazn'*', in Joachim T. Baehr and Norman W. Ingham (eds.), *Mnemozina: Studia litteraria russica in honorem Vsevolod Setchkarev* (Munich: Fink, 1974), 117–29.

Four Soviet Plays, ed. Ben Blake (Moscow: Co-operative Publishing Society of Foreign Works in the USSR, 1937).

Frank, Grace, *The Medieval French Drama* (Oxford: Clarendon Press, 1954).

Frank, Joseph, *The Idea of Spatial Form* (New Brunswick, NJ and London: Rutgers University Press, 1991).

Frank, Siggy, '"By Nature I am no Dramatist": Theatricality in Nabokov's Novels', in William Norman and Duncan White (eds.), *Transitional Nabokov* (Oxford and New York: Peter Lang, 2009), 167–84.

'Exile in Theatre/Theatre in Exile: Nabokov's Early Plays *Tragediia Gospodina Morna* and *Chelovek iz SSSR*', *Slavonic and East European Review*, **85**/4 (October 2007), 629–57.

Franklin, Jeffrey J., *Serious Play: The Cultural Form of the Nineteenth-Century Realist Novel* (Philadelphia: University of Pennsylvania Press, 1999).

Fromberg, Susan, 'The Unwritten Chapters in *The Real Life of Sebastian Knight*', *Modern Fiction Studies*, **13**/4, (1967–8), 427–42.

Garber, Marjorie, 'McGuffin Shakespeare', in her *Quotation Marks* (New York and London: Routledge, 2003), 147–75.

    Shakespeare's Ghost Writers: Literature as Uncanny Causality (New York: Methuen, 1987).

Garner, Stanton B., Jr, *The Absent Voice: Narrative Comprehension in the Theater* (Urbana: University of Illinois Press, 1989).

Gassner, John, 'Broadway 1941: Europe and the American Theatre', *The Atlantic Monthly*, March 1941, 329–37.

Gay, Penny, *Jane Austen and the Theatre* (Cambridge University Press, 2002).

Genette, Gérard, *Paratexts: Thresholds of Interpretation*, trans. Jane E. Lewin (Cambridge University Press, 1997).

Gessen, I. V., *Gody izgnaniia: Zhiznennyi otchet* (Paris: YMCA-Press,1979).

Gibson, Joy Leslie, *Squeaking Cleopatras: The Elizabethan Boy Player* (Stroud: Sutton, 2000).

Gogol, Nikolai, *Sobranie khudozhestvennykh proizvedenii*, 5 vols. (Moscow: Izdatel'stvo Akademii nauk SSSR, 1960–2).

Golub, Spencer, *Evreinov: The Theatre of Paradox and Transformation* (Ann Arbor, MI: UMI Research Press, 1984).

Goodman, Nelson, *Languages of Art: An Approach to a Theory of Symbols* (London: Oxford University Press, 1969).

'The Good Mr. Nabokov: Lolita's Father Neglects the Nymphets for Pushkin and Robbe-Grillet', trans. Maurice Couturier, *L'Express*, 5 November 1959 [posted on NABOKV-L, 'An interesting interview of Nabokov in French', 19 January 2011].

Grabes, Herbert, 'Nabokov and Shakespeare: The English Works', in Vladimir Alexandrov, (ed.), *The Garland Companion to Vladimir Nabokov* (New York: Garland, 1995), 496–512.

Grayson, Jane, *Nabokov Translated: A Comparison of Nabokov's Russian and English Prose* (Oxford University Press, 1977).

Green, Martin and John Swan, *The Triumph of Pierrot: The Commedia dell'Arte and the Modern Imagination* (New York: Macmillan, 1986).

Greenblatt, Stephen, *Shakespearean Negotiations: The Circulation of Social Energy in Renaissance England* (Berkeley: University of California Press, 1988).

Greenwood, Christopher, *Adapting to the Stage: Theatre and the Work of Henry James* (Aldershot: Ashgate, 2000).

Gregg, Richard A., 'Pushkin and Shenstone: The Case Reopened', *Comparative Literature*, **17**/2 (Spring 1965), 109–16.

Grossmith, Robert, 'The Twin Abysses of "Lik"', *The Nabokovian*, **19** (Fall 1987), 46–50.

Guerra, René, 'Ob odnoi zabytoi p'ese Vladimira Nabokova', in Vsevolod Sechkarev (ed.), *Otkliki: Sbornik statei pamiati Nikolaia Ivanovicha Ul'ianova (1904–1985)* (New Haven, 1986), 97–119.

    'Vladimir Nabokov v neprivychnoi ipostasi. Zametki o dvukh poslednikh p'esakh Nabokova-Sirina "Sobytie" i "Izobretenie Val'sa"', *Kontinent*, **45** (1985), 367–79.

Guicharnaud, Jacques, *Modern French Theatre from Giraudoux to Beckett* (New Haven: Yale University Press, 1961).

Gul', Roman, *Ia unes Rossiiu: apologiia emigratsii*, (New York: Most, 1981).

Halliday, F. E., *Shakespeare and His Critics* (London: Duckworth, 1949).

Hamilton, Clayton, *Studies in Stagecraft* (London, 1914).

Handke, Peter, *Theaterstücke* (Frankfurt am Main: Suhrkamp, 1992).

Hartnoll, Phyllis, *A Concise History of the Theatre* (London: Thames and Hudson, 1968).

Hassele, James E., *Russian Refugees In France and the United States Between the World Wars* (Philadelphia: American Philosphical Society, 1991).

Henke, Robert, *Performance and Literature in the Commedia dell'Arte* (Cambridge University Press, 2002).

Henry, Barbara, 'Theatricality, Anti-theatricality and Cabaret in Russian Modernism', in Catriona Kelly and Stephen Lovell (eds.), *Russian Literature, Modernism and the Visual Arts* (Cambridge University Press, 2000), 149–71.

Honigmann, E. A. J., *The Stability of Shakespeare's Text* (London: Arnold, 1965).

Horch, Franz (ed.), *Die Spielpläne Max Reinhardts 1905–1930* (Munich: R. Piper, 1930).

Huber, Martin, *Der Text als Bühne: Theatrales Erzählen um 1800* (Göttingen: Vandenhoeck und Ruprecht. 2003).

Ianovskii, V. S., *Polia eliseiskie: Kniga pamiati* (St Petersburg: Pushkinskii fond, 1993).

Inge, M. Thomas, 'Collaboration and Concepts of Authorship', *PMLA*, **116**/3 (2001), 623–30.

Innes, Christopher *Avant-Garde Theatre: 1892–1992* (London: Routledge, 1993).

'Iz dvukh uglov: Perepiska Nikolaia Evreinova s Iuriem i Iuliei Rakitinymi 1928–1938', in V. V. Ivanov (ed.), *Mnemozina: Dokumenty i fakty iz istorii russkogo teatra xx veka* (Moscow: GITIS, 1996–), vol. iii, 243–78.

Johnson, D. Barton, *Worlds in Regression: Some Novels of Vladimir Nabokov* (Ann Arbor, MI: Ardis, 1985).

Johnston, Robert Harold, *New Mecca, New Babylon: Paris and the Russian Exiles, 1920–1945* (Kingston: McGill-Queen's University Press, 1988).

'Paris: Die Hauptstadt der russischen Diaspora', in Karl Schlögel (ed.), *Der grosse Exodus: Die russische Emigration und ihre Zentren. 1917 bis 1941* (Munich: Beck, 1994), 260–78.

Jones, W. Gareth, 'Commedia dell'arte: Blok and Meyerhold, 1905–1917', in David J. George and Christopher J. Gossip (eds.), *Studies in the Commedia dell'Arte* (Cardiff: University of Wales Press, 1993), 185–97.

K[annak], E[vgenii], Review of Vladimir Nabokov, *Tragediia Gospodina Morna*, *Rul'*, 6 April 1924, 6.

Karlinsky, Simon, 'Illusion, Reality and Parody in Nabokov's Plays', in L. S. Dembo, *Nabokov: The Man and His Work* (Madison: University of Wisconsin Press, 1967), 183–94.

Karpalov, G., '"Izobretenie Val'sa"', *Pravda*, 20 December 1988, 3.

Kelly, Catriona, *Petrushka: The Russian Carnival Puppet Theatre* (Cambridge University Press, 1990).

Keynes, F. A., *By-Ways of Cambridge History*, 2nd edn (Cambridge: W. Heffer, 1956).

Khodasevich, Vladislav, 'O Sirine', *Vozrozhdenie*, 13 February 1937, 9. Reprinted in *Sobranie sochinenii v chetyrekh tomakh* (Moscow: Soglasie, 1996–7), vol. 11, 388–95.

'"Russkie zapiski", aprel – iiul', *Vozrozhdenie*, 22 July 1938, 9.

Sobranie sochinenii v chetyrekh tomakh (Moscow: Soglasie, 1996–7).

'"Sobytie" V. Sirina v Russkom teatre', *Sovremennye zapiski*, **66** (May 1938), 423–7. Reprinted in Mel'nikov, N. G. and O. A. Korosteleva (eds.), *Klassik bez retushi: Literaturnyi mir o tvorchestve Vladimira Nabokova* (Moscow: Novoe literaturnoe obozrenie, 2000), pp. 169–73.

Kimney, John, 'The Three Voices of *Despair*', *Russian Language Journal*, **34**/119 (Fall 1980), 101–8.

Knapp, Bettina L., *French Theatre 1918–1939* (London: Macmillan, 1985).

Krieger, Murray, *Ekphrasis: The Illusion of the Natural Sign* (Baltimore and London: Johns Hopkins University Press, 1992).

Langer, Susanne K., *Feeling and Form: A Theory of Art Developed from Philosophy in a New Key* (London: Routledge and Kegan Paul, 1953).

Leach, Robert and Victor Borovsky (eds.), *A History of Russian Theatre* (Cambridge University Press, 1999).

Lee, L. L., '*Bend Sinister*: Nabokov's Political Dream', in L. S. Dembo (ed.), *Nabokov: The Man and His Work* (Madison: University of Wisconsin Press, 1967), 95–105.

Lessing, Gottfried E., *Laokoon*, ed. Dorothy Reich (Oxford University Press, 1965).

Litavrina, M. G., 'Russkie dramaticheskie teatry v Parizhe (1924–1943 gg.)', in E. A. Shulepova (ed.), *Kul'turnaia missiia rossiiskogo zarubezh'ia: Proshloe i sovremennost'* (Moscow: Rossiiskii institut kul'turologii, 1999), 70–7.

Russkii teatral'nyi Parizh (St Petersburg: Aleteiia, 2003).

'Literaturnyi sud', *Dni*, 26 January 1923, 5.

Litvak, Joseph, *Caught in the Act: Theatricality in the Nineteenth-Century English Novel* (Berkeley and Oxford: University of California Press, 1992).

Livak, Leonid, *How It Was Done in Paris: Russian Émigré Literature and French Modernism* (Madison: Univerisity of Wisconsin Press, 2003).

L' vov, L., Review of Vladimir Nabokov's *Sobytie*, *Illiustrirovannaia Rossiia*, **12** March 1938, 14.

Maddox, Lucy, *Nabokov's Novels in English* (London: Croom Helm, 1983).

Markovskii, Evgen, *Ukraiinskii vertep: Rozvidki j teksti* (Kiev: Z drukarni Vseukraïns'koï akademii nauk, 1921).

Marshall, B., 'Sebastian Speaks: Nabokov's Narrative Authority in *The Real Life of Sebastian Knight*', *Style*, **23**/2 (1989), 213–24.

Masterworks of 20th Century Russian Literature and Illustration, Bloomsbury Auction Catalogue (Auction 21 May 2008, New York).

Matsekha, E., 'Nekto v serom zadaet zagadki: V. Nabokov na stsene Rizh. TIuZa', *Izvestiia*, 2 May 1989, 4.

Matthews, Brander, *Principles of Playmaking and Other Discussions of the Drama* (New York: C. Scribner's Sons, 1919).

Mayer, David III, *Harlequin in His Element: The English Pantomime, 1806–1836* (Cambridge, MA: Harvard University Press, 1969).

Medvedev, Aleksei, 'Perekhitrit' Nabokova', *Inostrannaia literatura*, **12** (1999), 217–29.

Meierkhol' d, Vsevolod, *Stat'i, pis'ma, rechi, besedy*, 2 vols. (Moscow: Iskusstvo, 1968).

Meisel, Martin, *Realizations: Narrative, Pictorial and Theatrical Arts in Nineteenth-Century England* (Princeton University Press, 1983).

Mel' nikov, N. G. and O. A. Korosteleva (eds.), *Klassik bez retushi: Literaturnyi mir o tvorchestve Vladimira Nabokova* (Moscow: Novoe literaturnoe obozrenie, 2000).

Meltzer, Francoise, *Hot Property: The Stakes and Claims of Literary Originality* (Chicago and London: University of Chicago Press, 1994).

Merkel, Stephanie, 'Vladimir Nabokov's *King, Queen, Knave* and the Commedia dell'Arte', *Nabokov Studies*, **1** (1994), 83–102.

Meshchanskii, A. Iu., '"Tragediia Gospodina Morna" kak predtecha russkoi azychnoi prozy V. V. Nabokova', *Voprosy filologii*, **11**/2 (2002), 100–8.

Morgan, Paul B., 'Nabokov and the Medieval Hunt Allegory', *Revue de littérature comparée*, **60**/3 (1986), 321–7.

Nabokov, Dmitri, 'Introduction [to Nabokov's lectures on drama]', in Vladimir Nabokov, *The Man from the USSR and Other Plays*, trans. Dmitri Nabokov (San Diego, New York and London: Harcourt Brace Jovanovich Publishers, 1984), 311–13.

'Introductory Note [to *The Event*], in Vladimir Nabokov, *The Man from the USSR and Other Plays*, tr. Dmitri Nabokov (San Diego, New York and London: Harcourt Brace Jovanovich Publishers, 1984), 125.

'Introductory Note [to *The Man from the USSR*], in Vladimir Nabokov, *The Man from the USSR and Other Plays*, trans. Dmitri Nabokov (San Diego, New York and London: Harcourt Brace Jovanovich Publishers, 1984), 33.

'Nabokov and the Theatre', in Vladimir Nabokov, *The Man from the USSR and Other Plays*, trans. Dmitri Nabokov (San Diego, New York and London: Harcourt Brace Jovanovich Publishers, 1984), 3–26.

Nabokov, Nikolas, *Bagázh: Memoirs of a Russian Cosmopolitan* (London: Secker and Warburg, 1975).

Nicol, Charles, 'The Mirrors of Sebastian Knight', in L. S. Dembo (ed.), *Nabokov: The Man and His Work* (Madison: University of Wisconsin Press, 1967), 85–94.

Nicoll, Allardyce, *Masks, Mimes and Miracles* (London: G. C. Harrap, 1931).

The World of Harlequin: A Critical Study of the Commedia dell'Arte (Cambridge University Press, 1963).

Novikov, R. V., '"Tragediia Gospodina Morna" V. Nabokova: k poetike "p'esy-snovideniia"', in L. F. Alekseeva and V. A. Skripkina (eds.), *Maloizvestnye stranitsy i novye kontseptsii istorii russkoi literatury XX v.: Materialy mezh-dunarodnoi konferentsii, Moskva, MGOU, 24–25 iiunia 2003 g.* (Moscow: Moskovskii gosudarstvennyi oblastnoi universitet, 2003), vol. i, 181–7.

O' Connor, Katherine Tiernan, 'Nabokov's *The Real Life of Sebastian Knight*: In Pursuit of a Biography', in Joachim T. Baer (ed.), *Mnemozina: Studia litteraria russica in honorem Vsevolod Setchkarev* (Munich: Fink, 1974), 281–93.

Ofrosimov, Iurii, *Teatr: Fel'etony* (Berlin: Volga, 1926).

Olcott, Anthony, 'The Author's Special Intention: A Study of *The Real Life of Sebastian Knight*', in Carl R. Proffer (ed.), *A Book of Things about Vladimir Nabokov* (Ann Arbor, MI: Ardis, 1974), 104–21.

Oreglia, Giacomo, *The Commedia dell'Arte* (London: Methuen, 1968).

Palamarchuk, Petr, 'Teatr Vladimira Nabokova', *Don*, **7** (1990), 147–53.

Paperno, Irina and Joan Delaney Grossman (eds.), *Creating Life: The Aesthetic Utopia of Russian Modernism* (Stanford University Press, 1994).

P[archevskii], K., 'Russkii teatr: "Sobytie" V. Sirina', *Poslednie novosti*, 6 March 1938, 5. Reprinted in N. G. Mel'nikov and O. A. Korosteleva (eds.), *Klassik bez retushi: Literaturnyi mir Vladimira Nabokova* (Moscow: Novoe literaturnoe obozrenie, 2000), 163–4.

Patterson, Richard R. 'Nabokov's *Bend Sinister*: The Narrator as God', *Studies in American Fiction*, **5**/2 (Autumn 1977), 241–53.

Pellérdi, Márta, 'Nabokov's *The Real Life of Sebastian Knight* or, What You Will', *Kodolányi Füzetek* (*Studies on the 20th Century English Novel, Working Papers*), 5 (1999) (www.mek.iif.hu/porta/szint/tarsad/irodtud/engnovel/engnovel.htm#2).

'Perepiska Vladimira Nabokova s M. V. Dobuzhinskim', ed. V. Stark, *Zvezda*, **11** (1996), 93–108.

Peters, Julie Stone, *Theatre of the Book, 1480–1880: Print, Text and Performance in Europe* (Oxford University Press, 2000).

Peterson, Dale, 'Nabokov's *Invitation*: Literature as Execution', *PMLA*, **96** (1981), 824–36. Reprinted in Julian W. Connolly (ed.), *Nabokov's* Invitation to a Beheading: *A Critical Companion* (Evanston, IL: Northwestern University Press, 1997), 66–92.

Pfister, Manfred, *The Theory and Analysis of Drama* (Cambridge University Press, 1988).

Pifer, Drury, 'Le théâtre et le monde', *Europe: revue littéraire mensuelle*, **791** (March 1995), 57–63.

Pirandello, Luigi, *Six Characters in Search of an Author and Other Plays* (London: Penguin, 1995).

Pogodin, Nikolai, *Sobranie dramaticheskikh proizvedenii v piati tomakh* (Moscow: Iskusstvo, 1960–1).

Puchner, Martin, *Stage Fright: Modernism, Anti-Theatricality, and Drama* (Baltimore and London: Johns Hopkins University Press, 2002).

Pushkin, Alexander, *Eugene Onegin: A Novel in Verse*, trans. Vladimir Nabokov (Princeton University Press, 1990).
  'Mozart and Salieri', trans. Vladimir Nabokov, *The New Republic*, **104** (21 April 1941), 559–65
Putrenko, T., 'Bednyi Nabokov', *Literaturnaia gazeta*, 14 December 1988, 8.
Quinn, B., 'Aspects of Nabokov's Transition to English Prose in *The Real Life of Sebastian Knight*', *Studies in English Language and Literature*, **40** (February 1990), 81–101.
Raeff, Marc, *Russia Abroad: A Cultural History of the Russian Emigration* (New York: Oxford University Press, 1990).
'Repertory: Nabokov in Embryo', *Time*, **24** January 1969.
Ricoeur, Paul, *Oneself as Author*, trans. Kathleen Blamey (University of Chicago Press, 1992).
Rimmon, Shlomith, 'Problems of Voice in Nabokov's *The Real Life of Sebastian Knight*', in Phyllis A. Roth (ed.), *Critical Essays on Vladimir Nabokov* (Boston: G. K. Hall, 1984), 109–29.
Rosenfield, Claire, '*Despair* and the Lust for Immortality', *Wisconsin Studies in Contemporary Literature* (Spring 1967), 174–92. Reprinted in L. S. Dembo, *Nabokov: The Man and His Work* (Madison: University of Wisconsin Press, 1967), 66–84.
Rouse, John, 'Textuality and Authority in Theatre and Drama: Some Contemporary Possibilities', in Janelle G. Reinelt and Joseph R. Roach (eds.), *Critical Theory and Performance* (Ann Arbor: University of Michigan Press, 1992), 146–57.
Rowe, William Woodin, *Nabokov's Spectral Dimension* (Ann Arbor, MI: Ardis, 1981).
Rudnitskii, Konstantin, *Rezhisser Meierkhol'd* (Moscow: Nauka, 1969).
Said, Edward, 'Reflections on Exile', in his *Reflections on Exile and Other Essays* (Cambridge, MA: Harvard University Press, 2000), 173–86.
Sand, Maurice, *The History of the Harlequinade*, 2 vols. (London, 1915).
Schechner, Richard, *Between Theater and Anthropology* (Philadelphia: University of Pennsylvania Press, 1985).
Scherr, Barry P., *Russian Poetry: Meter, Rhythm, and Rhyme* (Berkeley: University of California Press, 1986).
Schlögel, Karl, 'Berlin: "Stiefmutter unter den russischen Städten"', in Karl Schlögel (ed.), *Der grosse Exodus: Die russische Emigration und ihre Zentren 1917 bis 1941* (Munich: Beck, 1994), 234–59.
Schlögel, Karl, Katharina Kucher, Bernhard Suchy and Gregor Thum (eds.), *Chronik russischen Lebens in Deutschland 1918–1941* (Berlin: Akademie Verlag, 1999).
Schuman, Sam, '"Despair and Die", Nabokov and Shakespeare's Tragedies', *Notes on Contemporary Literature*, **12**/1 (January 1982), 11–12.
  'Nabokov and Shakespeare: The Russian Works', in Vladimir Alexandrov (ed.), *The Garland Companion to Vladimir Nabokov* (New York: Garland, 1995), 512–17.
  'Something Rotten in the State: *Hamlet* and *Bend Sinister*', *Russian Literature Triquarterly*, **24** (1991), 197–212.

Sedykh, Andrei, 'U V. V. Sirina' [interview with Vladimir Nabokov], *Poslednie novosti*, 3 November 1932, 2. Reprinted in Vladmimir Nabokov, *Sobranie sochinenii russkogo perioda v piati tomakh* (St Petersburg: Simpozium, 1999–2000), vol. v, 641–3.

Segel, Harold B., *Pinocchio's Progeny: Puppets, Marionettes, Automatons, and Robots in Modernist and Avant-Garde Drama* (Baltimore and London: Johns Hopkins University, 1995).

Seidel, Michael, *Exile and the Narrative Imagination* (New Haven: Yale University Press, 1986).

Senderovich, Savely, and Yelena Shvarts, 'Balagan smerti: Zametki o romane V. Nabokova "Bend Sinister"', *Kul'tura russkoi diaspory: Vladimir Nabokov – 100. Materialy nauchnoi konferentsii (Tallinn – Tartu, 14–17 ianvaria 1999)* (Tallinn: TPÜ Kirjastus, 2000), 356–70.

'The Juice of Three Oranges: An Exploration in Nabokov's Language and World', *Nabokov Studies*, **6** (2000–1), 75–124.

'The Tongue, That Punchinello: A Commentary on Nabokov's *Pnin*', *Nabokov Studies*, **8** (2004), 23–41.

Senelick, Laurence (ed.), *Wandering Stars: Russian Émigré Theatre, 1905–1940* (Iowa City: University of Iowa Press, 1992).

Shakespeare, William, *As You Like It* (Cambridge University Press, 2000).

Hamlet, Prince of Denmark (Cambridge University Press, 1985).

Othello (Cambridge University Press, 1984).

Twelfth Night Or What You Will (Cambridge University Press, 1985).

Shapiro, Gavriel, 'Nabokov and Early Netherlandish Art', in Gavriel Shapiro (ed.), *Nabokov at Cornell* (Ithaca, NY and London: Cornell University Press, 2003), 241–50.

The Sublime Artist's Studio: Nabokov and the Art of Painting (Evanston, IL: Northwestern University Press, 2009).

'Vladimir Nabokov and "The World of Art"', *Slavic Almanach: The South African Year Book for Slavic, Central and East European Studies*, **6**/9 (2000), 35–52.

Shapiro, Michael, *Gender in Play on the Shakespearean Stage: Boy Heroines and Female Pages* (Ann Arbor: University of Michigan Press, 1994).

Shik, Aleksandr, 'Russkie emigranty v mirovom teatre dramy i komedii', *Vozrozhdenie*, **213** (1969), 111–24.

Shikhovtsev, E., 'Teatr Nabokova', *Teatr*, **5** (1988), 163–4.

Shrayer, Maxim D., 'Vladimir Nabokov and Women Authors', *The Nabokovian*, **44** (Spring 2000), 52–63.

Shershow, Scott Cutler, *Puppets and 'Popular' Culture* (Ithaca, NY and London: Cornell University Press, 1995).

Sisson, J., '*The Real Life of Sebastian Knight*', in Vladimir Alexandrov (ed.), *The Garland Companion to Vladimir Nabokov* (New York: Garland, 1995), 633–43.

Six Soviet Plays, ed. and trans. Eugene Lyons (Boston: Houghton Mifflin, 1934).

Sizif [G. Adamovich], 'Otkliki', *Poslednie novosti*, 10 March 1938, 3.

'Skonchalsia I. S. Lukash', *Novoe russkoe slovo*, **29** May 1940, 2.

Smith, Gerald S., 'Nabokov and Russian Verse Form', *Russian Literature Triquarterly*, **24** (1991), 271–305.

'"Sobytie", p'esa V. Sirina (pis'mo v redaktsiiu)', *Poslednie novosti*, **10** March 1938, 4.

The Song of Igor's Campaign, trans. Vladimir Nabokov (Woodstock, NY and New York: Ardis, 1988).

Stark, Vadim, 'Voskresenie Gospodina Morna', *Zvezda*, **4** (1997), 6–8.

Stegner, Page 'The Immortality of Art: Nabokov's *The Real Life of Sebastian Knight*', *The Southern Review*, **2**/2 (1966), 286–96.

  Escape into Aesthetics: The Art of Vladimir Nabokov (London: Eyre and Spottiswoode, 1967).

Strandberg, Victor, 'Nabokov and the "Prism of Art"', in Steven G. Kellman and Irving Malin (eds.), *Torpid Smoke: The Stories of Vladimir Nabokov* (Amsterdam and Atlanta, GA: Rodopi, 2000), 189–202.

Stuart, Dabney, *Nabokov: The Dimensions of Parody* (Baton Rouge, LA and London: Louisiana State University Press, 1978).

  '*The Real Life of Sebastian Knight*: Angles of Perception', *Modern Language Quarterly*, **29** (1968), 312–28.

Suagee, Stephen, 'An Artist's Memory Beats All Other Kinds: An Essay on *Despair*', in Carl R. Proffer (ed.), *A Book of Things about Vladimir Nabokov* (Ann Arbor, MI: Ardis, 1974), 54–62.

S[urguchev], I[lya], '"Sobytie", p'esa Sirina', *Vozrozhdenie*, 11 March 1938, 12.

Sweeney, Susan E., 'Looking at Harlequins: Nabokov, The World of Art and the Ballets Russes', in Jane Grayson, Arnold McMillin and Priscilla Meyer (eds.), *Nabokov's World*, vol. II: *Reading Nabokov* (Basingstoke: Palgrave, 2002), 73–95.

  'Sinistral Details: Nabokov, Wilson, and *Hamlet* in *Bend Sinister*', *Nabokov Studies*, **1** (1994), 179–94.

Symonds, John Addington, *Shakespeare's Predecessors in the English Drama* (London, 1900).

Tammi, Pekka, *Problems of Nabokov's Poetics: A Narratological Analysis* (Helsinki: Suomalainen Tiedeakatemia, 1985).

  Russian Subtexts in Nabokov's Fiction (Tampere University Press, 1999).

Tekiner, Christina, 'Time in Lolita', *Modern Fiction Studies*, **25** (1979), 463–9.

Thomas, George R., *Ten Miracle Plays* (London: Arnold, 1966).

Tillis, Steve, *Toward an Aesthetics of the Puppet: Puppetry as Theatrical Art* (New York and London: Greenwood, 1992).

Timenchik, Roman, 'Chitaem Nabokova: "Izobretenie Val'sa" v postanovke Adol'fa Shapiro', *Rodnik*, **10** (1988), 46–8.

Toker, Leona, *Nabokov: The Mystery of Literary Structures* (Ithaca, NY and London: Cornell University Press, 1989).

Tolstaia, N. I., '"Polius" V. Nabokova i "Posledniaia ekspeditsiia Skotta"', *Russkaia literatura*, **1** (1989), 133–6.

Tolstoi, Ivan, 'Nabokov i ego teatral'noe nasledie', in Vladimir Nabokov, *P'esy*, ed. Ivan Tolstoi (Moscow: Iskusstvo, 1990), 5–42.

'Preodolenie steny: P'esy Vladimira Nabokova "Sobytie" i "Izobretenie Val'sa" v Leningrade i v Rige', *Zvezda*, **7** (1989), 203–6.

Tolstoy, Leo, *The Kreutzer Sonata and Other Stories*, trans. David McDuff (London: Penguin, 2004).

Sobranie sochinenii v dvadtsati tomakh, 20 vols. (Moscow: Gosudarstvennoe izdatel'stvo khudozhestvennoi literatury, 1960–5).

Tompa, Andrea, 'Staging Nabokov', *Nabokov Online Journal*, **2** (2008) (http://etc.dal.ca/noj/volume2/articles/09_Tompa.pdf).

Troubetzkoy, W., 'Vladimir Nabokov's *Despair*: The Reader as "April's Fool"', *Cycnos*, **12**/2 (1995), 55–62.

Vakar, N. P., '"Sobytie" – p'esa V. Sirina (beseda s Iu. P. Annenkovym)', *Poslednie novosti*, 12 March 1938, 4. Reprinted in N. G. Mel'nikov and O. A. Korosteleva (eds.), *Klassik bez retushi: Literaturnyi mir o tvorchestve Vladimira Nabokova* (Moscow: Novoe literaturnoe obozrenie, 2000), 165–6.

Vladimir Nabokov: Selected Letters, 1940–1977, ed. Dmitri Nabokov and Matthew J. Bruccoli (London: Weidenfeld and Nicolson, 1990).

Vlock, Deborah, *Dickens, Novel Reading, and the Victorian Popular Theatre* (Cambridge University Press, 1998).

'V. V. Nabokov i I. A. Bunin. Perepiska', ed. M. D. Shrayer and R. Davis, in R. Davis and V. A. Keldysh (eds.), *S dvukh beregov: Russkaia literatura xx veka v Rossii i za rubezhom* (Moscow: IMLI RAN, 2002), 167–219.

Volkovyskii, N[ikolai], 'O skvernykh zrelishchakh', *Dni*, 6 February 1923, 5.

Waugh, Patricia, *Metafiction: The Theory and Practice of Self-Conscious Fiction* (London and New York: Methuen, 1984).

Weber, Samuel, *Theatricality as Medium* (New York: Fordham University Press, 2004).

Weimann, Robert, *Author's Pen and Actor's Voice: Playing and Writing in Shakespeare's Theatre* (Cambridge University Press, 2000).

'Textual Authority and Performative Agency: The Uses of Disguise in Shakespeare's Theatre', *New Literary History*, **25** (1994), 789–808.

Wiles, David, 'Theatre in Roman and Christian Europe', in John Russell Brown (ed.), *The Oxford Illustrated History of Theatre* (Oxford University Press, 1995), 49–92.

Willett, John, *The Theatre of the Weimar Republic* (New York: Holmes and Meier, 1988).

The Theatre of Erwin Piscator: Half a Century of Politics in the Theatre (London: Eyre Methuen, 1978).

Williams, Robert C., *Culture in Exile: Russian Emigrés in Germany 1881–1941* (Ithaca, NY: Cornell University Press, 1972).

Wilson, John, 'Dies Borealis: Christopher Under Canvass, No. VI', *Blackwood's Edinburgh Magazine*, **67** (April 1850), 481–512.

'Dies Borealis: Christopher Under Canvass, No. VII', *Blackwood's Edinburgh Magazine*, **67** (May 1850), 622–39.

Wood, Michael, *The Magician's Doubts: Nabokov and the Risks of Fiction* (London: Pimlico, 1995).

Woodward, J. B., 'From Brjusov to Ajkhenvald: Attitudes to the Russian Theatre, 1902–1914', *Candian Slavonic Papers*, **1** (1965), 173–88.

Woolf, Virginia, *Orlando: A Biography* (London: Penguin, 1993).

Worrall, Nick, 'Meyerhold Directs Gogol's "Government Inspector"', *Theatre Quarterly*, **2**/7 (July–September 1972), 75–95.

Worthen, William B. *Shakespeare and the Authority of Performance* (Cambridge University Press, 1997).

'Drama, Performativity, and Performance', *PMLA*, **113**/5 (1998), 1093–107.

Wyllie, Barbara, *Nabokov at the Movies: Film Perspectives in Fiction* (Jefferson, NC and London: McFarland, 2003).

Zheleznov M., '"Sobytie" V. Sirina', *Novoe russkoe slovo*, 6 April 1941, 4.

Zimmer, Dieter E., *Nabokovs Berlin* (Berlin: Nicolai, 2001).

'Nachwort des Herausgebers'. in Vladimir Nabokov, *Gesammelte Werke*, xv/i (*Dramen*), ed. Dieter E. Zimmer (Reinbeck: Rowohlt, 2000), 563–78.

Zlochevskaia, A., 'Teatr N. V. Gogolia i dramaturgiia russkogo zarubezh'ia pervoi volny', *Voprosy literatury*, **2** (March–April 2005), 209–35.

Zunshine, Lisa (ed.), *Nabokov at the Limits: Redrawing Critical Boundaries* (New York and London: Garland, 1999).

Index